Linking Customer and Employee Satisfaction to the Bottom Line

Also Available from ASQ Quality Press:

Linking Customer and Employee Satisfaction to the Bottom Line

A Comprehensive Guide to
Establishing the Impact of Customer
and Employee Satisfaction on
Critical Business Outcomes

Derek R. Allen and Morris Wilburn

ASQ Quality Press
Milwaukee, Wisconsin

Linking Customer and Employee Satisfaction to the Bottom Line
Derek R. Allen and Morris Wilburn

Library of Congress Cataloging-in-Publication Data

Allen, Derek R., 1959–
  Linking customer and employee satisfaction to the bottom line: a
comprehensive guide to establishing the impact of customer and
employee satisfaction on critical business outcomes / Derek R. Allen
and Morris Wilburn.
      p. cm.
  Includes bibliographical references and index.
  ISBN 0-87389-501-0
  1. Consumer satisfaction. 2. Job satisfaction. 3. Industrial management.
4. Success in business. I. Wilburn, Morris, 1953– II. Title.

  HF5415.335 .A433 2002
  658.3'1422—dc21   2002001314

© 2002 by ASQ

10 9 8 7 6 5 4 3 2 1

ISBN 0-87389-501-0

Acquisitions Editor: Annemieke Koudstaal
Project Editor: Craig S. Powell
Production Administrator: Gretchen Trautman
Special Marketing Representative: David Luth

ASQ Mission: The American Society for Quality advances individual,
organizational, and community excellence worldwide through learning,
quality improvement, and knowledge exchange.

Attention Bookstores, Wholesalers, Schools, and Corporations: ASQ Quality
Press books, videotapes, audiotapes, and software are available at quantity
discounts with bulk purchases for business, educational, or instructional use.
For information, please contact ASQ Quality Press at 800-248-1946, or write to
ASQ Quality Press, P.O. Box 3005, Milwaukee, WI 53201-3005.

To place orders or to request a free copy of the ASQ Quality Press Publications
Catalog, including ASQ membership information, call 800-248-1946. Visit our
Web site at www.asq.org or http://qualitypress.asq.org .

Printed in the United States of America

 Printed on acid-free paper

American Society for Quality

Quality Press
600 N. Plankinton Avenue
Milwaukee, Wisconsin 53203
Call toll free 800-248-1946
Fax 414-272-1734
www.asq.org
http://qualitypress.asq.org
http://standardsgroup.asq.org
E-mail: authors@asq.org

Table of Contents

List of Figures

Foreword

A customer, Mr. Smith, buys a new automobile, his first new car purchase. Mr. Smith is just 21 years old. He likes the car's styling, the car has fewer breakdowns than his old used autos, and the car gets good mileage. The dealer, located in the city, provides good service and takes the time to answer Mr. Smith's questions. Service people who are committed to the dealership are friendly and helpful in all of their dealings with Mr. Smith. He finances the car through the auto finance company. The finance company gives Mr. Smith the loan at a competitive rate, and he arranges an automatic monthly payment procedure through his bank. Mr. Smith sees his car displayed in company advertising and is pleased that the auto company is innovative in bringing new and safer automobiles to the public using current technology. Mr. Smith thinks the auto company has offered *superior* value on all fronts. He relates his positive experiences with his car to 10 other people and influences five of them to visit the dealer's showroom. His wife buys a new car, a different model, from the same auto company and through the same dealer.

Sounds simple. This is the story of a loyal customer. The auto company now has a customer in Mr. Smith who will contribute a significant profit in his lifetime even though his name does not appear on the company's balance sheet. Corporate financial officers do not always see their balance sheets as the amalgamation of many individual customers with different levels of satisfaction and loyalty. They should. The story is the same whether you operate a retail store, run a financial institution, or manufacture business equipment.

The simplicity of the above linkages may be the reason they are often ignored. Today, unlike 30 years ago when customer satisfaction research was in its infancy, virtually every company conducts some form of customer satisfaction research and employee surveys. Customer satisfaction studies may range from simple comment cards to well-designed relationship and transactional surveys. Employee surveys range from old-fashioned job satisfaction surveys to comprehensive employee engagement/commitment surveys. However, even today, with the current explosion of knowledge in these areas, companies do not always put their feedback systems in a proper strategic context. Top management in many companies does not look at measurement systems from the point of view of customer segmentation and profitability.

This book by Dr. Derek R. Allen and Mr. Morris Wilburn makes a case to research practitioners and management to focus on linkages between customer satisfaction, employee satisfaction, and business profitability. By bringing together all of the theoretical knowledge and empirical work done to date on these issues, the authors encourage researchers to design these types of studies in an integrated fashion for the benefit of the company. One of the greatest failures in the current lack of integration is contributed by the silo structure inherent in any business where ownership of different surveys is diffused.

The book provides analytical guidance for researchers as well as conceptual guidance to managers to develop an integrated view of customer satisfaction and employee satisfaction and their link to business outcomes. The book is clear evidence of the elevation of customer feedback research to a professional discipline with significant intellectual rigor. It will serve as an excellent reference tool to allow loyalty managers to better use customer feedback information to a strategic advantage.

Dr. T. R. Rao
CEO/President
Market Probe

Preface

This book is intended for advanced service quality managers and marketing researchers with more than a modest exposure to statistical data analysis. Our objective is to provide the reader with a fundamental understanding of how customer satisfaction and employee attitudes may be empirically linked to substantive business outcomes such as profitability. Above all, this book is intended for the *practitioner* and, as such, relies upon numerous industry examples to illustrate key points.

The scope of this book ranges from a brief treatment of customer and employee satisfaction measurement to in-depth discussions concerning analytical approaches to linking customer satisfaction and profitability. We have avoided as much as possible an overly technical treatment of these subjects. Instead, a more descriptive, managerial approach was taken in an effort to facilitate an understanding of how sophisticated analytical techniques can be applied and, more important, what they can tell us about the data. Nonetheless, we cannot avoid some technical discussions since our objective is to demonstrate how to link customer and employee satisfaction data to key business measures.

We have attempted to include actual industry examples to illustrate how techniques were applied, how the results were interpreted, and, finally, how critical strategic marketing decisions were affected. We have also addressed some of the most problematic aspects of service quality data and internal business metrics, including data scaling and scaling variables such as customer profitability.

This book provides the advanced service quality manager or marketing researcher embarking on customer satisfaction research with a comprehensive overview of how these data may be related to critical business outcomes.

Perhaps more important, researchers with mature customer satisfaction measurement systems may use the techniques described in this book to maximize the value of their existing programs. Indeed, more and more frequently, researchers managing large customer and employee satisfaction programs are being required to demonstrate their systems' value. A more poignant question has been posed by senior management with increasing frequency: *What is the value of customer and employee satisfaction research?*

No technique or methodology can *guarantee* a strong link between customer satisfaction and key business outcomes. This book can, however, ensure that appropriate scales, variables, and assumptions are used. Further, we have included a wide variety of case studies that will facilitate an understanding of the types of variables one must consider when attempting to link business metrics to psychometric data. This book makes a concerted effort to address employee satisfaction and its role in the development of customer satisfaction and profitability, customer retention, and market share. As such, we feel it makes a unique contribution to the service quality management and human resources fields.

The first four chapters of the book introduce customer satisfaction, employee satisfaction, the Six Sigma approach to quality management, and the links between satisfaction, profitability, and customer retention. The fifth chapter introduces a unique application of survival analysis using customer attrition data. Chapter 6 provides a review of key business performance variables, and chapter 7 describes how data should be prepared for the type of analysis described in chapters 8 through 10. Chapter 8 introduces bivariate approaches to establishing empirical linkages between customer satisfaction, employee satisfaction, and financial performance measures. Chapter 9 introduces a series of multivariate dependence models beginning with multiple regression analysis and includes discussions on the use of logistic regression, principal components regression, and nonlinear regression. Chapter 10 introduces causal modeling with both manifest and latent variables.

The final chapter of this book describes a number of cutting-edge applications that have been used to link both customer and employee satisfaction to key business outcomes. Among these are decision support software and simulation packages that permit managers to pose "what if?" questions using their data. The use of this type of tool will facilitate the ability of managers and researchers alike to test the efficacy of models linking customer satisfaction to corporate profitability.

Theoretical Foundations: Chapters 1–4

Applications: Chapters 5–10

Summary: Chapter 11

Acknowledgments

This book would not have been possible without the theoretical and technical foundations laid by many applied and academic researchers over the past 25 years. The completion of this work was greatly facilitated by the administrative skills of Sandy Cummings, who produced all of the graphics and spent many hours ensuring that editorial changes were implemented. Maya Hughes provided insightful editorial input and project management during the development of this book, and to her we are extremely grateful.

A number of Market Probe project management staff helped proof this book. Among them were Amy Bastic, Jill Carnick, Deana Gillespie, Chandreyee Mittra, Megan Murphy, Heather Nagel, Bob Peterson, Lori Richards, Debashis Sengupta, Ron Sincere, and Barry Tochterman. We would also like to thank Karen Ethington for reviewing the accounting practices associated with the business performance metrics described in chapter 6. Thanks also go to the anonymous ASQ reviewers whose insights and valuable comments enhanced this volume's contribution to the customer satisfaction research literature. Special thanks to Leayn and Paul Tabili at New Paradigm for their outstanding prepress work. Finally, we would like to express our gratitude to ASQ Quality Press editorial staff members Annemieke Koudstaal and Craig Powell.

1
Why Customer Satisfaction?

INTRODUCTION

This book focuses on the relationships between customer satisfaction, employee satisfaction, and tangible business outcomes such as market share, revenue, and profitability. How customer satisfaction research developed and the role it plays in business are described in this chapter. As a construct, customer satisfaction enjoys an enviable niche in terms of its role in corporate incentive systems and other reward programs. The conventional wisdom is that since it is used so extensively in gauging performance, customer satisfaction must be indicative of business success . . . or the lack thereof. But this logic is somehow circular and fails to present scientific evidence for such a relationship.

In this book, we provide a synthesis of applied and academic research with the aim of empirically demonstrating the relationship between customer and employee satisfaction and substantive outcomes such as corporate profitability. In order to set the stage, we first treat customer satisfaction (chapter 1) and employee satisfaction (chapter 2). By establishing a sound understanding of these constructs and how they are measured, we can more effectively demonstrate how they affect key business outcomes such as profitability and market share.

That customer satisfaction is inexorably related to the quality revolution in the United States is practically incontrovertible. The formalization of customer satisfaction as a quality component in national competitions such as the Malcolm Baldrige National Quality Award has further validated the customer satisfaction research agenda. As shown in Figure 1.1, customer satisfaction constitutes a significant part of the Baldrige Award criteria.

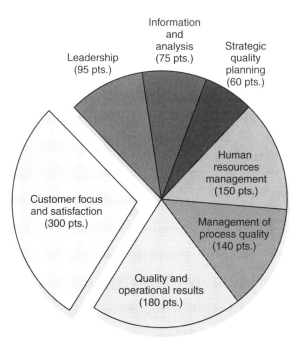

Figure 1.1 Malcolm Baldrige National Quality Award evaluation criteria.

This chapter provides a succinct history of customer satisfaction research and reviews more contemporary attempts to link satisfaction to retention and, ultimately, corporate profitability.

The first forays into the measurement of customer satisfaction occurred in the early 1980s. These typically involved assessing the drivers of satisfaction. Early works by Oliver (1980), Churchill and Surprenant (1982), and Bearden and Teel (1983) tended to focus on the operationalization of customer satisfaction and its antecedents. By the mid-1980s, the focus of both applied and academic research had shifted to construct refinement and the implementation of strategies designed to optimize customer satisfaction, according to Zeithaml, Berry, and Parasuraman (1996, 31).

Rigorous scientific inquiry and the development of a general service quality theory can be attributed to Parasuraman, Berry, and Zeithaml (1985). Their discussion of customer satisfaction, service quality, and customer expectations represents one of the first attempts to operationalize satisfaction in a theoretical context. Parasuraman, Berry, and Zeithaml proposed that the ratio of perceived performance to customer expectations was key to maintaining satisfied customers. The disparity between performance and expectations was presumed to take five forms, as shown in Figure 1.2.

Several years later, Parasuraman, Berry, and Zeithaml (1988) published a second, related discussion that focused more specifically on the psychometric aspects of service quality. Their multi-item SERVQUAL scale is considered to be one of the first attempts to operationalize the customer satisfaction construct. The SERVQUAL scale focused on the performance component of the service quality model in which quality was defined as the disparity between expectations and performance. The battery of items used in the SERVQUAL multi-item scale is still used today as a foundation upon which instrument development is often based. The primary areas considered in the scale are depicted in Figure 1.3.

The five primary components of the model each represent a distinct aspect of the customer relationship. For example, the *tangibles* dimension includes the appearance of facilities, equipment, personnel, and communication materials. Similarly, the *reliability* dimension addresses the service provider's ability to perform dependably and accurately. The *responsiveness* component of the SERVQUAL architecture involves the service provider's

Figure 1.2   Principal disparities affecting service quality.

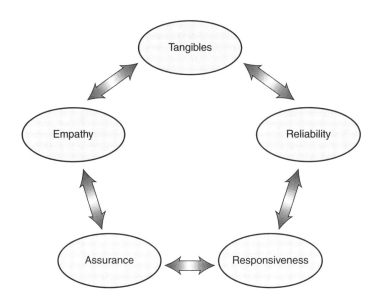

Figure 1.3   SERVQUAL scale dimensions.

willingness to help customers and provide prompt service. *Assurance* is identified as the knowledge base and courtesy of employees and their ability to instill trust and confidence. Finally, *empathy* relates to the service organization's caring and individualized service.

Throughout the 1980s, both applied and academic researchers focused on these (and other) issues and their effects on overall customer satisfaction according to Zeithaml, Berry, and Parasuraman (1996, 31). That is, the primary research question involved which of the five areas was most important vis-à-vis customer expectations. Much of the earliest applied work involving the derivation of attribute importance involved stated measures. It was not uncommon to encounter surveys in which for every item both importance and performance measures were sought. The gap between these two measures was considered instrumental in resource allocation. Large gaps demanded the most attention. It is important to note, however, that Parasuraman, Berry, and Zeithaml (1988) employed regression analysis to assess the effect of each dimension relative to a dependent measure in their introduction of the SERVQUAL model. The use of regression analysis and other dependency models to derive the importance of attributes relative to an outcome measure is now considered *de rigueur* and is described in detail in the following pages.

DERIVING ATTRIBUTE IMPORTANCE

Derived importance models represent a cornerstone of customer satisfaction research. The *derivation* of attribute importance currently represents the norm in the customer satisfaction research industry. Today, few if any consultants advocate the stated importance framework in which customers are asked to rate (or rank) the importance of service or product quality issues. Its shortcomings have been illustrated with the frequently cited airline safety example in which stated and derived importance metrics lead to disparate conclusions. In the airline safety example, we contrast the importance of five issues:

- Food quality

- Cleanliness

- Safety

- Attendant courtesy

- Comfort

When *asked* which of these issues is most important to them, most consumers will indicate that safety is their primary concern. After all, who would respond that food quality is more important than personal safety? As most who are familiar with this example will recall, the derived importance framework employs multiple regression to mathematically determine the impact of each issue on a single outcome variable: overall satisfaction with the airline.

There is some confusion surrounding the implication of the word *importance* in the dependence model, or multiple regression, context. Take, for example, the reaction of product managers at a world-class manufacturing company when told that product quality was not important. Their initial inclination was to dismiss the results and walk out! The simple fact is that the use of the term *importance* tends to cloud the true meaning of what we are trying to convey. In the regression context, importance implies the magnitude of impact on an outcome variable such as overall satisfaction or repurchase propensity. Once they understood this, the managers and engineers at the manufacturing company described above were actually quite pleased. Their products were—and still are—considered best in class and enjoy stellar customer satisfaction scores.

So, exactly what are we conveying when we say something is important in a dependence model context? It should be clear that derived importance results provide managers with road maps for *maximizing* an outcome variable such as overall satisfaction. In order to achieve the greatest increase in

Table 1.1   Hypothetical key drivers.

Service/Product Satisfaction	Quarter 1 Key Driver Status	Quarter 4 Key Driver Status
Teller courtesy	No	Yes
Competitive rates	No	No
Waiting time for teller	No	Yes
Statement accuracy	No	No
Parking space	Yes	No
Branch proximity	No	No

overall satisfaction (or any other outcome variable), we focus on the predictor variables that have the greatest effect on it. More accurately, we isolate the predictor variables that *covary* most strongly with the outcome variable. It is this covariation that is at the heart of derived importance models.

Derived importance models are probably erroneously labeled. A more appropriate name might be *marginal resource allocation* models. It is important that we consider only marginal resources since *reallocating* existing resources based upon a derived importance model will not necessarily yield the desired results. Consider the extreme example of a retail bank that blindly reallocates existing resources based upon its key driver analysis. Assume the simplified set of key drivers shown in Table 1.1.

If bank management erroneously decides to reallocate resources based upon the set of *first quarter* key drivers, it may choose to reduce the number (and quality) of the teller staff in order to free funds for the acquisition of adjacent land for parking. This reallocation of resources yields a completely different set of drivers in the *fourth quarter*. The new drivers reflect the effects of management's decision to reallocate *existing* rather than *marginal* dollars. Since teller staffing was cut back, waiting time increased and, as a result, customers became less satisfied with this aspect of their relationship with the bank. In fact, it appears from these data that the dissatisfaction was sufficiently acute to affect overall satisfaction. Such a turn of events underscores the *dynamic nature of key drivers*. It also illustrates why key driver analysis should really be considered as a marginal resource allocation tool.

MEASUREMENT ISSUES AND CUSTOMER SATISFACTION

When we consider the linkage between customer satisfaction and profitability, *how* we measure customer satisfaction emerges as a significant issue. Given our desire to establish a relationship between customer satisfaction and key business outcomes, the measurement of the former is a salient issue. If we fail to adequately measure satisfaction, our chances of establishing an empirical link with, for example, profitability or market share may be lessened.

Over the past 20 years or so, researchers have experimented with a wide variety of approaches to measuring customer satisfaction. Among these are gap measures, letter grade scales, expectation scales, and Likert-type numeric scales with anchored endpoints. Each approach has advocates who defend it tenaciously. It seems clear that the Likert-type numeric scale with endpoint anchors ("very satisfied" to "very dissatisfied") is favored by both academicians and researchers working in applied settings.

The multipoint scale yields more data variability than, for example, binary scales that elicit "yes" or "no" responses (Hayes 1998, 70–71). For organizations performing at stellar levels (for example, top-two-box scores of 90% or greater on a 5-point scale), it may be worth considering either a 7-point or 10-point scale. There are at least two reasons for this. Consider a hypothetical organization with 75 national sales districts. The company sells and services a premium product that is universally considered "best in class." Assume that this company has a mature customer satisfaction measurement (CSM) and tracking program that relies upon a 5-point scale. Feedback is provided on a quarterly basis at the sales district level. If most sales districts receive quarterly scores of better than 90%, differentiating performance levels among them will be difficult at best. It is the ability to discriminate between top performers and poor performers that adds tremendous utility to CSM programs that are linked to compensation and bonus plans. Clearly, if the reporting metric produces a distribution of scores so narrow that statistically differentiating performance levels is impossible, then the program will have only modest utility.

In reality, choice of measurement scales is frequently determined by univariate reporting requirements. A company that routinely receives 90% top-two-box scores on a 5-point scale will likely only enjoy about an 85% top-two-box score on a 7-point scale. On a 10-point scale, the same company would expect a score of only about 75%. In addition, the distribution of districts around the average top-two-box score will be more diffuse. The wider distribution of scores around the mean gives us more discriminating power. The enhanced discriminating power enables us more reliably to isolate poor performers.

The second reason a 7-point or 10-point scale is preferred involves *covariance*. In general, it is easier to establish covariance between two variables with greater dispersion, or variance, around their means. It is this covariance that is critical to establishing strong multivariate dependence models used in key driver assessments. It will also prove to be critical in our efforts to establish a strong link between customer satisfaction and key business outcomes such as profitability and market share. Thus, from a model development perspective, the 10-point scale is preferred. Sophisticated statistical software such as Jöreskog and Sörbom's LISREL 8 structural equation modeling package, for example, *assumes that data are ordinal* if five or fewer scale levels are present.

In an empirical review of several scale types, Wittink and Bayer (1994) concluded that a 10-point dependent measure was preferred. The authors also maintained that a 2-point *experiential* predictor variable scale should be adopted. This scale type solicits a yes or no response to statements involving specific service or product experiences. For example, "Did the service person provide you with an accurate invoice?" can only be answered with a yes or no. While the 10-point dependent measure is well accepted in both academic and industry research settings, the 2-point predictor variable scale has been met with some trepidation. One reason is that models based upon this measurement approach tend to have lower predictive (R^2) capacities.

Not surprisingly, the configuration that Wittink and Bayer advocated has not been widely adopted. Nonetheless, their comparison of the 5-point and 10-point dependent variable scales is valuable. Wittink and Bayer relied upon a total of 13 criteria. These included issues involving the respondent, such as simplicity and understandability, and statistical issues such as response bias, power, and sensitivity. Response bias involves the extent to which target respondents are excluded due to inability or refusal to participate. Power involves the extent to which the scale can detect changes over time (or differences among groups). Finally, sensitivity was defined as the degree of room for improving customer satisfaction. Given this set of criteria, Wittink and Bayer concluded that the 10-point endpoint-anchored measurement scale was preferred to the 5-point alternative.

We must concede that skewness remains a problem even with the 10-point scale; this problem may never be fully circumvented in customer satisfaction research. Nonetheless, there are ways to lessen the impact of skewed data. One simple approach is to provide extreme endpoints. Rather than a scale ranging from "satisfied" to "dissatisfied," we can make the anchor labels more difficult to achieve. For example, labeling the endpoints as "delighted" and "very disappointed" has been used with some success. Others have suggested a traditional 5-point scale ranging from "very dissatisfied" to "very satisfied" with the addition of a sixth point labeled separately as "delighted." This approach also seems to yield slightly less skewed distributions but poses the danger of losing interval-level properties. That is, it is a 6-point scale with three labels; the difference between a "5" rating and a "6" is ambiguous. Is the distance from "very satisfied" to "delighted" the same as the distance between a rating of a "4" and a "5"? An additional option that is (regrettably) infrequently employed in applied customer satisfaction research involves data transformation. While a wide variety of transformations are available, our interest focuses on the distribution that is highly skewed.

All things considered, most statisticians working with customer satisfaction research—particularly those involved in model development—advocate scales with more points. This is because of the increased variance and better chance of demonstrating covariance among key variables. The final scaling decision is frequently dictated by past measurements. A company with a stable tracking system that has used a 5-point scale for many years should consider carefully the implications of *losing continuity* in its search for *more variance*. Clearly, the two must be weighed judiciously; a company with stellar customer satisfaction ratings might be inclined to pursue more scale points in an effort to enhance its ability to differentiate top performers from poor performers. On the other hand, there would be few compelling reasons to explore an expanded scale for a company with more modest scores and little interest in multivariate statistical models.

There are no unequivocal answers when it comes to the number of points for a scale. Each case is characterized by the current distribution of scores, the need for tracking continuity, benchmarking, and, in many cases, personal preference. It should be clear that *fewer* than 5 points veers dangerously from the interval properties assumed by most of the multivariate statistical procedures described in this book. Similarly, more than 10 points is very uncommon and may be unmanageable for the respondent.

ALTERNATIVES TO CUSTOMER SATISFACTION

It should come as no surprise that in an effort to understand consumer behaviors some researchers have advocated alternatives to customer satisfaction. Ostensibly, these new constructs are better predictors of critical outcomes such as repeat purchases and, inevitably, corporate profitability. The two principal alternatives to customer satisfaction include customer value perceptions and customer loyalty. The former measure involves consumer evaluations of product (or service) price and quality. The ratio of these two perceptions (price and quality) yields a value assessment. Customer loyalty measurement involves more emotive measures and is considered to be dependent upon customer satisfaction. Each is discussed in more detail in the following pages.

CUSTOMER VALUE VERSUS CUSTOMER SATISFACTION

Customer value perceptions have been offered as a viable alternative to customer satisfaction. Gayle (1994, 8–11) proposed that consumers' value perceptions represented a natural extension of customer satisfaction. The reason companies win or lose customers, Gayle argued, lies in those customers' value perceptions.

Ostensibly, the two primary advantages of customer value management include the ability to link customer value perceptions to market share and the measurement context. With respect to the latter, customer value perceptions are measured in the market as a whole. That is, consumers assess a company's products or services *relative to those of other competitors*. This measurement framework naturally permits comparisons among key competitors.

Gayle operationalized value as the ratio between price and quality, as shown in Figure 1.4. The two axes of the figure represent perceived price and perceived quality. The center diagonal line represents the fair market value. Being above the line is indicative of worse value. Conversely, a company whose product or service is encountered below the line represents a better value.

In the example shown in Figure 1.4, ABC Microchips represents a worse value. Not only is it perceived to have lower-quality products, it is also

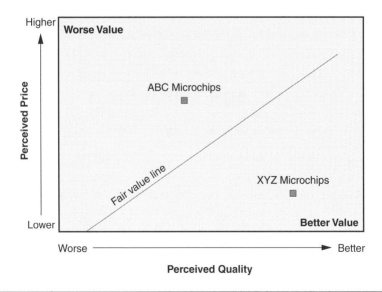

Figure 1.4   Customer value map.

assumed to be considerably more expensive. As a result, it is positioned above the fair value line and presumably would enjoy a much lower share than its competitor, XYZ Microchips. It should be clear that this type of analysis solicits evaluations of all competitors from respondents. While this is certainly appropriate in an industrial setting, wherein a purchasing agent is familiar with various suppliers, it is not clear how well value analysis works with consumers who have little knowledge of competitors' prices and quality. It could be argued that only *perceived* price and quality are required; however, this may change as consumers engage in information gathering. Still, customer value management has a significant following and appears to represent both a challenge and complement to customer satisfaction research.

CUSTOMER LOYALTY VERSUS CUSTOMER SATISFACTION

As the customer satisfaction research environment has matured, a variety of rival and complementary constructs have emerged. Among these is customer loyalty. There appears to be no consensus among researchers concerning the operationalization of loyalty. A large part of loyalty may involve an attitudinal state. It is not, for example, exclusively a *behavior*. Dick and Basu (1994) suggested that customer loyalty is a combination of behaviors and attitudes. In short, the authors maintained that loyal customers are those who had *both* a favorable attitude *and* repeated purchases. Such an approach allows for "spurious loyalty," which arises when purchases are made repeatedly by a customer who does not have a particularly favorable attitude toward the brand.

When considered exclusively as an attitudinal state, loyalty certainly has many desirable behavioral outcomes, such as higher repurchase and lower attrition (customer defection) rates. Repurchase activities or switching behaviors may be *manifestations* of loyalty. The behaviors are not loyalty, but they may be an outcome of loyalty. An aversion to switching and high repurchase rates do not necessarily mean that a customer base is *loyal* per se. Clearly, many other factors can cause these desirable behaviors, including proximity and price, as shown in Figure 1.5.

If loyalty is not a behavior, nor the same as satisfaction, what exactly is it? Recent developments in the operationalization of loyalty have yielded attitude scales designed specifically for the industrial buyer and consumer markets. Loyalty may have two primary dimensions: affective and rational, as shown in Figure 1.6. The *affective* dimension of loyalty has emotional underpinnings and involves human interaction. In contrast, the *cognitive* dimension of loyalty includes evaluations of the business relationship that involve price, proximity, timeliness, and so on.

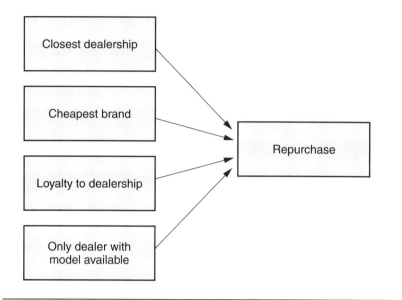

Figure 1.5   Reasons for automobile repurchase.

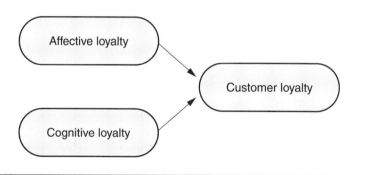

Figure 1.6   Affective and cognitive dimensions of loyalty.

Very few applied customer satisfaction programs currently accommodate a fully-developed operationalization of loyalty. Fewer still attempt to differentiate between the affective and cognitive components of loyalty. Table 1.2 presents a summary of several questionnaire items we have used in an effort to capture both dimensions of loyalty. These were developed based upon qualitative and quantitative experiences across a diverse range of industries in both consumer and business-to-business settings.

In most cases, customer satisfaction is a necessary, but not sufficient, condition for loyalty. We believe that satisfaction and loyalty are two different constructs. Satisfaction is directed specifically at product or service attributes and may be a relatively more dynamic measure. In contrast, loyalty is a broader, more static attitude toward a company in general. As described earlier, it may subsume both rational and emotional elements and is clearly affected by satisfaction.

As shown in Figure 1.7, a causal chain is suggested. First, brand image, service quality, product quality, and price are four critical predictor variables.

Table 1.2   Questionnaire items relating to loyalty.

Cognitive Component Items

"For our firm, staying in the relationship with XYZ Co. is a matter of necessity."

"Discontinuing our relationship with XYZ Co. would result in a loss of business for our company."

"Our company stays in its relationship with XYZ Co. because of the rewards and benefits it brings us."

Affective Component Items

"The people at XYZ Co. are just like us."

"XYZ Co. staff have our best interests at heart."

"A lot of the employees at XYZ Co. are my friends."

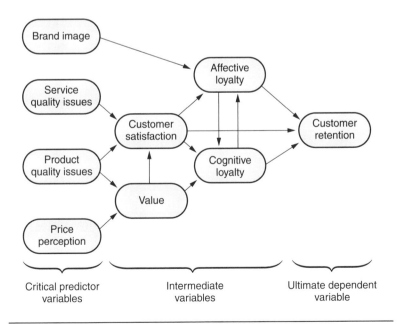

Figure 1.7   Relationship between loyalty and satisfaction.

The first set of intermediate variables involves value and customer satisfaction. Value is shown to be a function of both product quality and price perceptions and directly affects customer satisfaction. The second set of intermediate variables involves the two dimensions of loyalty described earlier. Note that brand image perceptions directly affect the emotional component of loyalty, while value perceptions and customer satisfaction have an impact on the more rational aspects of loyalty. Finally, customer satisfaction and the two loyalty measures directly affect customer retention.

Customer retention is typically measured as an attitudinal item. That is, one or more questionnaire items relating to the respondent's probable future behavior frequently serve as a measure for customer retention. In some industries, it is becoming increasingly common to encounter actual measures of retention in models similar to that depicted in Figure 1.7. Clearly, behavioral measures of retention and its tangents (that is, share of wallet) require a mature customer database that captures actual customer loss.

The implication of Figure 1.7 is that customer retention is dependent upon a complex intermingling of effects. It is likely, for example, that some level of reciprocal causation exists between the affective and cognitive components of loyalty. In effect, they cause one another. The final outcome of the hypothetical causal chain shown in the figure is customer retention. In some instances customer retention has been used as a surrogate for profitability. Whenever possible it is preferable to use individual-level profitability metrics. For example, banks typically track profitability at the household level. Unfortunately, most companies rarely have this type of information at the customer level. However, this situation is changing. Financial services organizations typically have mature profitability measures in place and can gauge the future worth of virtually any customer. One result of this advantage is that the financial services industry has experienced a tremendous increase in activity with respect to the development of models aimed specifically at linking customer satisfaction and profitability. On the other hand, organizations that have little contact with their customers are in a much less appealing situation.

It will be especially interesting to assess the relative effects of customer loyalty and customer satisfaction with respect to key business outcomes. Whether, for example, customer loyalty emerges as a more potent predictor of profitability than customer satisfaction will be of great importance. Of course, in the framework presented in Figure 1.7, customer satisfaction is an antecedent of customer loyalty. As such, it is likely that customer satisfaction will enjoy an important role in the development of corporate profitability even if it is not as strong a predictor as loyalty. This is pure conjecture at this point, unfortunately, since there is no evidence to suggest that the relative impact of these constructs has been tested.

Figure 1.7 is not only a conceptual schematic of how loyalty and customer retention develop. The relationships posited in the figure can actually be tested using a broad class of techniques known as *causal modeling*. This analytical approach permits us to develop complex causal sequences involving multiple dependent variables. Sophisticated reciprocal relationships like the one depicted between affective and cognitive loyalty are possible, and can be tested statistically. We will never be able to establish causality using cross-sectional data, but the causal modeling techniques introduced later in this book allow us to test whether the causal relationships we posit are consistent with the data.

THE FUTURE OF CUSTOMER SATISFACTION RESEARCH

The future of customer satisfaction research will most likely be to continue to establish empirical relationships with key business outcomes. The measurement of customer profitability and its surrogates will play an important role in future research. Customer retention appears to be emerging as a viable surrogate for profitability when the value of individual customer relationships cannot be quantified. Similarly, actual customer behaviors represent a reasonably good substitute for the types of profitability measures that, for example, the financial services industry enjoys. The extent to which these metrics reside in a common data warehouse will largely determine the ease with which these data can be integrated and related to both retention and profitability.

Many companies have developed robust models that permit management to test the effects of changes in customer and employee satisfaction on customer retention and profitability. These tools may include cost–benefit analyses that match the cost of increasing customer (or employee) satisfaction to the resulting increased profits. To the extent possible, customer satisfaction researchers should have such a tool in mind when developing their survey instruments. In this framework, customer satisfaction research is part of a bigger picture in which the intent is more explicit: to increase corporate profits. After all, the corporate interest in customer satisfaction is not happenstance; there is an implicit assumption that increasing customer satisfaction will yield greater profits. And yet, without an empirical link between customer satisfaction and key business measures such as profitability, this relationship remains a mystery.

There have been numerous attempts to produce simulation applications that permit 'what if?' scenarios using customer satisfaction data. One of the most comprehensive studies was conducted by Dillon, White, Rao, and

Filak (1997) using American Express data. The authors' simulation model permitted managers to assess the impact of changing customer satisfaction on overt behaviors like share of spending, card retention, and spending volume. Once a structural equations model was developed and tested, it was migrated to a spreadsheet environment. Using a series of simple commands, managers could test the effects of changing satisfaction with various product and service quality issues. Retention, spending volume, and share of wallet were outcome variables that changed as the service and product quality issues were manipulated in the simulation.

The remainder of this book focuses on techniques that can be used to develop statistical models for predicting key metrics such as retention or profitability. We include a chapter on employee satisfaction because it appears to be an issue of substantive importance with respect to corporate profitability in particular. This is followed by a detailed discussion of the Six Sigma process that was developed at Motorola. Interestingly, customer satisfaction enjoys an important role in the Six Sigma architecture. Chapter 4 addresses current research aimed at linking customer satisfaction and key business outcomes. Chapter 5 and chapter 6 focus on customer retention and the isolation of key business metrics, respectively. These are followed by a detailed discussion of data preparation in chapter 7. Chapters 8, 9, and 10 introduce increasingly rigorous techniques used to link customer satisfaction and employee satisfaction to financial performance measures. These three chapters introduce bivariate measures, multiple regression techniques, and causal modeling, respectively. Finally, chapter 11 presents a futuristic view of customer satisfaction research and describes simulation software advances, decision support systems, and problems associated with global data collection.

2

Employee Satisfaction and Related Phenomena

INTRODUCTION

The earliest employee satisfaction research took place in the 1930s (Hoppock 1935; Kornhauser and Sharp 1932; Roethlisberger and Dickson 1939). Since that time, a substantial amount of progress has been made, both in applied contexts and on theoretical fronts. As early as the mid-1950s, some of the larger companies were conducting employee satisfaction studies on a more or less regular basis. By the 1970s, several research suppliers had developed standardized employee satisfaction questionnaires that were being used widely (Spector 1997). Employee satisfaction has been a key area of research among industrial and organizational psychologists, and hundreds of articles on it have been published in academic journals and trade publications.

Historically, the motivation behind this research was the belief that employee satisfaction influenced employee productivity, absenteeism, and retention. In the early 1980s, an additional issue arose: the influence of employee satisfaction on customer satisfaction in predominantly service-oriented settings.

Concern about these business outcomes also prompted work outside of employee satisfaction, in the areas of employee commitment and company culture and climate. Company culture and climate are outside the scope of this chapter, but we will cover two topics from those areas: market orientation and service climate.

As a result of this work, businesses today that are concerned with employee satisfaction and related attitudes are in a fortunate position in that many of the necessary research tools already exist. Not all research issues have been resolved, of course, but it is usually possible to design and execute a study that will provide a great deal of guidance to management.

POTENTIAL EFFECTS OF EMPLOYEE SATISFACTION

Studies have usually found a relationship between employee satisfaction and productivity (Iaffaldano and Muchinsky 1985; Petty, McGee, and Cavender 1984). The implications of these results, however, are uncertain because this relationship may be partly attributable to causation "going the other way," that is, productivity may influence employee satisfaction.

There have also been studies of the relationship between employee satisfaction and employee turnover (Crampton and Wagner 1994; Michaels and Spector 1982; Mobley, Horner, and Hollingsworth 1978; Hulin, Roznowski, and Hachiya 1985). In many cases, relationships were found.

Scott and Taylor (1985) reviewed the findings of 114 studies and discerned that, on average, the correlation between employee satisfaction and absenteeism was $r = -.15$. However, this analysis probably understates the relationship, because many of those studies did not make a distinction between justified and unjustified absences. Also see Brooke and Price (1989).

Studies have also investigated the relationship between employee satisfaction and customer satisfaction in service-oriented businesses (Rucci, Kirn, and Quinn 1998; Heskett, Sasser, and Schlesinger 1997; Johnson, Ryan, and Schmit 1994; Ryan, Schmit, and Johnson 1996; Tornow and Wiley 1991; Wiley 1996; Wiley and Brooks 2000; Bernhardt, Donthu, and Kennett 2000). In many cases, relationships were found.

SOME ADDITIONAL COMMENTS ON PREVIOUS WORK

As stated earlier, by the 1970s several research suppliers had developed standardized employee satisfaction questionnaires. The one most commonly used was the 72-question Job Descriptive Index (JDI), developed by Smith, Kendall, and Hulin (1969).

The authors conceptualized the drivers of overall satisfaction as falling into five categories:

1. Work
2. Pay
3. Promotion
4. Supervision
5. Coworkers

Another commonly used questionnaire was the Minnesota Satisfaction Questionnaire (MSQ), developed by Weiss, Dawis, England, and Lofquist (1967). It came in two forms, one with 100 questions and one with 20. These authors conceptualized the drivers of overall satisfaction as falling into 20 categories, shown in Figure 2.1:

Of course, a practical limitation of the JDI and the MSQ is that the texts of the actual questions are copyrighted by their respective developers, and a fee is required for their use.

- Activity
- Independence
- Variety
- Social status
- Human relations aspects of supervision
- Technical aspects of supervision
- Moral values
- Security
- Social service
- Authority

- Ability utilization
- Company policies and practices
- Compensation
- Advancement
- Responsibility
- Creativity
- Working conditions
- Coworkers
- Recognition
- Achievement

Figure 2.1   Elements of the Minnesota Satisfaction Questionnaire.

Overview

Disregarding proprietary approaches, it can be said that at the broadest conceptual level, four categories of drivers of overall employee satisfaction have been studied, as follows:

- The employee
- The job itself
- The company
- The environment in which the person and the company exist

As one might expect, applied research pays much more attention to the company than to the other three areas, especially the employee and the environment. The reason for this is practicality: the company has little influence over the environment in which it and the employees exist. Although a company can certainly exercise control over some employee characteristics (such as personality traits) through its hiring process, hiring is typically outside the scope of an employee satisfaction initiative. Readers interested in alternative conceptualizations of the categories of drivers should read Locke (1976).

DIMENSIONS OF SATISFACTION

At the next broadest conceptual level, questions used today typically fall into the following categories:

- Initial preparation of the employee for the job
- Ongoing training opportunities
- The nature of the work performed
- Conflicting requests
- Role ambiguity
- Stress
- Working conditions
- Tools and equipment
- Materials and supplies
- Workload

- Immediate supervisor
- Company policies and procedures
- Pay
- Benefits
- Opportunity to contribute to the company
- Consideration of opinions by the company
- Opportunities for promotion
- Security
- Recognition
- Appreciation
- Coworkers
- Demographics (age, gender, and education)
- Tenure

The Job Itself

A job has the following characteristics, or attributes:

- Routinization
- Role ambiguity
- Conflicting job requirements
- Overload
- Number of different skills used
- Task identity (whether an employee does an entire job or a piece of a job)
- Significance within the company
- Autonomy

Analysis of the relationship between some of these characteristics and overall satisfaction is complicated by the fact that the effects of the characteristics may vary from one individual to another, depending upon their personalities (Hackman and Oldham 1976).

The Company

Typically, most of the questions in the questionnaire fall into this category, particularly in the area of immediate supervisor (for example, the manager respects employees, treats everyone fairly, does what he or she says he or she will do). One of the reasons for this emphasis is that the employee's overall relationship with his or her immediate supervisor is often strongly related to overall employee satisfaction.

The Individual

A large number of factors have been studied in this area, including the importance of work in general to the employee (Kanungo 1982; Mannheim, Baruch, and Tal 1997), personalities that are generally positive or negative (Agho, Mueller, and Price 1993), overall satisfaction with life (Liou, Sylvia, and Brunk 1990), involvement in kinship groups in the local community (Price and Mueller 1981), health status (Ware 1976), demographics, and tenure with the company.

Academic research has shown that many of these factors influence overall employee satisfaction, but for reasons of practicality few are usually included in applied studies. In spite of this practice, we recommend that to the extent possible certain of these factors be included in the analysis. Our reason is that some of these factors can influence employees' responses to some of the attitudinal questions in the questionnaire and therefore can improperly influence the results of driver analyses if excluded (for example, if gender is excluded from the analysis, and if gender influences a given attitudinal question more than it influences others, the apparent effect of that attitudinal question on overall satisfaction will actually be the effect of gender to some extent).

The Environment

Most of the academic research in this area has focused on the effect of the environment on job characteristics, but the environment's direct effect upon employee satisfaction has also been examined to some extent. Perhaps the most notable finding of this research is that the employee's perception of the number of job opportunities outside the company is negatively related to the employee's overall satisfaction. That is, the perception of more job opportunities is associated with less job satisfaction.

OVERALL EMPLOYEE SATISFACTION

Typically, overall employee satisfaction is not measured using just one question. One common approach is to combine the responses to three or four summary questions; the questions most commonly used today are shown in Figure 2.2.

In the JDI questionnaire mentioned earlier, overall satisfaction was measured by combining the responses to three questions: those regarding satisfaction with work, satisfaction with coworkers, and satisfaction with supervision.

There are two advantages of combining responses to multiple questions as opposed to using only one question. One is that the concept of overall satisfaction is so broad that it cannot be measured with only one question. Another advantage, seldom discussed but still very important, has to do with measurement error. That is, the mean of the responses to two or more questions usually has less measurement error than the response to any one of the questions individually.

Note that each of the questions being combined here is broad in scope. An alternative approach that is sometimes used is to combine all of the *narrow* questions in the questionnaire (for example, my manager does what they say they will do). We have two reservations regarding this approach. One is that it requires that we deal with the difficult issue of how much weight should be given to each of the questions. Making this determination is difficult because the questions are interdependent in the "real world," not just intercorrelated in the data. Another reservation is that this approach yields an accurate measure of overall satisfaction only to the extent that the battery of questions is complete, meaning that we have identified all of the

---

1. Overall, I am satisfied with my job.

2. Overall, I am satisfied with X as a place to work.

3. I am proud to work at X.

4. I would recommend X to a relative or friend as a place to work.

5. Even if I had the opportunity to get a similar job at the same salary and benefits with another company, I would stay at X.

Figure 2.2   Summary of employee satisfaction questions.

drivers of overall satisfaction. Admittedly, this approach does have the advantage of an overall satisfaction measure that is usually somewhat "easier to move."

COMMITMENT

There is a lack of consensus on the appropriate definition of commitment. Perhaps the best definition was developed by Mowday, Porter, and Steers (1982), as "the relative strength of an individual's identification with and involvement in a particular organization." Notice that there are three characteristics of commitment so defined: a strong belief in and acceptance of the organization's goals and values, a willingness to exert considerable effort on behalf of the organization, and a strong desire to maintain membership in the organization. A good overview of this literature can be found in Mowday, Porter, and Steers (1982).

Commitment differs from overall satisfaction in that commitment is broader. There is also a difference in emphasis, with commitment involving more emphasis on the organization and overall satisfaction involving more emphasis on the job. Also, it is reasonable to believe that commitment is more stable over time.

Porter and Smith (1970) and Mowday, Steers, and Porter (1979) developed a battery of commitment questions, shown in Figure 2.3. Note that by design these questions reflect the three characteristics of commitment cited earlier.

A summary measure of commitment is obtained by taking the simple average of these 15 questions.

The reason for the attractiveness of employee commitment to companies and managers is obvious, of course. We would expect that commitment would be related to business outcomes that are traditionally measured (such as productivity and absenteeism) as well as to less tangible behaviors (such as good corporate citizenship). As often as not, a relationship is found. In spite of this encouragement and the fact that many companies conduct commitment studies, problems are often encountered in applied work. The difficulty is that developing driver questions for the questionnaire is much more difficult than is the case with, say, customer loyalty questionnaires. That is, customer loyalty questionnaires often contain questions at three levels of specificity (for example, overall satisfaction with the bank, overall satisfaction with the teller, and courtesy of the teller), whereas commitment questionnaires often contain questions at only one level of specificity: the general level exemplified by the questions in Figure 2.3.

1. I am willing to put in a great deal of effort beyond that normally expected in order to help this organization be successful.

2. I talk up this organization to my friends as a great organization to work for.

3. I feel very little loyalty to this organization. (R)

4. I would accept almost any type of job assignment in order to keep working for this organization.

5. I find that my values and the organization's values are very similar.

6. I am proud to tell others that I am part of this organization.

7. I could just as well be working for a different organization as long as the type of work were similar. (R)

8. This organization really inspires the very best in me in the way of job performance.

9. It would take very little change in my present circumstances to cause me to leave this organization. (R)

10. I am extremely glad that I chose this organization to work for over others I was considering at the time I joined.

11. There's not too much to be gained by sticking with this organization indefinitely. (R)

12. Often, I find it difficult to agree with this organization's policies on important matters relating to its employees. (R)

13. I really care about the fate of this organization.

14. For me this is the best of all possible organizations for which to work.

15. Deciding to work for this organization was a definite mistake on my part. (R)

An "R" denotes a negatively phrased item (which must be reverse-coded).

Figure 2.3 Commitment questions.

Source: Mowday, R., R. Steers, and L. Porter. 1979. "The Measurement of Organizational Commitment." *Journal of Vocational Behavior* 14: 224–47. Used with permission.

MARKET ORIENTATION AND SERVICE CLIMATE

By definition, market orientation is an organizational culture, defined as "the pattern of shared values and beliefs that help individuals understand organizational functioning and thus provide them with the norms for behavior in the organization" (Deshpandé and Webster 1989). But there is not a consensus in the literature on the object(s) of those values and beliefs, namely, "what the culture is about." Some early authors stressed the customer, while other authors stressed the gathering of information on the market and dissemination within the organization. Still other authors included the competition.

Not nearly as much work has been done in this area as in employee satisfaction, and most of the work that has been done is academic in nature. The most discussed batteries of questions are those developed by Narver, Jacobson, and Slater (1993), Kohli, Jaworski, and Kumar (1993), and Deshpandé, Farley, and Webster (1997). These batteries are found in Figures 2.4, 2.5, and 2.6. Narver and Slater conceived of market orientation as having three components: customer orientation, competitor orientation, and interfunctional coordination. Kohli, Jaworski, and Kumar conceived of market orientation as comprising intelligence generation, intelligence dissemination, and responsiveness.

Deshpandé and Farley (1999) conducted an analysis in which the questions from these three batteries were examined together, with the goal of eliminating those that were redundant or otherwise not needed. Their elimination process left 10 questions. However, this was only one analysis, and therefore this finding should be regarded as preliminary.

Some of the questions from these three batteries have been examined with respect to their empirical relationship with business outcomes. Pelham (1999) conducted a study of 229 industrial manufacturing companies and found that market orientation was more strongly related to business outcomes than either company environment (such as intensity of competition) or company strategy. Narver and Slater (1990) conducted a study of 140 strategic business units from the forest products division of a major corporation and found that market orientation was strongly related to business outcomes, even after the effects of industry environment were controlled for.

It will be encouraging if the results of these early studies are confirmed by later work. Even if they are, though, the future of market orientation research in applied settings is uncertain. One reason for this uncertainty is that measures of market orientation will probably exhibit a great deal of inertia and, as such, improved performance on these measures will be difficult to achieve.

In our strategic business unit:

1. Our salespeople regularly share information within our business concerning competitors' strategies.

2. Our business objectives are driven primarily by customer satisfaction.

3. We rapidly respond to competitive actions that threaten us.

4. We constantly monitor our level of commitment and orientation to serving customers' needs.

5. Our top managers from every function regularly visit our current and prospective customers.

6. We freely communicate information about our successful and unsuccessful customer experiences across all business functions.

7. Our strategy for competitive advantage is based on our understanding of customers' needs.

8. All of our business functions (marketing/sales, manufacturing, R&D, finance/accounting, and so on) are integrated in serving the needs of our target markets.

9. Our business strategies are driven by our beliefs about how we can create greater value for customers.

10. We measure customer satisfaction systematically and frequently.

11. We give close attention to after-sales service.

12. Top management regularly discusses competitors' strengths and strategies.

13. All of our managers understand how everyone in our business can contribute to creating customer value.

14. We target customers where we have an opportunity for competitive advantage.

15. We share resources with other business units.

Figure 2.4 Items proposed by Narver, Jacobson, and Slater.

Source: Narver, J., R. Jacobson, and S. Slater. *Market Orientation and Business Performance: An Analysis of Panel Data.* Working paper, Marketing Science Institute. Report Number 93-121. Used with permission.

1. In this business unit, we meet with customers at least once a year to find out what products or services they will need in the future.

2. In this business unit, we do a lot of in-house market research.

3. We are slow to detect changes in our customers' product preferences. (R)

4. We poll end users at least once a year to assess the quality of our products and services.

5. We are slow to detect fundamental shifts in our industry (such as in competition, technology, and regulation). (R)

6. We periodically review the likely effect of changes in our business environment (such as regulation) on customers.

7. We have interdepartmental meetings at least once a quarter to discuss market trends and developments.

8. Marketing personnel in our business unit spend time discussing customers' future needs with other functional departments.

9. When something important happens to a major customer or market, the whole business unit knows about it within a short period.

10. Data on customer satisfaction are disseminated at all levels in this business unit on a regular basis.

11. When one department finds out something important about competitors, it is slow to alert other departments. (R)

12. It takes us forever to decide how to respond to our competitors' price changes. (R)

13. For one reason or another we tend to ignore changes in our customers' product or service needs. (R)

14. We periodically review our product development efforts to ensure that they are in line with what customers want.

15. Several departments get together periodically to plan a response to changes taking place in our business environment.

continued

Figure 2.5   Items proposed by Kohli, Jaworski, and Kumar.

Source: Reprinted with permission from the *Journal of Marketing Research,* published by the American Marketing Association. A. Kohli, B. Jaworski, and A. Kumar, 1993, 30:467–77.

continued

16. If a major competitor were to launch an intensive campaign targeted at our customers, we would implement a response immediately.

17. The activities of the different departments in this business unit are well coordinated.

18. Customer complaints fall on deaf ears in this business unit. (R)

19. Even if we came up with a great marketing plan, we probably would not be able to implement it in a timely fashion. (R)

20. When we find that customers would like us to modify a product or service, the departments involved make concerted efforts to do so.

An "R" denotes a negatively phrased item (which must be reverse-coded).

Figure 2.5   Items proposed by Kohli, Jaworski, and Kumar.

Source: Reprinted with permission from the *Journal of Marketing Research,* published by the American Marketing Association. A. Kohli, B. Jaworski, and A. Kumar, 1993, 30:467–77.

1. We have routine or regular measures of customer service.

2. Our product and service development is based on good market and customer information.

3. We know our competitors well.

4. We have a good sense of how our customers value our products and services.

5. We are more customer focused than our competitors.

6. We compete primarily based on product or service differentiation.

7. The customer's interest should always come first, ahead of the owner's.

8. Our products and services are the best in the business.

9. I believe this business exists primarily to serve customers.

Figure 2.6   Items proposed by Deshpandé, Farley, and Webster.

Adapted from *Factors Affecting Organizational Performance: A Five Country Comparison* by R. Deshpandé, J. Farley, and F. Webster. Marketing Science Institute, Cambridge, MA, 1997.

1. My branch manager supports employees when they come up with new ideas on customer service.

2. My branch manager sets definite quality standards of good customer service.

3. My branch manager meets regularly with employees to discuss work performance goals.

4. My branch manager accepts the responsibilities of his or her job.

5. My branch manager gets the people in different jobs to work together in serving branch customers.

6. My branch manager works at keeping an orderly routine going in the branch.

7. My branch manager takes time to help new employees learn about the branch and its customers.

Figure 2.7   Items proposed by Schneider, Parkington, and Buxton.

Adapted from "Employee and Customer Perceptions of Service in Banks" by B. Schneider, J. Parkington, and V. Buxton. *Administrative Science Quarterly* 25 (1980): 252–67.

Schneider, Parkington, and Buxton (1980) developed a battery of questions measuring service climate. These questions are found in Figure 2.7. Note that although the discussions in the literature suggest that these questions were developed independently of the market orientation questions we have discussed, there is some overlap between the two concepts.

DISCUSSION

Market orientation is studied much less frequently than either employee satisfaction or commitment. This may appear strange to the reader, as we would intuitively expect the questions used to measure market orientation to be positively related to business outcomes, and therefore of interest to managers. We would expect this partly because many of these questions focus on the company's attention to customers and competitors, which is strongly stressed in marketing theory. In addition, common sense would lead us to expect that interdepartmental communication and cooperation would increase operational efficiency.

There are several reasons for this disparity in the frequency of research. One is the relative lack of validation studies of market orientation research. The results of the validation studies that have been conducted are impressive, but relatively few such studies have been conducted.

Another reason is that managers at lower and middle levels within the company have less ability to influence market orientation and therefore have less practical interest in it. Similarly, management steps to influence market orientation are more difficult to identify and implement.

Service climate is also studied much less frequently than employee satisfaction and commitment. This disparity is more difficult to explain, as the reasons cited above apply less to service climate. In addition, the service climate questions we discussed earlier focus on the behaviors and attitudes of the employee's immediate manager, which is one of the main focuses of employee satisfaction questionnaires.

Industry Differences

An issue that has not received much discussion in the literature is the existence of industry differences: the relative importance of the attributes under study, or even their presence, may differ from one industry to another. For example, intuitively we would expect that the relative importance of the ingredients of market orientation would differ between high-technology and traditional manufacturing industries.

An Additional Basis on Which Companies Can Compete

Companies in many product categories in developed countries are faced with the problem of simultaneously encountering high consumer expectations and strong competition. Even when a company competes in a narrowly defined segment, it often encounters three or four strong competitors that may have products very similar to those of the company's.

Companies in this situation are therefore faced with the difficult question "How can we differentiate ourselves from our competitors and give customers a reason to choose us over them?" One way is to differentiate on the basis of service quality. An additional benefit of this is that it may be more difficult for competitors to copy, to the extent that the service quality is driven by company culture or climate. That is, company culture or climate may be more difficult to replicate than the capability to manufacture a particular product.

3

The Six Sigma Approach

INTRODUCTION

While customer satisfaction measurement enjoys a substantial position as a criterion in the Malcolm Baldrige National Quality Award (see Figure 1.1), it is even more integral in other quality programs. The "Six Sigma" system developed at Motorola, for example, relies heavily upon customer satisfaction measurement and tracking. This approach involves defect minimization and employs the normal distribution to assess the impact of quality improvement efforts. Breyfogle (1999) provides a comprehensive review of Six Sigma and its implementation.

The Six Sigma approach to management science can be attributed to Robert W. Galvin, who, as CEO of Motorola, laid the foundation in the 1980s for what is now a highly structured measurement and analysis program, according to Love (2000, 1–4). Motorola's focus on quality yielded dramatic results, including winning the Malcolm Baldrige National Quality Award.

In an excellent article outlining Six Sigma, Blakeslee (1999) describes the system as being empirically driven, placing emphasis on root cause analysis and closed-loop business processes. The primary objective of the Six Sigma process is to reduce variance around critical business measures relating to service or product quality. Reducing process variation yields improved products and services. Indeed, services or products that are produced at the optimum Six Sigma level yield a mere four defects per million.

Figure 3.1 illustrates the type of process variance reduction that the Six Sigma approach tries to achieve. The left portion of the figure depicts the distribution of time spent waiting to see a bank teller at a typical suburban branch. Waiting in line for more than four minutes is considered unacceptable

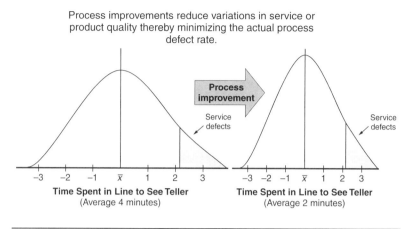

Process improvements reduce variations in service or product quality thereby minimizing the actual process defect rate.

Process improvement

Service defects

Service defects

−3 −2 −1 $\bar{x}$ 1 2 3
Time Spent in Line to See Teller
(Average 4 minutes)

−3 −2 −1 $\bar{x}$ 1 2 3
Time Spent in Line to See Teller
(Average 2 minutes)

Figure 3.1   Six Sigma process variance reduction.

by most customers. In the Six Sigma context, customers who wait in line for four minutes or more have experienced a service defect. The left-hand side of Figure 3.1 presents a distribution in which a significant proportion of bank customers experience defective service levels.

One of Six Sigma's *operational* objectives is to reduce process variance and provide zero defect services and products. Perhaps more important is that at the *strategic* level Six Sigma is intended to keep the organization focused on and aligned with customer needs. The right-hand side of Figure 3.1 presents an improved process. The distribution of waiting time is now markedly more peaked. This is reflected in the smaller standard deviation around the mean waiting time. Clearly, fewer customers experience defective service levels in this distribution as well.

A focus on customer needs and expectations at the strategic level means gathering marketplace information. Competitive intelligence plays a key role at the strategic level. Knowing how satisfied competitors' customers are and what drives their satisfaction is crucial in the Six Sigma framework. This type of information can help identify trends, opportunities, and service or product quality gaps.

One of the most appealing aspects of the Six Sigma approach involves the closed-loop relationship between business process improvements and financial accountability. That process improvements should be linked to financial outcomes is a basic requirement of the Six Sigma approach. It is likely, in fact, that this aspect of Six Sigma precipitated additional academic and applied research into linking customer satisfaction and corporate profitability.

This book focuses on establishing empirical links between customer satisfaction, employee satisfaction, and critical business outcomes such as market share and profitability. In this regard, Six Sigma is of special interest. One of the core philosophies of the Six Sigma program is to demonstrate the bottom-line benefits of process improvements. Indeed, Six Sigma teams are typically expected to complete four or more projects each year with a bottom-line contribution of at least $500,000, according to Breyfogle (1999, 8). Fuller (2000, 312), for example, reported that savings of over $100 million were realized at Seagate within the first 18 months after adopting the Six Sigma approach. Hoerl (2000, 318) reported phenomenal savings at some of the country's largest companies. Motorola, for example, was cited as having saved nearly $1 billion in three years. Similarly, Allied Signal saved over $2 billion after adopting Six Sigma. Finally, GE was reported to have realized savings of over $1 billion in 1998 and $2 billion in 1999.

It is easy to see how improving quality by reducing defective products or service interactions simultaneously yields more satisfied customers and reduces costs. Figure 3.2 illustrates the dual effects that may be realized when the Six Sigma process has been fully embraced. Benefits such as customer satisfaction, market share, and complaint de-escalation have been referred to as "soft" dollar results by Fuller (2000, 312). They are differentiated from "hard" dollar returns such as reduced costs for material and less rework. With respect to quality programs in general, it is safe to say that few so explicitly require that projects yield hard dollar returns.

Programs such as Six Sigma are important because they can help us increase both customer and employee satisfaction. The premise of this book

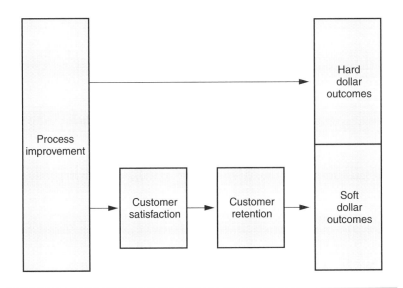

Figure 3.2   Hard dollar and soft dollar outcomes of process improvement.

is that increasing customer and employee satisfaction has a positive effect on critical business outcomes such as market share and profitability. Take the case of Blue Sky Airlines, which tracks both customer and employee satisfaction, as shown in Figure 3.3. To simplify this example, we have selected only three customer satisfaction and three employee satisfaction issues.

Figure 3.3 is characterized by a left-to-right causal sequence. Business processes and systems make up the heart of any organization's operations. They are also presumed to affect both customer and employee satisfaction. Figure 3.3 presents a simplification of customer and employee satisfaction. The former is measured as satisfaction with three variables: the reservation system, baggage handling, and check-in waiting time. Customers' satisfaction with these three aspects of Blue Sky Airlines affects their overall satisfaction. In a similar fashion, overall employee satisfaction has three antecedents: satisfaction with pay, coworkers, and job variety.

Customer satisfaction and employee satisfaction have a reciprocal relationship. As shown in Figure 3.3, satisfied employees tend to produce satisfied customers and vice versa. Finally, note that customer satisfaction affects profitability through customer retention. Employee satisfaction similarly affects profitability through lower turnover rates.

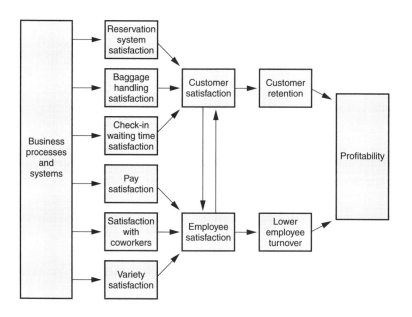

Figure 3.3 Blue Sky Airlines: relationship between customer and employee satisfaction and profitability.

The entire model depicted in Figure 3.3 suggests that business processes and systems affect specific aspects of customer and employee satisfaction. These in turn exert influence on customer retention and employee turnover. Higher rates of customer retention and lower turnover rates yield greater profits. The figure does not accommodate the direct impact of changing business processes and systems on profitability. For example, making a process such as check-in registration more streamlined could result in a decreased need for staff. This would directly affect Blue Sky Airlines' cost structure inasmuch as "hard" dollar savings can be quantified. In short, the relationships in Figure 3.3 are highly constrained and limited to "soft" savings as described earlier and by Fuller (2000, 312).

THE SIX SIGMA PROCESS

As shown in Figure 3.4, the Six Sigma process can be broken into five stages: definition, measurement, analysis, improvement, and control. The definition phase involves articulating the nature of problematic process components and forecasting the benefits of correcting or improving them. In the case of Blue Sky Airlines, this could mean determining why check-in lines tend to be slow. For example, it might be determined that some passengers wait in the line even though they are already checked in. A sign indicating that check-in is not required for passengers with preassigned seating might solve the problem. Similarly, Blue Sky managers might

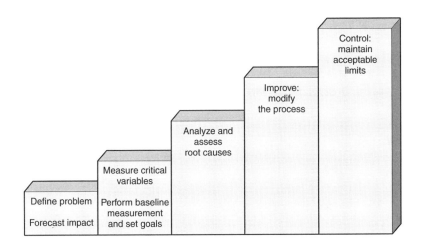

Figure 3.4   Steps in the Six Sigma process.

determine that their problem with misrouted baggage is attributable to junior grounds crew members who are still somewhat unfamiliar with some procedures. Again, the definition step requires only that the problem be spelled out.

The measurement phase of the Six Sigma process entails defining which process variables should be quantified and tracked. In the case of Blue Sky Airlines, this means operationalizing the key variables: the percentage of baggage misrouted and the average time spent waiting in the check-in line. The measurement phase also requires some baseline measurements and goal setting with respect to desired quality levels. In the case of missing baggage, the measurement phase requires that Blue Sky management track the daily proportion of missing baggage complaints for a month. Similarly, if the problem involved check-in waiting time, personnel could unobtrusively observe and record line length at key points during the day.

An understanding of the root causes underlying problematic processes is the core of the analysis stage of the Six Sigma process. It involves developing a good picture of why certain problems exist. In short, the root cause of baggage loss may be untrained handlers. Similarly, the root cause of the long lines at the Blue Sky Airlines terminal may very well involve uninformed passengers rather than staffing problems. The analysis stage requires us to assess system problems in these terms.

The improvement phase involves an assessment of how changing specific process variables will affect the critical outcome variable. For example, periodic training sessions for new baggage handlers could be assumed to have an impact on the critical outcome variable: the average daily proportion of bags reported missing. Lack of information is the likely cause of waiting line length, so some form of consumer education and signage could yield significant changes in the average check-in waiting time.

The final step in the Six Sigma process involves control. This maintenance step requires us to ensure that the modified system operates at the desired level. For example, once Blue Sky Airlines institutes training programs for baggage handlers, it must continue to monitor lost baggage complaint levels and ensure that they stay within the prescribed window. Should baggage complaints suddenly skyrocket, a new root cause analysis would be warranted.

The focus of Six Sigma has, over time, broadened. What was initially a program focused on manufacturing processes has gradually expanded to include a substantive customer focus. As Hahn, Doganaksoy, and Hoerl (2000, 319) noted, Six Sigma now has an explicit goal to "wow" the customer. In recent years this new customer focus has precipitated an emphasis on product and service improvements that directly affect customers.

Product (or service) reliability has become an important aspect of Six Sigma programs. Product or process reliability is considered to be a primary antecedent of customer satisfaction.

SIX SIGMA TOOLS

Six Sigma is a highly data-driven process. The Six Sigma manager's toolbox is packed with powerful statistical techniques. These range from simple distribution plots to more sophisticated tools such as multiple regression analysis. This section provides a review of the tools available to the Six Sigma manager. The techniques presented in this section can be considered in three categories: univariate statistics, bivariate statistics, and multivariate statistics.

Six Sigma places considerable emphasis on univariate statistics. In particular, measures of dispersion and central tendency play important roles. Means, trimmed means, and variances are cornerstones of the Six Sigma measurement process. Correlations and simple linear regression represent the most important bivariate statistics used in Six Sigma. Finally, multiple regression enjoys a prominent position in more advanced Six Sigma analysis. A variety of regression diagnostics including residual analysis and collinearity assessment are included in the Six Sigma analysis toolbox.

Perhaps the most intriguing tools available in the Six Sigma toolbox are the numerous graphical techniques employed to synthesize data. The statistical process control chart is an integral part of the Six Sigma measurement process. Figure 3.5 presents an example of a control chart. As shown, the upper and lower confidence levels (UCL and LCL) are depicted above and below the center line, which depicts the mean. The

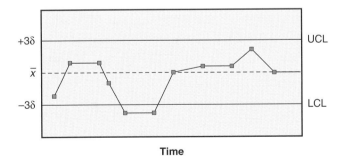

Figure 3.5 Six Sigma control chart.

UCL and LCL lines are set at three standard deviations above and below the mean. When the measurement crosses the UCL or LCL line, a significant change in the process may have occurred. Breyfogle (1999, 161–62) suggests that the process should appear random. That is, there should be no systematic patterns in the process control chart. Nonrandom patterns suggest instability.

Other process shifts can be detected by observing nonrandom patterns in the data points. For example, Breyfogle (1999, 162) suggests that having 10 out of 11 data points on the same side of the center line suggests a shift in the process. Many other heuristics exist for statistical process control chart diagnostics. The main benefit of this type of display is that it clearly depicts points that are significantly above or below the mean rating.

Product reliability testing represents a significant portion of system assessment in the Six Sigma program. The sequential reliability test summarizes failure rates for a given product. Figure 3.6 presents hypothetical data for three products. The x axis of the figure depicts cumulative hours of testing, and the y axis presents the number of failures. As shown, Product A was associated with only about 5 failures in 5000 hours of testing. It is shown in the "passed test" section of the figure. Product B, on the other hand, yielded 15 failures in 3000 hours of testing. In this case, the product is maintained in the testing process. Finally, Product C was associated with about 20 failures in only 2000 hours and was considered to have failed the test.

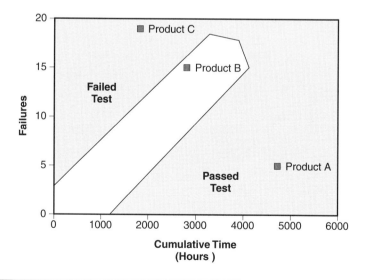

Figure 3.6 Six Sigma sequential reliability test.

QUALITY FUNCTION DEPLOYMENT

Quality function deployment (QFD) is a set of quality management tools that is very customer oriented. It is frequently referred to as the "house of quality" because the primary diagram used by this approach resembles a house. Figure 3.7 illustrates the extent to which customers and their needs drive the quality management process. QFD helps organizations to convert customer needs into process or product designs. Its customer focus makes it of special interest in this chapter.

Breyfogle (1999, 243–46) provides an excellent summarization of how the QFD chart is completed. First, customer requirements must be operationalized. These are typically revealed through qualitative efforts such as focus groups or more formal quantitative survey research. Care should be taken to ensure that the customer requirements listed in the QFD chart closely approximate the language used by customers. Failing to do so could yield erroneous results when the QFD chart is interpreted.

The second component of the QFD chart that we address involves the importance of customer requirements. Typically, importance ratings are of the "stated importance" sort. That is, respondents rate how important each product or service feature is to them on a Likert-type scale. This might

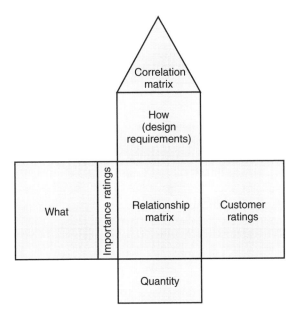

Figure 3.7   Quality function deployment.

involve having respondents rate the importance of each feature in the customer requirements list on a 5-point scale. Interestingly, there has not been a concerted effort to employ *derived* importance metrics in the QFD chart's feature importance section. For example, conjoint analysis could be used to yield the derived importance of various features.

Next, customer perceptions of the existing design and specific competitors must be measured for each of the service or product issues discussed earlier. Respondents rate the attractiveness of the existing design relative to that of each of several competitors. The results of this exercise make up the right-hand side of the QFD chart shown in Figure 3.7.

Design requirements are presented at the top of the QFD chart. These are typically produced by engineers in manufacturing environments or quality experts in service industries. The design requirements are generated specifically to address the customer requirements described earlier. For example, if travelers who fly Blue Sky Airlines indicate they want more legroom, engineers might consider changing the seat-back position, increasing the space between seat rows, or expanding the first-class section. All of these represent designs that could address a very specific customer requirement.

The "roof" of the house of quality is composed of "correlations" among the design requirements, as shown in Figure 3.8. These are really simply an assessment of the degree to which each design requirement is related to the others. The correlations are not empirically based.

The main relationship matrix reflects the interrelationships between the design requirements and the customer requirements. A judgment must be made by the quality manager with respect to the relationship between design and customer requirements. These are summarized in the main body of the QFD chart; the relationship matrix portion of the chart summarizes how customer and design requirements can be interwoven.

The house of quality's "basement" comprises objective tests relating to the design requirements. Competitors' products are included. These are typically presented in raw form. For example, if the design requirement were "minimal time for check-in," then the entries in this section of the QFD chart would be in minutes. Similarly, if the design requirement were "more legroom," then the entries would be in inches. It is also important to rate each design requirement in terms of difficulty. This information is typically presented above the objective tests described earlier.

Figure 3.8 illustrates a completed QFD chart prepared for Blue Sky Airlines. At first glance the myriad symbols and entries in the chart are perplexing. Indeed, the QFD chart subsumes a great deal of information. Notice that the customer requirements are separated into two areas: seat functionality and seat comfort. Design requirements range from adding individual seat temperature adjustments to increasing seat width.

The "roof" of the house of quality is made up of design requirement intercorrelations. Four levels of significant association are included. The absence of one of the four symbols indicates a lack of correlation between two design requirements. Note that these correlations are not empirically obtained; they are estimated by the QFD chart creator in collaboration with process improvement team members. The QFD chart in Figure 3.8 suggests that there is a strong relationship between the individual temperature adjustment and the upgraded seat package. This is because the latter includes a rudimentary temperature adjustment function.

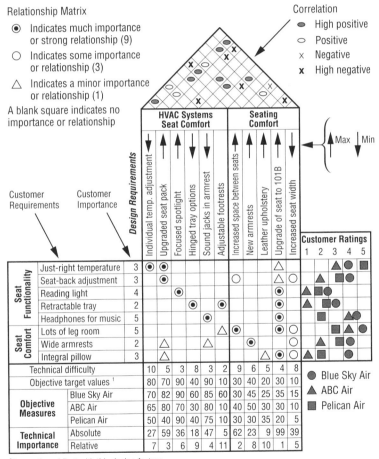

Figure 3.8   The house of quality: Blue Sky Airlines.

The actual customer ratings of Blue Sky Airlines and two competitors are depicted at the far right of the figure. Survey respondents were asked to rate all three companies with respect to the eight customer requirements on the far left of the figure. The customer rating data suggest that Blue Sky Airlines performs very well relative to the two competitors. In nearly every case, Blue Sky Airlines is rated better than the two competitors.

The central relationship matrix linking customer requirements and design requirements is associated with one of four entries. The first symbol (◉) indicates a strong relationship between the customer and design requirements. A lower level of importance is denoted by another symbol (○). A trivial level of importance is indicated using a third symbol (△). Finally, a blank square indicates a lack of association between a design and a customer requirement.

The relationship matrix shown in Figure 3.8 suggests the following. First, each of the eight customer requirements is associated with at least one design requirement. For example, the customers' desire for an integral pillow in the seat is related to four design requirements: upgraded seat pack, leather upholstery, upgrade of seat to 101B, and increased seat width. Note that the relationships differ in magnitude, as depicted by the three different symbols.

The technical difficulty of achieving each design requirement is provided under the primary relationship matrix. Difficulty ratings use a 10-point scale, with higher numbers indicating greater difficulty.

At the bottom of the QFD chart are objective target values. In this application, the entries indicate the proportion of the Blue Sky Airlines fleet that would *ideally* have each design requirement. These estimates are followed by objective measures of the current fleet status. Objective measures of the competitors' fleets are also included. For example, we would ideally like to see 80% of the fleet with individual temperature controls on each seat. Blue Sky Airlines has this feature on 70% of its fleet, while its two main competitors (ABC Air and Pelican Air) have 65% and 50%, respectively.

The bottom of Figure 3.8 presents the absolute and relative technical importance metrics for each design requirement. The absolute importance of a design requirement is calculated by multiplying the relationship matrix value entries by the customer importance rating. For example, the absolute technical importance of the first design requirement (individual temperature adjustment) is 27 (9×3). This calculation is completed for each design requirement until all 11 have technical importance metrics. Finally, the relative technical importance number is simply a rank ordering of the 11 technical importance metrics. The seat upgrade design requirement emerges with the highest technical importance, since its absolute value (99) far surpasses that of any of the other options.

Combined, the customer, competitive, and design components of the QFD chart provide an integrated perspective on process or product improvement. One improvement that can be made to the QFD chart involves the customer importance ratings. This is a stated rather than derived metric. The latter approach to ascertaining the importance of customer requirements involves using a statistical technique known as conjoint analysis. In conjoint analysis, respondents are asked to rate or rank various product configurations. The product configurations are selected in such a way that every feature is tested with respect to desirability. Derived importance metrics reveal which feature will have the greatest effect on propensity to purchase or, more generally, desirability.

The chasm between stated and derived importance metrics is significant. While derived importance metrics quantify the effect of a product feature on its desirability, stated importance metrics are more problematic. They have come into disfavor primarily because customers say *everything* is important to them. More to the point, what customers say is important may, in reality, not be an area that management should focus on. Allen and Rao (2000, 69–72) provide a comprehensive review of the differences between stated and derived importance.

The tools presented in this chapter are important because they go beyond simple customer satisfaction measurement and reporting. Indeed, Six Sigma and the QFD approach are *systemic* approaches to organization management. The key is that while many organizations track their customer satisfaction, fewer make a concerted effort to address the service and product quality issues that drive satisfaction. Process and product quality improvement programs are necessary to push customer satisfaction levels higher. A customer satisfaction program that does not subsume process or product quality initiatives may yield stagnant results.

Invariably, customer satisfaction surveys encompass a wide variety of specific service and product quality items. Key driver analysis is typically employed to isolate the issues that have the greatest impact on overall customer satisfaction. Implicit in the key driver framework is that processes or product characteristics will be improved in an effort to maximize overall satisfaction. It should be clear from the reviews of both the Six Sigma and QFD approaches that—if at all possible—customer satisfaction data should be integrated with competitive data, customer requirements, and product or process performance metrics.

This book is consistent with the philosophy just described. That is, customer satisfaction is treated as one component of a larger strategic vision. As such, its relationship with other business variables is of great interest. In particular, how customer satisfaction relates to customer loyalty, employee satisfaction, customer retention, and overall corporate profitability will be the focus of our ensuing discussions.

LINKING SIX SIGMA TO
FINANCIAL PERFORMANCE

One aspect of Six Sigma that makes it of particular interest to this discussion is that there have been attempts to link process improvement explicitly to profitability. Earlier, we demonstrated that process improvements can yield both hard dollar outcomes and soft dollar outcomes. The former involves financial enhancement directly linked to the process. Such would be the case when, for example, a complex process is simplified. The simplification might involve time savings that could be linked directly to hourly wages. When even a modest time savings in a complex process is achieved, the cumulative savings over the course of a year could be considerable. Hard dollar outcomes attributable to Six Sigma initiatives are very easy to quantify and are most typically encountered in success stories. Figure 3.9 provides a high-level perspective on how Six Sigma yields financially desirable outcomes.

As Eckes (2001, 6) reports, in the mid-1990s under the guidance of CEO Jack Welch, General Electric enjoyed substantive hard dollar returns attributable to Six Sigma. Among these were inventory turns that escalated to 9.2 from 5.8. Further, the ratio of plant and equipment expenditures to depreciation dropped dramatically. This ratio is a reflection of manufacturing efficiency, and its change confirmed that under Six Sigma GE was becoming a more streamlined company that significantly reduced hidden costs associated with reworking products and services.

Naumann and Hoisington (2001, 26) suggest that organizations striving to link their Six Sigma initiatives to hard dollar returns rely upon an activity-based cost (ABC) accounting system. This, according to the authors, facilitates establishing an unambiguous relationship between the process improvement and its dollar impact. The ABC accounting architecture permits management to quantify the costs of labor, material, and support associated with specific activities. A set of activities may be subsumed by a single process. Naumann and Hoisington concede, however, that few organizations have this form of accounting system. In its absence, the authors suggest using one of several "less refined" approaches.

One less sophisticated approach to activity-based cost accounting involves an assessment of staffing. An examination of total workforce hours may have utility. The authors suggest that activities that require 40% or more of the total should be scrutinized; it is likely that these activities can be streamlined. Labor savings are clearly one major benefit of Six Sigma initiatives. If at all possible, workforce hours should be linked to specific activities within a process. By doing this, management can directly measure the effect of process improvements in terms of labor hours.

Another approach to approximating the ABC accounting method involves an examination of material costs. Tracking material use as it

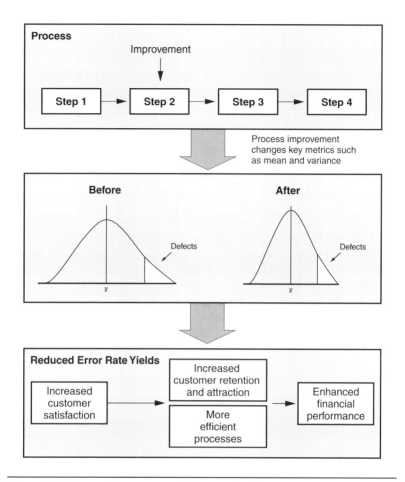

Figure 3.9   Process improvement link to profitability.

relates to processes should be performed. Six Sigma programs often yield tremendous savings in reduced waste and scrap and further enhance inventory control, shrinkage rates, and acquisition costs.

Naumann and Hoisington (2001, 156) suggest that yet another alternative or adjunct to the highly desirable ABC accounting approach involves scrutinizing processes designed to produce customized products or services. While mass production processes are typically continuously improved throughout their lifetimes, processes that focus on custom products and services often do not benefit from formal optimization efforts. Instead, custom processes often remain inefficient because of their idiosyncratic nature. Since there is ostensibly little room for standardization, fewer efforts to streamline custom processes are made.

Clearly, there are numerous approaches to quantifying the hard dollar outcomes associated with Six Sigma programs. The most sophisticated programs can differentiate between labor and materials benefits. Recording time and material expenditures and linking them to specific processes—or even subprocesses—is imperative if an accurate assessment of a Six Sigma initiative is to be made. Large, complex organizations may actually be more capable in this regard than smaller organizations. The latter may not have sophisticated cost-accounting systems in place. In order to link labor and material expenditures to specific processes, fundamental data must be captured.

Establishing soft dollar outcomes associated with Six Sigma programs requires the adoption of a theoretical framework for understanding the sometimes tenuous relationships that reflect *consumer behaviors*. Compared with the hard dollar costs of labor and materials, soft dollar benefits involving customer perceptions and their behavioral consequences are more difficult to establish. It is clear that one critical variable in the soft dollar outcome mix is customer satisfaction. Process improvements are presumed to yield enhanced services and products that result in more satisfied customers. For example, customers who spend an average amount of time in a line to see a bank teller will tend to be more satisfied if this time is shortened. Similarly, if the proportion of customers who encounter a product defect drops from 8% to 5%, we would expect overall customer satisfaction to increase. Streamlined processes and lower product defect rates result in happier customers or, at least, fewer *dissatisfied* customers.

If we assume that process improvements can affect customer satisfaction, then we must turn our attention to the relationship between customer satisfaction and key business outcome measures such as profitability, market share, and share of wallet. There is no lack of anecdotal evidence that links customer satisfaction and desirable financial outcomes. As Fornell (1999) suggested, the relationship between customer satisfaction and profitability seems almost requisite:

> This is a sign of a well-functioning market economy. If firms were not rewarded financially for satisfying their customers, the structure of the economy, or parts thereof, would need to be examined. By the same token, if companies that cause dissatisfaction among their customers were not punished by consumer and investor rejection, one would have to question the structure of the market.

In their book focusing on establishing empirical relationships among customer attitudes, Six Sigma process improvements, and financial results, Naumann and Hoisington (2001, 17–37) provide numerous examples in which increased customer satisfaction yielded desirable business outcomes.

Of particular interest are the results presented by the American Customer Satisfaction Index (ACSI) project, which is sponsored by the American Society for Quality (ASQ) and the University of Michigan Business School's National Quality Research Center.

The ACSI is based on quarterly data and over 50,000 interviews conducted annually with customers of measured companies. The index measures customer satisfaction with 164 companies and 30 government agencies. It relies upon a 100-point scale; benchmarking against it is problematic without access to the raw data and proprietary data-handling tools used to manage the huge ACSI database.

The 164 companies account for approximately 40 percent of the U.S. GDP. This is the only cross-industry set of national metrics that explicitly attempts to link customer satisfaction to financial outcomes such as profitability. The effects of customer satisfaction on profitability, however, are not broken down with respect to soft dollar and hard dollar returns. Nevertheless, the data are intriguing because they strongly confirm a relationship between customer satisfaction and financial outcome variables. As Naumann and Hoisington (2001, 28) report, companies with high ACSI scores enjoyed an average increase in stock price of 4.6 percent. In contrast, companies with low ACSI scores had, on average, a decrease in stock price of 0.4 percent. Similarly, companies in the top 50 percent ACSI score group generated an average $24 billion in value, while those firms in the bottom half of the distribution created only $14 billion in shareholder value.

Again, the ACSI program does not explicitly address the difference between hard dollar and soft dollar returns. It seems clear, however, that both are assumed. As Fornell (2001) suggested, companies with high customer satisfaction levels probably enjoy benefits that include higher retention rates with respect to customers, employees, and repeat business:

> A test for a well-functioning market economy would be the extent to which buyers can reward sellers that satisfy them and penalize those who don't. Eventually, these rewards and penalties should show up in corporate earnings. High levels of customer satisfaction are indicators not only of repeat business, which typically accounts for an overwhelming portion of a company's profit, but also of the general health of a company. A company with satisfied customers often has motivated and loyal employees, good products, and effective management.

It seems reasonably clear that improved processes will yield more satisfied customers. In turn, there appears to be unambiguous evidence to uphold the belief that companies with more-satisfied customers will, on average, do better financially than companies with less-satisfied customers.

The linkage between better products or services and customer satisfaction and the subsequent relationship between customer satisfaction and financial outcomes represent the soft dollar return on the Six Sigma process.

The next two chapters focus more closely on the relationship between service and product quality, customer satisfaction, and profitability. Chapter 4 introduces the notion of "return on quality" and isolates customer retention as a key intermediate variable in the causal sequence linking quality, customer satisfaction, and profitability. Thus, chapter 4 is concerned with the soft dollar effects of service and product quality. Chapter 5 suggests that while customer retention may be the critical link between customer satisfaction and profitability, it is important to differentiate the retention of highly profitable customers from the retention of those who are less profitable. In effect, chapter 5 focuses on how to optimize the relationship between customer satisfaction, retention, and profitability by focusing exclusively on the retention of individually profitable customers.

4

The Customer Satisfaction–Profit Link

INTRODUCTION

It should come as no surprise that very few companies even consider the relationship between customer satisfaction and profitability. Establishing an empirical link between customer satisfaction and key business outcomes such as profitability and market share assumes that a number of criteria are met. Of greatest concern is the organization's maturity. Companies with relatively unsophisticated or very new customer satisfaction programs are not likely to pursue the types of analysis described in this book.

The desire to link customer satisfaction to important business indicators is becoming a more salient topic in many organizations today. More and more often, managers of quality programs are being called upon to demonstrate the bottom-line financial impact of their programs. Keiningham and Zahorik (1995, 7) suggested that since 1991 there has been "an explosion of interest" in linking customer satisfaction to important business performance indicators.

For many years, corporate America was immersed in the "religion of quality." Few would question the implicit assumption that greater quality meant more profits. This chapter reviews the literature and focuses on research that explicitly attempts to link quality improvement or customer satisfaction improvements to changes in key business metrics such as profitability and market share.

Bhote (1996, 3–19) describes how companies mature with respect to their customer focus, management, tools, and organizational structure. The four stages of development are presented in Table 4.1. The first stage is referred to as "innocent," and the second stage, characterized by immaturity,

Table 4.1 The four stages in the evolution of customer loyalty.

Characteristic	Stage 1: Innocent	Stage 2: Awakened	Stage 3: Progressive	Stage 4: World-Class
1. Scope	Inward preoccupation	Cost reduction driven	Competition driven	Adding value to customer
2. Focus	Commodity	Technology/quality	Customer satisfaction	Customer loyalty
3. Customer segmentation	No differentiation	Elimination of "dog" customers	Internal customer and company stakeholders	Core customers
4. Management	Bureaucratic, dictatorial	Micro-management	Coach	Vision, inspiration, leadership
5. Organization	Vertical management	Matrix management	Delayering; flat pyramid	Cross-functional teams; CCO
6. Goals	Fighting "forest fires"	Making the budget	Meeting customer expectations	Delighting customers
7. Customer requirements	Determined by management/ engineering	Determined by market research	Determined by conjoint analysis, other techniques	Determined by QFD
8. Customer measurements	Maximize sales, profits	Minimize complaints	Maximize market share	Maximize customer retention
9. Analysis of feedback	Little or no follow-up	Survey instruments never changed	Customer satisfaction index (CSI)	Former and non-customers analyzed
10. Improvement tools	Seven tools of QC	Brainstorming and statistical tools	Creative tools: VE and force field analysis	Business process reengineering

Source: Beyond Customer Satisfaction to Customer Loyalty: The Key to Greater Profitability (AMA Management Briefing), by Keki R. Bhote. Copyright © 1996, AMACOM, a division of the American Management Association, New York. Reprinted with permission.

is referred to as "awakened." The third and fourth stages are referred to as "progressive" and "world-class," respectively.

As shown, the four stages of development are increasingly sophisticated. For example, in its infancy an organization's scope is very introspective. In contrast, as a company matures it becomes more externally focused and finally emphasizes providing value to customers. In a similar vein, a company's focus moves from a commodity mind-set to customer satisfaction and finally to customer loyalty.

The most immature companies tend not to segment their markets. As they reach their pinnacles, however, customer segmentation systems become quite sophisticated and even differentiate between core and peripheral customers. Similarly, companies in their infancy tend to have bureaucratic management styles. This is in stark contrast to the mature world-class organization, which has a management style characterized by vision, inspiration, and leadership.

Structurally, companies in various stages of the maturation process differ substantively. For example, it is frequently the case that young companies have bureaucratic or dictatorial styles. As they mature, companies with this management structure tend to become flatter and eventually have cross-functional teams. The goals of companies at different stages of the maturation process also differ significantly. Young companies tend to specialize in "fighting forest fires," while more mature world-class companies focus on meeting customer expectations and, finally, on delighting customers.

Interestingly, customer requirements for companies in their infancy tend to revolve around products and engineering. As they grow older, these companies will become more customer focused, and eventually some may employ tools such as QFD to determine goals. With respect to measurement tools, the infant company is likely to gauge success in terms of sales and profit maximization. The company that grows and reaches world-class status, however, focuses instead on maximizing customer retention.

Customer feedback is treated very differently depending upon which stage a company is in. Companies in their infancy do little to follow up on customer feedback, while mature, world-class companies frequently employ statistical models to isolate customers at risk of leaving. Finally, quality improvement tools differ across the maturation process. For example, young companies typically focus on quality control, while those that meet world-class standards frequently employ business process reengineering.

It should be clear that not all companies are ready to link customer satisfaction to business outcome variables such as profitability and market share. Indeed, the approach outlined in this book may be appropriate only for world-class companies that have the management structures, quantitative tools, and data structures in place. A company need not be a multibillion-dollar conglomerate to employ the tools described in this book. However, it should meet most of the criteria in Table 4.1 that are associated with world-class performance.

The remainder of this chapter presents a series of studies conducted primarily in the 1990s. Each attempted to link customer satisfaction to return on investment or some other financial outcome. Some of these studies linked customer satisfaction to financial outcomes via a third, intervening variable such as customer retention. Nonetheless, the studies presented in the remainder of this chapter all attempted to empirically establish a relationship between certain desirable financial outcomes and customer satisfaction.

LINKING SATISFACTION TO THE BOTTOM LINE

That some businesses are interested in maximizing customer satisfaction doesn't necessarily reflect their corporate altruism. Indeed, an interest in customer satisfaction is almost always self-centered. After all, why should businesses measure, track, and attempt to improve customer satisfaction if there is no tangible benefit? The underlying premise, especially before the early 1990s, was that satisfied customers yielded greater profits. Companies with more satisfied customers would be more successful and more profitable. And yet there was only limited empirical evidence to support this notion. Buzzell and Gale (1987), for example, produced evidence to link market share growth and service quality; however, the lack of more substantive evidence supporting the contention that customer satisfaction was instrumental in ensuring corporate profitability led the Council on Financial Competition to issue the following indictment in 1989:

> Service quality as an issue is seriously overrated; service certainly is not as important as the mythic proportions it has taken on in industry trade publications and conferences.

This type of skepticism likely precipitated a flurry of academic and industry research aimed at linking customer satisfaction to corporate profitability and market share. Rust and Zahorik (1993), for example, focused on the retail banking industry. Their research related customer satisfaction, retention, and profitability. The authors concluded that retention rates drive market share and that customer satisfaction was a primary determinant of retention. Rust and Zahorik's model permitted them ". . . to determine the spending levels of each satisfaction element which will maximize profitability, subject to the assumptions of the model and accuracy of parameter estimation" (1993, 212).

Rust and Zahorik (1993, 211) suggested a number of ways companies could improve customer satisfaction and thereby increase retention rates, which drive profitability. Among these were "training programs to help personnel to be more responsive to customers, upgraded facilities, better data-handling systems, customer surveys and newsletters." The authors further suggested that companies with weak customer service cultures may need to fundamentally change the way they do business.

AN INTERVENING VARIABLE: CUSTOMER RETENTION

More recent efforts by authors such as Zeithaml, Berry, and Parasuraman (1996) have also attempted to refine the link between customer satisfaction and profitability by focusing on an intervening variable: retention. The authors presented four objectives associated with the study:

- A synthesis of existing research that links service quality and behavioral outcomes

- A hypothetical model that relates service quality to certain behaviors that precede defection

- The presentation of empirical evidence connecting service quality and behavioral intentions

- The development of a fundamental research agenda that will link individual-level behaviors to outcomes such as sales and customer retention

Using a mail-survey methodology, the authors achieved a 25 percent response rate and reported a total of 3069 returned surveys. The survey itself included several operationalizations of service quality. The first involved the SERVQUAL scale originally introduced by Parasuraman, Berry, and Zeithaml in 1988. The second battery included a set of refined items intended to reveal five dimensions of service quality: reliability, responsiveness, assurance, empathy, and tangibles.

Behavioral intentions were developed in an effort to capture the full range of possible outcomes. A 13-item battery, partially based on previous research by Cronin and Taylor (1992) and Boulding et al. (1993), was developed. It ostensibly measured a wider range of behavioral intentions. Some of the unique survey content involved the likelihood of paying a price premium and behavioral loyalty despite price increases.

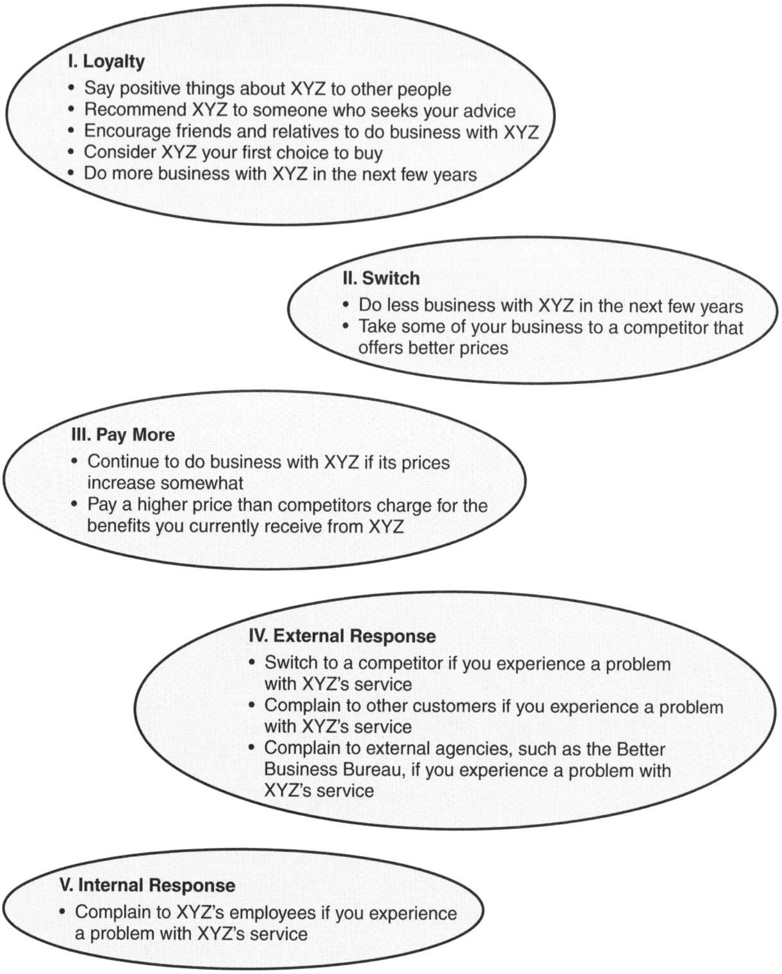

I. Loyalty
- Say positive things about XYZ to other people
- Recommend XYZ to someone who seeks your advice
- Encourage friends and relatives to do business with XYZ
- Consider XYZ your first choice to buy
- Do more business with XYZ in the next few years

II. Switch
- Do less business with XYZ in the next few years
- Take some of your business to a competitor that offers better prices

III. Pay More
- Continue to do business with XYZ if its prices increase somewhat
- Pay a higher price than competitors charge for the benefits you currently receive from XYZ

IV. External Response
- Switch to a competitor if you experience a problem with XYZ's service
- Complain to other customers if you experience a problem with XYZ's service
- Complain to external agencies, such as the Better Business Bureau, if you experience a problem with XYZ's service

V. Internal Response
- Complain to XYZ's employees if you experience a problem with XYZ's service

Figure 4.1   Five dimensions of behavioral intention.

The data were analyzed using a factor analytic approach. The 13-item battery was reduced using this method. Figure 4.1 summarizes the five-factor solution the authors presented. As shown, the five factors encompassed five dimensions of behavioral intent.

When the behavioral intention measures were regressed on the SERVQUAL scale, the results strongly confirmed the authors' hypotheses. In short, the following propositions were supported:

- Customers who do not experience service problems have the best behavioral intention scores

- Customers who do experience problems and have them favorably resolved have moderately favorable behavioral intention scores

- Those with unresolved problems were associated with the least favorable behavioral intention scores

Zeithaml, Berry, and Parasuraman concluded that the relationships between service quality, retention, and profitability were anything but straightforward. Nonetheless, their study strongly confirmed the intuitively appealing notion that service quality significantly affects behavioral intentions.

THE IMPACT OF CUSTOMER SATISFACTION IN A HEALTHCARE SETTING

Other researchers focused on operationalizing actual consumer behaviors and their attitudinal antecedents. In a study involving 15,000 patients discharged from 51 related hospitals, Nelson and Rust (1992) focused on questions such as the following:

- What constitutes quality healthcare?

- How can costs be cut while increasing quality?

- Does quality drive hospital costs?

- How does quality affect profitability?

Nelson and Rust focused on two issues in particular. First, they were interested in the relationship between customer satisfaction and profitability. Next, their attention turned to the individual effects of specific quality dimensions on profitability.

Participants were mailed a questionnaire that consisted of 41 items spanning 10 categories of hospital quality. Content areas included admissions, nursing service items, housekeeping items, living arrangements, and the discharge process. Averaging the scores of items within each of the 10 categories yielded 10 distinct summary measures:

- Admissions

- Daily care

- Information exchange

- Nursing service

- Physician service

- Auxiliary medical service

- Housekeeping

- Living arrangements

- Discharge

- Billing

Indicators of hospital financial performance were gleaned from industry standards and were available to the parent company that oversaw all 51 hospitals. The financial performance variables included the following:

- Earnings before depreciation, interest, and taxes per bed

- Net revenue per bed

- Return on assets

In order to reduce the complexity of the analysis and circumvent collinearity, the authors relied upon principal components analysis to simplify the set of 10 hospital quality ratings. This method trimmed the field of predictor variables to four:

- Factor 1: Medical and billing

- Factor 2: Daily care, information, and nursing

- Factor 3: Admissions

- Factor 4: Discharge

The authors employed multiple regression analysis to assess the effect of the hospital quality dimensions on the financial outcome variables. Of particular interest was how much variance in each of the three financial outcomes could be accounted for by the set of quality issues. A separate multiple regression analysis was conducted for each of the three financial outcome variables. Each one of the regression models yielded statistically significant results. With respect to explanatory power, the adjusted R^2 values ranged from .10 to .29. At first these values might appear to be abysmal. However, when we consider the nature of the dependent variables, the models' efficacy is noteworthy. In effect, Nelson and Rust's analysis suggests that up to 29 percent of the variation in these financial outcomes can be accounted for by the four quality dimensions.

In terms of the individual dimensions of hospital quality and their effect on the three financial outcome variables, the authors were surprised at one result in particular. The regression analyses confirmed that factor 2 (daily care, information, and nursing) was not a statistically significant antecedent of any of the three financial outcome variables. The authors concluded that one explanation for this could be that high-quality nursing and daily care services produced more rapid recoveries among patients which, in effect, lowered profitability. The reason for this may be that shorter stays in less-intensive care situations yield fewer profits for the hospital.

CUSTOMER SATISFACTION, SHARE, AND PROFITABILITY

Anderson and Fornell (1994) studied a large data set of Swedish companies in their quest to produce empirical evidence that customer satisfaction pays off with greater profits. The authors presented five hypotheses relating customer satisfaction to attractive financial outcomes. The five hypotheses are presented in Figure 4.2.

The first hypothesis suggests that economic returns are one outcome of customer satisfaction. In short, higher levels of customer satisfaction are presumed to yield greater economic returns.

- H_1: Customer satisfaction is a positive correlate of economic returns

- H_2: Perceived quality should have a positive effect on satisfaction

- H_3: Market perceptions of quality will positively affect satisfaction

- H_4: Market expectations of quality are adaptive; the size of the adaptive updating will be small

- H_5: With respect to customer satisfaction, the impact of perceived quality will be stronger than the effect of quality expectations

Figure 4.2 Hypotheses relating customer satisfaction to economic returns.

Despite its apparent simplicity, this first hypothesis captures a myriad of possible relationships between two key variables. For example, if increasing customer satisfaction yields a greater return on investment, at what point does this relationship begin to falter? Diminishing returns must come into play at some point. Similarly, how much should a company invest in its effort to increase customer satisfaction in hopes of reaping bigger and bigger financial rewards?

The second hypothesis summarized in Figure 4.2 suggests that *market-perceived quality* will have a positive effect on overall satisfaction. This is an intuitively palatable statement that accommodates the accumulation of sentiment (good or bad) relative to a company's goods or services. Past experiences with a company's product will be associated with a "half-life" of unknown duration. One *recent* bad experience, for example, may more strongly affect quality perceptions than a similarly negative experience in the distant past.

The third hypothesis links *quality expectations* in the market to customer satisfaction. Anderson and Fornell proposed that a customer's experience in period X_{t-1} would influence expectations in the current period X_t. In short, past experience will drive current expectations. The authors referred to this phenomenon as "adaptive expectations." This experiential information is constantly updated in the marketplace; its effects are felt on both the production and consumption sides of the equation.

Customers in mature, stable industries have more experience with suppliers' quality. The implication is that in more mature industries' adaptive expectations, the most recent (X_{t-1}) experiential information will have a lesser effect on current assessments of quality than in less mature industries. In other words, recent experiences will have a smaller impact on marketplace quality judgments compared with the cumulative effect of past information. Again, customers in mature markets will have greater experience with quality and, as a result, recent and perhaps anomalous variations in quality will carry less weight. Adaptive expectations are at the core of Anderson and Fornell's final hypothesis. They suggested that the marketplace has adaptive expectations involving suppliers' goods. The relative weight given to the most recent information concerning quality will, they argued, be considerably less than the weight of all past historical information.

The study of Swedish industrial data yielded some very interesting results. Both quality and expectations had a positive effect on customer satisfaction. Quality had a stronger effect on customer satisfaction. The authors concluded that a substantive "carryover effect" supported the proposition that customer satisfaction is cumulative. The effect of quality expectations on customer satisfaction were also statistically significant.

The financial outcome variables produced strong statistical models. In fact, return on investment (ROI) was strongly linked to customer satisfaction. There was also evidence to support the contention that customer satisfaction is a cumulative phenomenon that develops over time. The implication is that short-term variations in quality will not necessarily affect overall customer satisfaction.

Interestingly, this study suggested that as market share increased, customer satisfaction declined. A modest ($r = -.25$) but statistically significant correlation between the two variables was encountered. The authors found that an increase in market share from one year to the next was often associated with a *decrease* in customer satisfaction. One explanation for this phenomenon is that as companies grow, they are less able to meet the idiosyncratic needs of certain customers. They are no longer able to focus on the individual customer and must instead make products that will appeal to a broader mass market.

In an effort to demonstrate the efficacy of the ROI model, the authors presented an empirical prediction of the value of a one-point increase in customer satisfaction. When projected for five years, the results were startling. Consider applying the Swedish industrial model to a sample of U.S. firms with average assets of $7.5 million and average ROI of 11%. The results would be considerable: ". . . the cumulative incremental return associated with a continuous one-point increase in satisfaction over a five-year span would be $94 million, or 11.4% of current ROI" (Anderson and Fornell, 67).

Clearly, the Anderson and Fornell study represents a significant contribution to the growing literature linking customer satisfaction to business outcome variables. Their explicit illustration linking actual revenues to changes in customer satisfaction is noteworthy. As the body of research treating customer satisfaction as an antecedent of critical business outcome variables becomes more mature, it is likely that some general heuristics will be developed. For example, these might be very general guidelines with respect to the impact that service versus product satisfaction variables have on profitability.

A "RETURN ON QUALITY" MODEL

That many companies have not yet quantified the financial benefits of their quality programs led Rust and Zahorik (1995) to focus specifically on linking service and product quality with financial outcome variables. The fact that many companies were disappointed with their quality programs led

Rust and Zahorik to focus their attention on a quantitative measure that they termed "return on quality," or ROQ.

The ROQ approach, according to the authors, makes four fundamental assumptions. The first of these is that quality is an investment not unlike other investments in plant production, human resources, or office equipment. Unfortunately, most companies don't take this tack. Instead, the modal approach to the quality investment equation is a leap of faith that it will produce returns at some point. Few companies explicitly link their quality investments to actual dollars earned or saved.

The second fundamental assumption of the ROQ approach is that quality efforts must be financially driven. This is consistent with the first assumption that quality is an investment. The third assumption suggests that it is possible to spend too much on quality. For example, it is possible to spend too much on a given initiative or to focus funds on inappropriate improvement areas, according to Rust and Zahorik. Implicit here is that not all quality improvement programs are valid. The authors' fourth ROQ assumption suggests that some quality initiatives may have questionable efficacy. Indeed, too often the "religion of quality" has permitted programs of questionable value to flourish.

In their effort to quantify the impact of service quality improvements on profitability, Rust and Zahorik posited a chain of effects beginning with a hypothetical quality improvement effort. If effective, the quality improvement effort yields increased perceived quality, increased customer satisfaction, and possibly reduced costs. Increased customer satisfaction then exerts a positive effect on customer retention and also on word-of-mouth advertising. The latter is important because most authors have not explicitly acknowledged that word-of-mouth advertising is a benefit of service quality initiatives. Based upon the increased customer retention and positive word-of-mouth advertising, revenues and market share are presumed to go up. The decreased marketing costs combined with the increase in the customer base lead to greater profitability, according to the Rust and Zahorik model.

Accountability is a cornerstone of the ROQ quality improvement model. Rust and Zahorik outlined a series of five steps, shown in Figure 4.3. These steps are critical to the ROQ process. The first step involves information gathering. Industry trends, competitive positioning, and customer satisfaction data should all be examined in the information-gathering stage. The second step in the ROQ quality improvement process involves the articulation of ROQ outcomes using the information gathered in the first step. This step should yield projections involving the financial implications of the quality improvement process. These might include, for example, estimates of market share.

1. Preliminary information gathering

2. Explication of possible outcomes

3. Limited improvement testing

4. Empirically based financial projections

5. Rollout of quality improvement program

Figure 4.3   The five steps of the ROQ quality improvement process.

The third stage in the ROQ quality improvement process involves limited testing of improvements. For example, if a national pizza chain were interested in the effects on customer satisfaction of a drive-through service, it would be prudent to test the enhancement in a limited number of stores. This testing process would permit management to predict with greater certainty the outcome of a national rollout.

The fourth step in the ROQ process involves financial projections based on empirical data. These might involve a cost–benefit analysis wherein the costs of the drive-through service could be contrasted with the marginal increase in sales attributable to the new service. Finally, the fifth stage involves a full rollout of the quality improvement effort.

The link between customer retention and profitability appears unequivocal to some authors. Reichheld and Sasser (1990, 105), for example, concluded that retention was a stronger predictor of corporate success than "scale, market share, unit costs, and many other factors usually associated with competitive advantage." By focusing on the link between customer satisfaction and an intervening variable (retention) known to affect profitability, Zeithaml, Berry, and Parasuraman (1993) were able to build a strong case for the importance of service quality.

Danaher and Rust (1996) also focused on the financial benefits of service quality. Their study took a slightly different tack. Rather than focus on increased profitability as a result of lower attrition rates, Danaher and Rust emphasized the utility of service quality in *attracting* new customers and increasing the usage rates of existing customers. Of particular importance was the benefit of word-of-mouth advertising attributable to high service quality levels.

The effect of customer satisfaction on profitability may be exerted through an intervening variable such as retention. Rust, Zahorik, and

Keiningham's (1994) effort to establish an ROQ measure, for example, linked customer satisfaction to customer retention, which in turn was used as a predictor of market share. Based upon a set of assumptions that included the possibility that a company could spend too much on customer satisfaction, the authors developed a computer application that would permit users to forecast the profit implications of service quality improvement efforts.

Reichheld (1996, 33–62) also discusses the relationship between customer retention and company revenue. Essentially, he argues that three relationships, paraphrased below, work together in such a way that a small improvement in the customer retention rate can have a surprisingly large effect on company revenue.

- The customer *retention rate* has a strong effect on average customer *tenure*. (The other determinant is the customer acquisition rate).

- In many product categories, there is a relationship between customer *tenure* and *purchase behavior*, with a customer who has more tenure spending more per year on average.

- A small change in the customer *retention rate* may, if maintained, have a substantial effect on the *number of customers* possessed by the company. This is an example of the phenomenon of "compound interest." For example, if a company's customer attrition rate is five points lower than its customer acquisition rate, its customer base will by definition grow at 5% a year, thereby doubling in absolute size every 14 years.

An improvement in the customer retention rate has direct and indirect effects on company revenue, according to Reichheld. The direct effect is the customer retention rate's effect on the number of customers possessed by the company. The indirect effect occurs through the customer retention rate's effect on the average customer tenure, and the average customer tenure's effect on the yearly spending of the average customer.

THE ACSI STUDY

As noted in chapter 3, one of the most compelling empirical linkages between customer satisfaction and profitability involves the American Customer Satisfaction Index, which was launched in 1994. The ACSI initiative has at least three primary objectives:

- Measurement—to quantify the quality of economic output based upon subjective consumer input

- Contribution—to provide a conceptual framework for understanding how service and product quality relate to economic indicators

- Forecasting—to provide an indicator of future economic variability by measuring the intangible value of the buyer–seller relationship

To recap, this program, which is operated jointly by the National Quality Research Center at the University of Michigan and the American Society for Quality (ASQ), is based on quarterly data and over 50,000 interviews conducted annually with customers of measured companies. The ACSI measures customer satisfaction with 164 companies and 30 government agencies. The index, which relies upon a 100-point scale, is updated on a rolling basis with new measures for two economic sectors replacing data from the prior year.

The ACSI survey process involves collecting data at the individual customer level. Telephone surveys are conducted using random samples. Since its inception, the ACSI program has conducted more than 250,000 consumer interviews. The resultant database is immense and provides a wealth of information; thus far, the program has published 20 quarterly national indices and less frequent annual indices at the company, industry, and sector levels.

Each quarter, the ACSI data are aggregated at the company level in order to create the company-level scores. Industry indices are calculated as well and are weighted by the sales of each company within a given industry. A further rollup is available at the sector level. Sector indices subsume industry indices and are also weighted by sales. The sectors are based on the one-digit Standard Industrial Code (SIC) classifications.

The theoretical framework underlying the ACSI program is depicted in Figure 4.4. As shown, the causal sequence begins with customer expectations and perceived quality measures that are presumed to affect, in order, perceived value and customer satisfaction (the ACSI metric). Customer satisfaction, as measured by the ACSI, has two antecedents: customer complaints and, ultimately, customer loyalty. The latter is measured in terms of price tolerance and customer retention. One fundamental assumption of the model is that for most companies repeat customers are a considerable profit source. Customer retention, which is estimated as *reported repurchase probability*, is a strong predictor of profitability. Using this structure, researchers at the University of Michigan are able to treat a company's customer base as an asset and calculate its net present value over time.

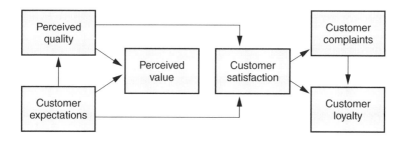

Figure 4.4 The ACSI model of customer loyalty.

The ACSI project has resulted in dozens of papers that confirm the relationship between quality, customer satisfaction, and financial performance. Anderson and Fornell (2000) provide a good background treatment of the ACSI program that facilitates an understanding of the types of data that are involved. An earlier work by Fornell et al. (1996) also provides considerable detail with respect to the ACSI. Anderson and Fornell's collaboration with Rust (1997) provides an excellent treatment of the relationship between customer satisfaction, productivity, and profitability. The authors examine the relationship in both products and services. Although their focus is not the relationship between customer satisfaction and financial performance, Bryant and Cha (1996) discuss the expectation measures that are part of the ACSI questionnaire. Fornell (1995) provides a more general discussion of the relationship between the quality of economic output and market share.

The size of the ACSI database and the fact that 50,000 interviews are conducted annually has facilitated investigations of the relationship between customer satisfaction and financial performance at the industry level. For example, several researchers have concentrated on the automotive industry. Johnson, Herrmann, and Gustafsson (1997) focused specifically on the relationship between quality, satisfaction, and retention in the automotive industry. Auh and Johnson (1997) also focused on customer retention in the automotive industry. These authors, too, linked quality, satisfaction, and retention.

The ACSI program represents one of the few research projects to collect *longitudinal* data relating customer satisfaction, retention, and financial performance. Since the ACSI project involves quarterly data collection and has been running continuously since the fourth quarter of 1994, there will be about 40 quarters of data available when the program celebrates its 10-year anniversary. This will permit even more robust inferences concerning the relationship between the index and key financial performance metrics by industry.

WHAT IS LOYALTY?

One shortcoming of many of the studies that operationalize customer retention based upon respondent input is that the relationship between the respondent's assessment of his or her likelihood to repurchase a given product or service and the actual *behavior* is often tenuous. Frequently, three or four questionnaire items are used to measure repurchase intention or, more generally, loyalty:

- How likely are you to *purchase* this product/service again in the next three months?

- How likely are you to *recommend* this product/service to a friend or colleague?

- Overall, how *satisfied* are you with this product/service?

Often a composite of these three items is used as a general measure of loyalty or repurchase likelihood. In other cases, only the first item, which relates directly to repurchase likelihood, is used. Some survey programs consider only those customers who score in the top 10 percent of each of these items to be likely repeat customers and, therefore, highly desirable. A score of a "9" or "10" on each of these items when measured on a 10-point scale is a reasonable reflection of repurchase intent.

We feel strongly that while repurchase behavior is a highly desirable outcome of customer satisfaction, the *behavior itself is not loyalty*. Rather, repurchase behavior is a manifestation of an attitudinal state we call loyalty. Loyalty is an attitude a consumer has about a service or product that leads to a long-term relationship and customer retention. Loyalty is not the repurchase behavior itself. Just because a customer repurchases regularly from a supplier does not necessarily mean he or she is loyal, per se. There may be a wide variety of other reasons the customer purchases repeatedly from the supplier. Figure 4.5 confirms that repeat purchases can be the result of widely varying circumstances.

As shown in Figure 4.5, repeat customers—or, more generally, customer retention—may be the result of any number of seemingly fortuitous circumstances. For example, a customer may lease a new car from the same dealer every two years over the course of a decade or more. To the dealer, this is a loyal customer. It is quite possible, however, that the customer's repeat business is due only to the dealer's proximity to his home. Similarly, repeat purchase may be due to mere habit or be based solely on price. Other examples exist in which the repeat purchase is made by error. Take, for example, the case of a purchasing agent who thinks he has switched suppliers from Company A to Company B but is actually still buying from Company A due to a

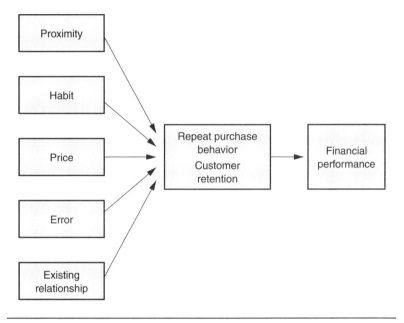

Figure 4.5 Reasons for repurchase behavior.

paperwork problem that he is unaware of. In this case the buyer may appear to be loyal but in actuality is not even aware he is a customer.

The importance of the preceding information is that should circumstances change, many ostensibly loyal customers may defect. In the case of the proximate dealership, if a competitor should move in closer to the customer, he might switch his allegiance based solely on proximity. Similarly, customers who repeatedly purchase a product or service based solely on price may quickly defect if a lower price alternative emerges. And, of course, the purchasing agent who erroneously concludes he is purchasing from Company B may recognize his mistake and correct it.

As shown in Figure 4.6, the attitude we refer to as loyalty may be defined as having two distinct dimensions. The first is considered to be the *affective* dimension and reflects the emotional attachment a consumer may develop for a product or service provider. Emotional ties may interweave relationships with the brand, its image, or the company's employees.

A second dimension of loyalty involves *cognitive* drivers. These are more rational in nature and may involve the consumer's critical assessment of his or her relationship with the supplier. These evaluations may involve attitudes toward the supplier's product quality, price, problem resolution, or distribution structure. It seems reasonable to conclude that compared with customer satisfaction, attitudinal loyalty is much less dynamic. While customer satisfaction may rise and fall based on service or product quality experiences, customer loyalty changes more slowly.

Of course, a myriad of other phenomena may affect an individual's decision to repurchase a product or service. Figure 4.7, for example, suggests a framework in which customer loyalty, customer satisfaction, customer value

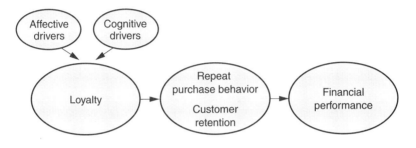

Figure 4.6   The affective and cognitive dimensions of loyalty.

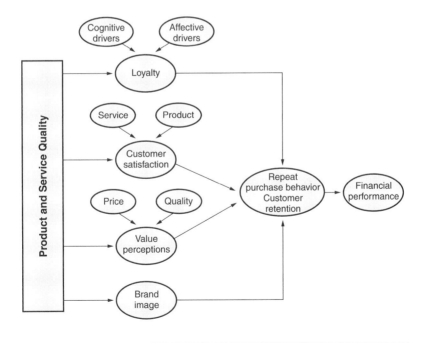

Figure 4.7   Quality and its effect on customer retention.

perceptions, and brand image all interact to affect repurchase behavior, which in turn drives financial performance. All four intermediate variables are presumed to be affected by product and/or service quality. It is important to note that these four constructs are considered to be interrelated; we have not explicitly linked them in the figure in the interest of clarity. Needless to say, though, loyalty, satisfaction, value, and image are strongly related.

As noted above, customer loyalty and brand image perceptions are probably not as dynamic as either customer satisfaction or value perceptions. In the latter case, a substantial increase in price could yield a precipitous decline in value perceptions. Similarly, if product quality begins to slip, it is very likely that customer satisfaction will decline accordingly. In both cases, we would expect loyal customers—those with strong emotional and cognitive ties to the product or service—to continue repurchasing despite the adversities of increased price and lower product quality. Of course, even highly loyal customers as defined here will lose their patience if these problems are long-term or particularly acute. The point is that customers who are strongly loyal in the attitudinal sense will be more likely to weather adversities than customers who are not, despite high levels of customer satisfaction and positive value perceptions.

Customer retention clearly plays an integral role in the relationships between product or service quality, customer satisfaction, and financial performance. The next chapter introduces a more explicit way to examine customer retention. Rather than rely upon respondent introspection to guide our assessment of retention, chapter 5 introduces an approach that links actual behavior with profitability. The methodology focuses our attention on a unique group of "at-risk" customers who are highly profitable.

5

Retention:
A Behavioral Strategy

INTRODUCTION

In both the applied and academic settings, customer retention is frequently operationalized using self-reported measures such as likelihood of repurchase. Considerable thought has gone into linking these self-reported measures to actual behaviors. One anecdotal approach is to estimate that roughly 10% of the respondents who report they are "very likely" to repurchase actually will do so. Such estimates are important because they are the only link between the survey data and actual behavior. Still, they are relatively primitive estimates in terms of their ability to predict behavior.

There are a number of approaches to this problem. One involves surveying customers with respect to their repurchase likelihood at time t_1 and then surveying the same sample at time t_2 to focus on their repurchase behavior. When customers are known and tracked in a database, more sophisticated approaches are possible. For example, one technique entails an initial survey regarding repurchase propensity followed by a database analysis aimed at determining the respondents' actual behavior.

In a few industries, customers are tracked quite closely with respect to their behaviors. The financial services industry is particularly fortunate to have a wealth of customer data. Furthermore, this information tends to be quite dynamic. While other industries have considerable customer information, it tends to be somewhat static. For example, insurance companies have very detailed personal information about their customers, but the relationship tends not to change much over time. The opportunities for interaction with the customer once a policy has been sold are few. On the opposite end of the spectrum, the advent of consumer "savings" cards in grocery stores has enabled researchers to track customer behavior on a weekly or even more frequent basis. Clearly, there are tremendous opportunities here to link psychographic data to actual purchase behaviors.

The financial services industry is especially interesting to researchers involved in linking customer retention to financial performance because, more and more frequently, banks are calculating and tracking profitability at the *customer level*. From a customer satisfaction measurement perspective, this lets us examine performance levels across profitability strata. In our financial services customer satisfaction research, we have encountered results that strongly suggest that the most profitable customers are the most difficult to satisfy. Conversely, the least profitable customers are nearly always highly satisfied and loyal—in terms of both attitude and behavior. This is a most disconcerting finding for most bank managers; the customers with the lowest net present value are also the most satisfied and most likely to remain customers in the future.

The availability of longitudinal behavioral and cross-sectional demographic data has led to efforts that focus exclusively on customer retention without regard for customer satisfaction or attitudinal measurements of loyalty. Frequently, when a vast database of 1 million or more households is under consideration, it is not possible to collect attitudinal data. Instead, we focus on the data that are available. Two categories of data are typically considered: demographics and product ownership profile. With respect to the former, comprehensive demographic data are generally not provided by consumers except when mortgage and home equity products are considered. Even then, however, this information often is not incorporated into the institution's general customer database. The best way to populate a comprehensive set of demographic variables is to use block-level census data. While these data are not at the household level, a good case can be made for the appropriateness of block-level demographic data when self-reported demographics are not available. The most substantive rationale for using block-level data involves the strong probability that people with similar demographics will reside in proximity to one another. Again, there is frequently no alternative to block-level data. When household-level demographics are available, they are typically associated with a specific product such as a mortgage. As a result, analyses must be restricted to those households with the product in question, which has limited utility.

This chapter focuses specifically upon the behavioral measurement of customer retention. Rather than relying upon customer introspection to establish probable retention rates, this analysis establishes measures of actual behavior. The behavior of greatest interest is the antithesis of retention: attrition. Instead of focusing entirely on longtime customers, the approach detailed in this chapter directs our attention to a behavior that is strongly related to retention rates. That is, we focus on customer attrition and how it can be predicted.

The methodology used in this example is quite novel. It employs a sophisticated statistical modeling approach to estimate the likelihood that a given household will terminate its relationship with a given bank. The model is based upon the behaviors of 100,000 households and then applied to a customer database of over 1 million households. Since customer satisfaction and loyalty data were not available for every household, the model was developed using behavioral (product-usage profile) and demographic (block-level census) data. As a result, each of the 1 million households was assigned an attrition risk ranging from 0 percent to 100 percent. A higher score indicates a higher risk of attrition.

With every household assigned an attrition risk level, the next step involved overlaying household-level profitability data. Collapsing the data into two categories with respect to profitability and attrition risk yielded four groups of customers: (1) high risk, high profit; (2) high risk, low profit; (3) low risk, high profit; and (4) low risk, low profit. From a managerial perspective, the customers of greatest concern are those in the high risk, high profit group. We introduce a series of increasingly efficacious intervention techniques aimed at permanently forestalling the departure of these especially valuable customers.

AN INTRODUCTION TO SURVIVAL ANALYSIS

The lifecycle of all organisms is characterized by birth, a life of varied duration, and ultimately death. Epidemiologists focus on understanding and predicting death rates in populations using a body of techniques known collectively as *survival analysis*. This family of multivariate statistical analyses is traditionally employed to facilitate an understanding of mortality rates in various populations. Marketing researchers have recently discovered that the methods employed in epidemiology have significant utility in applied customer research settings because, just as living things do, our *customer relationships* are born, live, and eventually die. Understanding why customers leave and, more important, predicting when they will leave make up the essence of this chapter.

Various populations under varying circumstances may have different attrition risk profiles. Consider the data presented in Figure 5.1, for example. This figure presents two risk profiles. The first is for wireless communications product purchasers, and the second reflects the risk profile for purchasers of vertical telephone services such as call waiting and call forwarding. As shown,

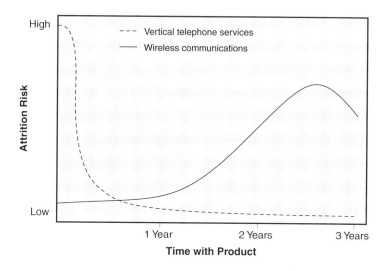

Figure 5.1   Illustration of attrition risk profiles.

users of vertical telephone services are at greatest risk of attrition during the first few months following purchase. Wireless communications product users, in contrast, have a higher attrition risk after nearly three years of use, due perhaps to their contractual obligation to keep their service for a fixed period—typically 24 or 36 months. Clearly, customer attrition risk differs depending upon a variety of circumstances including the type of product and its lifecycle.

This discussion will emphasize the use of survival analysis to address applied business problems. Our interest is the application of these techniques to *customer retention problems.* Increasingly, these techniques are used to predict attrition behaviors among customer populations. In this framework, mortality is the loss of the customer. Our primary objective is to identify "at risk" customers *before* they leave.

THE TECHNICAL ASPECTS OF SURVIVAL ANALYSIS

This section provides a limited technical treatment of proportional hazards regression models. A full understanding of the details of the models is not necessary to follow the case study presented in this chapter. Readers interested in in-depth discussions of the family of survival analysis models should turn to Lee (1992), Allison (1995), and Li (1995). These authors provide varying discussions of survival analysis. Li presents a case study using AT&T data, and Allison's book focuses on conducting survival analysis using the SAS System. Lee's 1992 book is a comprehensive, technical review of the techniques collectively known as survival analysis.

Survival analysis takes the same general form as multiple regression analysis. That is, there is a single dependent measure and a series of predictor variables. Technically, logistic regression, which accommodates a binary dependent variable, is a closer parallel to survival analysis than ordinary least squares regression. However, logistic regression can only address binary variables; there is no provision for time dependence. What sets the survival analysis framework apart from ordinary regression models is (1) its ability to accommodate "censored" data and (2) a dependent variable that contains two pieces of information: the termination of the customer and the age at which the termination occurred. These two requirements are discussed in greater detail below.

One of the most commonly used survival analysis techniques is known as proportional hazards regression. The method was first proposed by Cox in 1972. Allison (1995) noted that Cox's paper "Regression Models and Life Tables" had been cited over 800 times—more often than any other paper in the statistical literature. Further, Garfield (1990) noted that the Cox article was among the top 100 papers in all of science based on its cumulative citation count.

One unique aspect of survival analysis data is that it involves duration history. In terms of customer data, this means that our data set will include information concerning the duration of the relationship. That is, the data will reflect the relationship's inception through its termination. This is where "censoring" comes into play. Consider a typical customer relationship data set formatted for survival analysis for ABC Bank. If we define our study window as ranging from time t_1 through t_2, there will be a range of customers within this period. For example, some customers will have started their relationship with the bank *before* t_1 and others will have started their relationship some time after t_1 but before t_2. Similarly, there will be customers who terminate their relationship with the bank after t_2 and those who terminate before t_2. These situations are defined with specific terms in survival analysis. When a customer's "birth" preceeds time t_1, the record is said to be left-censored. In a similar fashion, when a termination occurs after time t_2, the record is considered to be right-censored.

At first glance, it would seem that the appropriate course of action concerning censored observations would be to discard them as we would in the case of observations with missing values in any other type of multivariate analysis. In survival analysis, however, we would not take this tack because to do so would bias the data. Removing cases that emerged before t_1 would effectively delete long-term customers. Similarly, removing customers who do not terminate their relationships before t_2 would discard many current customers and those whose termination date did not fall between t_1 and t_2. In survival analysis, left- and right-censored data are retained and considered to be missing only at the point of the censoring. As Li (1995, 19) noted, "In survival analysis, the philosophy regarding censoring is to utilize fully the information each censored case contributes up to the point when it is censored and not categorically discard it entirely from the observation set."

Cox's contribution can be considered in two parts. First, he proposed a model referred to as the *proportional hazards model*. Of additional importance, Cox introduced a new estimation technique known as *maximum partial likelihood*. To understand Cox's proportional hazards model, it is useful to consider the nature of a hazard function in survival analysis. The hazard function corresponds directly to the risk of event occurrence (such as death) at any point t. A hazard function can illustrate how the risk of event occurrence changes over time. Hazard functions typically allow for the influence of a set of covariates $x_1, x_2, \ldots, x_k$, so that in the case of coronary bypass surgery, for example, the risk includes variables such as age, weight, smoking history, gender, and cholesterol level. Note that proportional hazards models can accommodate *time dependent* covariates—these are predictor variables that vary over time as would be the case for an individual's savings account balance.

The key to the proportional hazards model is that different individuals have hazard functions that are proportional to one another. As Lee (1992, 250) notes, we can assume that $h(t|x_1)/h(t|x_2)$, which implies that for two individuals with covariates $x_1 = (x_{11}, x_{21}, \ldots, x_{p1})$ and $x_2 = (x_{12}, x_{22}, \ldots, x_{p2})$ the ratio of the hazard functions does not vary with time t. The basic model without time dependent covariates can be written as

$$h_i(t) = \lambda_0(t)\exp\{\beta_1 x_{i1} + \ldots + \beta_k x_{ik}\}$$

This means that for an individual i at time t, the hazard of event occurrence is the product of two factors:

1. The baseline hazard function $\lambda_0(t)$

2. The exponentiated linear function of covariates $(x_{i1} - x_{ik})$

Much like the intercept term β_0 in multiple regression analysis, the baseline hazard function $\lambda_0(t)$ can be considered to be the hazard function for a respondent whose covariate set is all zeros. Again, the proportional hazards model gets its name from the mathematical relationship between the hazard of event occurrence at time t for any two individuals. As Allison

(1995, 114) demonstrates for two individuals i and j, the relationship between their hazard functions is

$$\frac{h_i(t)}{h_j(t)} = \exp\left\{\beta_1\left(x_{i1} - x_{j1}\right) + \ldots + \beta_k\left(x_{ik} - x_{jk}\right)\right\}$$

Since $\lambda_0(t)$ cancels out of the numerator and denominator, the ratio of the hazards is constant over time. When we graph log $h_i(t)$ and log $h_j(t)$ over time, the lines will be exactly parallel.

Earlier we noted that one of Cox's significant contributions involved the development of a new estimation procedure known as the partial likelihood method. A substantive treatment of this technique is beyond the scope of this book. The most appealing characteristic of this estimation technique is that it decomposes the proportional hazards model into two pieces: $\lambda_0(t)$ and β. Partial likelihood effectively ignores the baseline $\lambda_0(t)$ and focuses exclusively on β. The benefit of this, according to Allison (1995, 115), is robustness: ". . . the estimates have good properties regardless of the actual shape of the baseline hazard function."

In order to illustrate how customer retention forecasting systems work, this chapter presents an actual case study. It involves a superregional bank with offices throughout North America. The research objective focused on reducing the rate of attrition among the customer base. With over one million households as customers, the client was not sure how to proceed with respect to reducing the rapidly increasing outflow of customers. The case study is presented below and is followed by a summary discussion of how intervention processes may be implemented to minimize customer loss. The results have been modified slightly based on the proprietary nature of the data.

CASE STUDY BACKGROUND

Facing tremendous competition from numerous "niche players," this financial services company faced a staggeringly high rate of customer attrition. The purpose of the study was to uncover the attributes associated with customers who defected to alternative financial services providers. To accomplish this, epidemiological modeling techniques were used to develop a statistical profile of customers at high risk of defection. The survival analysis approach was therefore employed to predict *mortality* among the customer base.

The rationale underlying this effort was grounded in the strategic and operational uses of the resulting model. In short, if a small set of accessible variables could be used to predict customer attrition, a variety of uses for the model could be considered. There are a wide variety of applications for an accurate attrition forecasting model. Of paramount interest is the ability to identify customers who are at risk of leaving. If "at-risk" customers can be identified, then steps may be taken to ensure that they remain long-term customers. The bottom line is that it is significantly less expensive to retain existing customers than to attract new ones.

The system presented in this case study was directly implemented at the mainframe database level. In short, the predictive model was set up to run monthly using the entire loan customer database. Customers identified as being at a high risk of leaving were subjected to a number of intervention measures. The primary objective of the intervention measures was to retain these existing customers. The following steps were taken to achieve this goal:

Stage 1: Quantify the differences between lost customers and current customers

Stage 2: Develop a predictive model to identify "at-risk" customers

Stage 3: Test the predictive model with customers who were not used in the model development process

Stage 4: Produce a user-friendly demonstration of the model that will illustrate its applications

The objectives were interrelated; each was determined by its immediate predecessor. Stage 4, for example, would be unnecessary without an accurate predictive model.

METHODOLOGY

This study relied upon contrasting two groups: current customers and defectors. Differences between these two groups were of special interest. Whether the high-mortality-risk group was younger, less affluent, or more likely to live in rural areas than loyal customers was the cornerstone of this project.

A wide variety of variables were reviewed in our effort to predict customer mortality. The project was constrained, however, by the number of missing values associated with certain variables. An exhaustive review of each variable's distribution and characteristics yielded a subset that was used to develop the final model. Of these, some were not statistically significant predictors; others were and have been retained in the model.

Initially, the analysis included both demographic and account variables. Of these, the demographic variables tended to be poor predictors of group membership. Customers with a high mortality risk did not differ significantly from long-term customers in terms of any one demographic variable. For example, customers who defected tended to be of the same age and gender as those who remained with the bank. Account history data, on the other hand, emerged as strongly predictive of whether a customer would remain with the company or defect. This is discussed in greater detail in the next section.

MODEL DEVELOPMENT

For each household in the sample (n = 100,000), both *static* and *dynamic* data were provided. Static data are those that remain relatively constant, such as income and household composition. In contrast, dynamic data include loan openings and closings, payment history, and account inquiries. These data, both static and dynamic variables, were used to develop models capable of accurately predicting customer attrition.

The model development stage was an iterative one; many successive variations were tried until the best, most reliable, most accurate, and most understandable model was developed. Thus, while there were many other competing models that could predict customer mortality, the final model tended to produce the most *accurate* predictions. It also did so with a minimal number of variables. As such, it was the most *parsimonious* model.

The final statistical model was composed of six variables. Of these, only one (combined monthly income) was a demographic variable. The remaining variables represented characteristics of the account relationship. Table 5.1 summarizes the model's significant variables in order of predictive impact.

Table 5.1   Summary of the predictive model.

Variable Description	Relation to Groups	Predictive Strength
Average loan balance	Higher balances suggested lower mortality risk.	Very strong
Average savings balance	Higher balances suggested lower mortality risk.	Very strong
Postal solicitation	Response to postal solicitation was related to lower mortality risk.	Very strong
Length of relationship	Tenure and mortality risk were inversely related.	Strong
Combined income	Customers with higher incomes had a higher mortality risk.	Moderate
Account closure	Customers who had closed any account in the preceding three months had a higher mortality risk.	Strong

THE SIGNIFICANT PREDICTOR VARIABLES

As shown in the table, the strongest predictors involved the customers' average loan and savings balances across all past and present accounts. The higher either balance, the lower the customer's mortality risk. Interestingly, the third predictor suggested that customers who had responded to postal solicitations (such as offers for additional loan monies) were more likely to remain loyal customers. The implications for this advertising channel are clear: consumers who respond to postal solicitations are more likely to be long-term customers. The fourth predictor variable shown in Table 5.1 involved customer tenure. This *momentum effect* is not unusual and is encountered across a wide variety of industries. Quite simply, it suggests that as relationship length increases, customers are more likely to stay. This may be attributed to their comfort and familiarity or simply to an inability to find suitable (proximate) alternatives.

The remaining two variables, while significant predictors of customer mortality, are not as strong as the variables discussed above. Combined income, for example, exerts moderate strength in the model. A parallel empirical investigation of this phenomenon confirmed that as customers' incomes increased, they were more likely to become targets of competitors. Finally, Table 5.1 suggests that a customer who had closed any type of account with the bank within the past three months was at considerable mortality risk.

MODEL VALIDATION

The model was highly successful in terms of its ability to predict attrition among the customer base used to construct the model. However, we employed a more rigorous validation procedure to test the model. This involved assigning a risk level to each of 100,000 customers who were *not* used in the model development process. Beginning in December 1998, these 100,000 customers were prospectively tracked over the course of 11 months. The results were very encouraging.

For simplicity's sake, the customers were assigned to 10 *deciles* based upon the model's assessment of their mortality risk. As shown in Figure 5.2, by October 1999 fully 98.6% of those in the lowest risk decile were still customers. However, customers in the highest risk decile experienced a much higher mortality rate. In fact, customers in the high-risk group had an attrition rate *many times higher* than those in the low-risk group; only 51.1% remained by the end of October 1999.

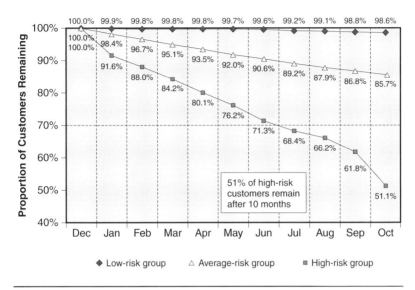

Figure 5.2 Attrition rates by risk decile.

MODEL IMPLEMENTATION

The cornerstone of the model development project was the need to iden-tify "at risk" customers before they left. Customers vary in terms of their worth, and clearly some "at risk" customers were of greater concern than others. Specifically, *profitable* customers whom the model isolated as being at significant risk for attrition were of greatest interest. Figure 5.3 depicts the integration of individual profitability and risk data. As shown, four quadrants emerge from the integration of profitability and attrition risk data.

The horizontal axis of the quadrant diagram presented in the figure represents attrition risk. As one moves to the right, mortality risk increases. The vertical axis of the quadrant diagram reflects customer prof-itability. Customers in the top-right quadrant of Figure 5.3 are of great concern to most organizations. These customers are both very profitable and associated with a significant mortality risk. Clearly, intervention efforts aimed at circumventing the predicted attrition would have signifi-cant utility if successful.

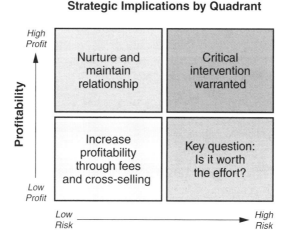

Figure 5.3   Attrition risk and profitability.

INTERVENING TO SAVE PROFITABLE CUSTOMERS

Our intervention efforts focused on the high-risk, profitable customer group. These customer households were associated with an attrition risk score of greater than 65%. The predictive equation was executed monthly to identify profitable, high-risk customers. Intervening in an effort to retain the high-risk customers was the next step. Intervention took several forms and was subject to field experiment and cost-benefit analyses wherein the optimal communications channel was tested.

The research design took the form of one control group and three experimental treatment groups. Five hundred customers were assigned to each of the four groups. Each of the experimental groups was subjected to intervention methodologies of varying (presumed) efficacy. While members of the control group were not contacted, two experimental groups received small gifts and the third received a personal telephone call from a branch manager.

Table 5.2 depicts the experimental and control groups associated with our efforts to optimize the intervention cost–benefit ratio. The table's rows relate to the four sample groups associated with the intervention analysis. The first row represents the control group of high-value, high-risk

Table 5.2 Cost-benefit analysis for interventions: experimental and control groups.

High-Value, High-Mortality-Risk Customers

Intervention Type	Unit Cost	Base	After 1 Year	Marginal Benefit	Cost per Saved Household
Control group	$0.00	500	260		
Mail pack 1	$0.75	500	311	51	$7.35
Mail pack 2	$1.00	500	345	85	$5.88
Telephone call	$1.40	500	390	130	$5.38

customers for whom no intervention efforts were made. These customers represent the baseline against which the various experimental interventions were contrasted. After one year, only 260 of the original 500 control group customers remained. Compare this with the next three rows presented in Table 5.2. Each introduces an ostensibly more effective (and costly) appeal to the customer. In every case, the intent is to strengthen the relationship between the bank and the customer through either a simple gift or a direct telephone call from a manager.

Table 5.2 suggests that while it was the most costly on a per unit basis ($1.40), the direct telephone call to high-risk, profitable customers yielded the lowest cost per saved household. That is, it was the most effective method of stemming the tide of defecting customers. While most expensive in the aggregate, it produced the lowest unit cost per saved household.

The intervention step is clearly critical; the magnitude of the intervention can vary greatly. This step need not be limited to three experimental groups, of course. A wide variety of intervention types may be tested, including the following:

- A personalized letter
- A telephone call from a branch manager
- A small token gift with the bank name
- A free money management course
- A complimentary portfolio review
- Reduced APR on loan products
- Increased yield on deposit products
- Reduced ATM charges
- A free safe-deposit box

In each case, the cost of the intervention is readily calculated. This is important because in order to produce a cost–benefit analysis across all interventions, it is necessary that a unit cost be known. This may be more difficult to calculate when the intervention involves reduced-rate loan products or increased-yield deposit products, but with some averaging, a good estimate can be produced. The key, of course, is to quantify the cost per saved household for each intervention strategy.

The actual profitability of each household, as described above, is known in actual dollars. The profitability of the most valuable profit decile was approximately $400 per year. The top decile comprised approximately 100,000 households. The profit contribution of these customers as a group was roughly $40 million per year. Of the 100,000 households in the top *profitability* decile, 10,000 were in the top *risk* decile. These 10,000 households with a total profit contribution of $4 million annually became the object of intense scrutiny.

It should be noted that *unprofitable* customers tended to have much higher attrition risk rates, as shown in Figure 5.4. Unprofitable customers tended to be younger, have fewer products with lower balances, and have shorter relationships with the bank. On the other hand, the most profitable customers tended to have more loan and deposit products with greater balances and long-term relationships with the bank. Thus, the *breadth* (number of products), *depth* (dollar balance), and *length* of their relationships were

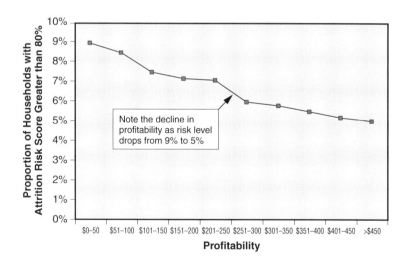

Figure 5.4   Relationship between high attrition risk and profitability.

considerably greater. A profitable customer was assigned a high attrition rate risk based upon a very specific set of circumstances. Generally, this involved account closure combined with a very high income. These two variables tended to be predictive of attrition.

This case study dramatically demonstrates that customer retention is related to financial performance. Higher retention rates are often associated with increased breadth, depth, and length of the relationship with the customer. We have found that in a variety of industries a type of inertia often drives retention. In short, as the customer relationship matures, the likelihood of attrition diminishes. Conversely, we often find that the highest attrition rates occur among new customers.

Had customer satisfaction data been available for all of the households used in the initial modeling, we could have assessed its relative impact with respect to the demographic and behavioral variables. This was not possible for two reasons. First, the difficulty and expense of collecting customer satisfaction data for the entire sample of 100,000 households that were used to generate the statistical model would have been prohibitive. An appealing alternative would have involved taking a *sample* of households from each risk decile and providing a mean level of satisfaction for each risk stratum. The second reason customer satisfaction data were excluded from the model was that bank management wanted a system that relied entirely upon data that were immediately available in the customer household database. The management wanted to avoid a situation in which customer satisfaction levels would be required for every customer household in order to produce a risk classification.

The approach to attrition modeling presented in this chapter can be implemented in any organization with longitudinal data. It is important that interactions with customers be recorded in the database. These "touchpoints" represent predictor variables in the attrition model. Financial services organizations enjoy a wealth of *dynamic* customer variables, such as account openings and closures and changes in balance levels, in addition to more *static* data such as age, income, and household life stage. Other organizations do not have such useful data, often because interaction with customers is very infrequent. Such is the case for insurance companies, whose customer interactions typically only involve claims processing.

It has been our experience that data sets that span longer periods of time with more frequent data capture intervals yield the best predictive models. Our best experiences have involved data sets spanning more than 10 years with *monthly* data updates. Of course, such a vast data repository does not guarantee a strong model. We have, in fact, generated viable models with as little as one year of monthly data, as the case study presented in this chapter so aptly illustrates.

6

Key Business Outcome Metrics

INTRODUCTION

This chapter is focused on a discussion of key business outcome measures. In it we describe a series of metrics that can be used to tie internal (employee) satisfaction and external (customer) satisfaction to the "bottom line." A variety of business outcome measures are available to companies interested in linking their customer satisfaction results to financial performance. Industries differ widely, however, in terms of the types of outcome measures available. For example, many financial services organizations— banks and brokerages, in particular—have implemented sophisticated systems that calculate profitability (net income after tax) at the household level. In contrast, many producers of consumer packaged goods have difficulty linking external satisfaction to profitability because their customers are largely anonymous. Companies that do not (or cannot) capture customer information at the time of purchase often have to resort to using panel data or other syndicated data sources to link customer satisfaction to business outcome variables.

This chapter focuses exclusively upon objective measures of financial performance. We purposely avoid self-reported measures that ostensibly reflect business outcomes. For example, we do not discuss survey data relating to the likelihood of future purchases, the likelihood of recommending to a friend, or share of wallet. The latter reflects what proportion of a consumer's investments are with a particular financial institution. The trouble with these data is that it is difficult to build a substantive bridge between these self-reported measures and actual behaviors. We are frequently asked to provide an estimate of the proportion of respondents who will *actually purchase* based upon their responses in a survey. Market potentials are often calculated in this somewhat tenuous fashion. After seeing an actual product or even a picture of one, respondents are often asked how likely they would be to purchase the product. Of those who indicate they "would definitely" purchase the product, only a subset actually do. Of course, the actual proportion of respondents who do purchase a product after indicating that they would in a survey situation varies by product category, price, and respondent profile. Hughes (1973, 167–99) presents an interesting discussion of the role of psychological theory, models, and measures relevant to demand analysis.

The focus of this chapter includes variables presumed to be the result of internal and external satisfaction, such as profitability, revenues, market share, and share of wallet. These four interrelated variables are among the most often used in efforts to present the bottom-line effects of customer and employee satisfaction. The remainder of this chapter focuses on measurement issues surrounding two of these key business outcome variables: market share and profitability. Before introducing these key outcome measures, however, we will consider an issue that is often overlooked in assessing customer retention and profitability: the cost of customer acquisition. Estimating the cost of customer (and employee) acquisition may be even more problematic than calculating customer profitability.

THE COST OF CUSTOMER ACQUISITION

Although technically subsumed by some measures of profitability, the cost of customer acquisition is discussed here to emphasize the importance of customer *retention*. The costs of acquiring new customers vary considerably across industries. For example, a marketing research firm might consider advertising costs, trade show expenses, sales commissions, travel, and other costs associated with the acquisition of a new customer. In its efforts to market ATM cards to its retail customers, a bank might incur a wholly different set of customer acquisition costs. Consider the costs of direct mail campaigns, statement stuffers, and blanket advertising. A successful direct mail program might generate a conversion rate of five percent. A consumer packaged goods producer may have to consider the costs of all advertising efforts, including broadcast, trade press, POS displays, periodicals, and so on.

The important thing to consider when evaluating customer loss is that the departure of a customer involves the loss of future revenue streams as well as the costs required to replace the lost customer. When a brokerage loses a customer, for example, it loses all future commissions related to the customer's trades. In order to replace the lost revenue stream, the brokerage must find another customer. The costs of this may involve direct mail programs, advertising, and telephone solicitations.

One consideration that is often overlooked is the probability that highly profitable customers are more costly to replace. For a bank, replacing a customer who has only a small savings balance is relatively easy. Of course, the profitability of this type of customer is very low, too. In contrast, the cost of replacing a more profitable customer is much greater. While the costs most certainly will include those associated with direct mail, advertising, and perhaps telephone solicitations, the bank may also have to attract the prospective profitable customer with higher-yield deposit product offers or low-interest loans. Often customers are profitable not only because of the depth (dollar value) or breadth (number of products) of their relationship with a producer but also because the *costs* associated with the relationship are very low. This situation is typically associated with long-term customers who require very little interaction and have streamlined their relationships. Thus, these customers are desirable because of the length of their relationship with the producer and because the relationship requires so little input.

RESEARCH DESIGN AND MEASUREMENT IMPLICATIONS

Linking financial performance to customer and employee satisfaction results can involve two types of research design: time series and cross-sectional analysis. The type of design that is selected can affect how certain financial performance metrics are captured. The first approach involves the measurement of customer and employee satisfaction and financial performance measures simultaneously and at equal intervals. For example, one could track customer satisfaction, employee satisfaction, and a financial performance measure such as market share on a monthly basis and plot these data in a manner similar to that depicted in Figure 6.1.

The data presented in Figure 6.1 suggest that the company has focused on a time series approach to evaluating the relationships between customer satisfaction, employee satisfaction, and market share. This may be attributable to a number of circumstances. It is possible, for example, that the organization has no logical subunits across which cross-sectional data could be gathered. That is, disaggregating based upon sales district, geography, or another unit may not be possible. As a result, the organization may be forced to conduct its evaluation at the corporate level using time series data.

With a sufficient number of observations, time series models using sophisticated techniques such as autoregressive moving average (ARMA)

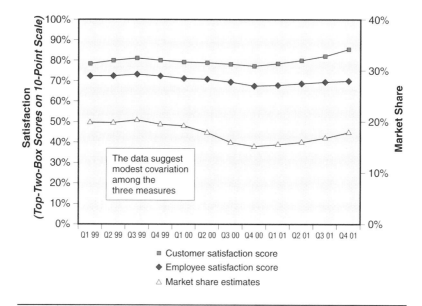

Figure 6.1   Plot of time series data relating customer and employee satisfaction to market share.

may be built. Many organizations' products are tied to macroeconomic indicators. Products that are used in new homes, such as fireplace inserts, sinks and bathtubs, and even lumber, are often subject to the vagaries of the national economy. Many manufacturers of this type of product forecast sales volumes based upon data such as the number of new housing starts on a monthly basis. Techniques such as ARMA time series models use a series of such predictor variables to forecast some critical business variables, such as unit sales, sometimes at the SKU level. Customer satisfaction and employee satisfaction data can also be used in this type of model. The introduction of *lags*, in which the effect on the outcome variable is delayed by, for example, one quarter, is also possible. The most problematic aspect of this tack, unfortunately, involves the availability (or paucity) of customer satisfaction and employee satisfaction data on a quarterly or more frequent basis.

In contrast to the time series approach to modeling financial performance data, the second approach, cross-sectional analysis, is more straightforward. Two types of cross-sectional analysis are possible. In the first, the profitability and satisfaction of individual customers are known. The second involves a situation in which the organization can be disaggregated into subunits such as sales districts, counties, or some other geographic unit. Both entail the development of statistical models based on data collected in one time period and reveal relationships such as those depicted in Figure 6.2.

The first type of cross-sectional model involves a situation in which the financial performance variable is available at the customer level. Such is often the case with banking data, wherein the approximate profitability of a *household* is known. In this case, it is a relatively easy matter to collect customer satisfaction data by surveying a sample of households. Of course, introducing *employee satisfaction* data in this scenario is somewhat tricky. One approach is to code the level of employee satisfaction at the branch visited most frequently by the household member(s). Thus, in every household record we would have access to data relating to (1) profitability, (2) customer satisfaction, and (3) employee satisfaction at the branch most frequently visited.

The second form of cross-sectional model involves a situation in which the organization is disaggregated into its naturally occurring subunits. Once the subunits (such as sales districts or counties) have been identified, disparate data sources may be combined at the subunit level. For example, average customer satisfaction and employee satisfaction scores can be calculated and assigned to each subunit. These data can be supplemented with financial performance metrics at the subunit level. The relationship among these variables is then assessed using a data set with as many observations as there are subunits. This is described in greater detail in subsequent chapters.

Figure 6.2   Cross-sectional data analysis: bivariate relationships.

THE ROLE OF CUSTOMER RETENTION

Chapter 4 focused on the link between customer satisfaction and financial performance outcomes. One conclusion that appeared to have been reached by a number of researchers involved the important role played by customer retention. In effect, there seemed to be a consensus that many of the desirable outcomes associated with positive customer satisfaction were due to its effect on customer retention. Many researchers have maintained that customer retention leads to superior financial performance. This is because firms with high customer retention rates tend to have lower costs, maintain more profitable long-term relationships, and enjoy substantial word-of-mouth advertising.

Of course, in many cases it is more difficult to measure customer retention than it is to measure some of its outcomes, such as profitability, market share, and share of wallet. This is particularly true when consumer packaged goods or other low-involvement products are considered. Even in some business-to-business relationships, it is difficult to measure customer retention despite the fact that market share statistics are readily available. We must stress at this point that many of the positive outcomes associated with high levels of customer satisfaction are exerted through customer retention.

While self-reported measures of customer retention are relatively easy to obtain, measuring behavioral customer retention is often problematic. In consumer packaged goods environments, it is especially difficult to quantify customer retention since customers frequently are anonymous. As was demonstrated in chapter 5, many financial services organizations are much better equipped to measure retention. When behavioral measures of retention are integrated with profitability metrics, the results can be very powerful.

The remainder of this chapter focuses on some of the key financial performance outcome measures that are often linked to customer satisfaction. Of particular importance are measures of profitability and market share. Customer satisfaction can be linked to these outcome measures with either the cross-sectional or time series approach, as described earlier in this chapter.

CUSTOMER SATISFACTION AND MARKET SHARE

Maximizing market share has historically been an unambiguous business objective. Its relationship to profitability is traced to the benefits of substantial market share. The main benefit of superior market share is related to cost, according to Jain (1990, 226–27). Market share affects cost in terms of scale and experience. Market leaders are presumed to have lower costs than their competitors as a result of their experience and the scale of their operations. However, as Jain noted, while maximizing market share is a reasonable goal for businesses, there are some caveats. Of greatest concern are the company's ability to:

- Finance the market share objectives

- Withstand antitrust actions

Jain (1990, 227) wrote that fear of antitrust actions led a number of companies to reevaluate their market share dominance objectives. Companies such as Kodak, Gillette, Xerox, and IBM were cited as examples of this reconsideration of maximum market share as a business objective. This reality led researchers such as Bloom and Kotler (1975, 63) to conclude that while growing market share is a reasonable goal, the objective should be refined to *optimizing* market share. The optimal market share, the authors suggested, should be based on the following:

- An estimation of the relationship between market share and profitability

- An estimation of the risk associated with increasingly high market share levels

- The determination of a market share level at which increases can no longer yield enough profit to compensate for the added risk exposure

As Jain (1990, 227) conceded, companies with low market share do not necessarily flounder. Indeed, certain niche players compete only in market segments where they excel. According to Hammermesh, Anderson, and Harris (1975), companies that are effective despite low market shares tend to compete only where they have distinctive competencies, make use of relatively low R&D budgets, avoid growth simply for the sake of growth, and have innovative leaders.

The role of market share in the relationships between service or product quality, customer and employee satisfaction, retention, and financial performance is complex. Barsky (1999, 107), for example, maintained that higher market share means *lower* customer satisfaction, which presumably leads to deflated financial performance. His reasoning was that mass producers are less able to satisfy customers in the way that niche players can. This may be true in some cases, but it stands to reason that sophisticated corporations that practice market segmentation and can differentiate their product offerings and marketing communications based on this strategy will be able to satisfy customers despite their dominant market share.

There appears to be a general consensus regarding the important role that market share plays with respect to profitability. Heskett, Sasser, and Schlesinger (1997, 20–21), for example, cited the 1970s Profit Impact of Market Share (PIMS) study and its conclusion that market share was one of the most important predictors of profitability. Customer retention appears to play a significant role in this relationship.

It is not hard to envision the impact of customer retention on market share; it would be difficult to grow market share in the face of high rates of customer attrition. Note that market share is often cited as an intermediate variable that predicts profitability. Figure 6.3 suggests that one causal chain may begin with enhanced service or product quality and management practices. These, in turn, yield higher customer and employee satisfaction, which positively affects customer retention. Higher customer retention levels lead to greater market share, which, finally, results in greater profitability.

There are a variety of ways to measure market share, which differ considerably with respect to cost. For example, some companies use panel data to estimate market share, and others use warehouse-withdrawal data. Both methods are relatively inexpensive. In contrast, larger companies with more resources tend to maintain their own market share estimation programs. These usually involve a telephone survey methodology wherein consumers are picked at random from a national sample and asked about their past product purchases and current ownership. In a consumer or retail setting, this might involve random digit dialing from a computer-generated sample of telephone numbers. When a business-to-business setting is involved, the sample is typically acquired from a supplier such as Dun & Bradstreet and the most appropriate respondents are identified through screening questions at the beginning of the survey. In either case, respondents are asked about

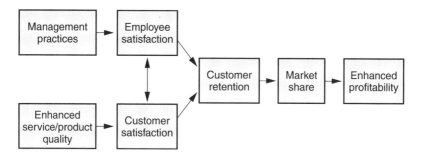

Figure 6.3   Causal sequence leading to profitability.

their past purchase behavior and the brands and models of products they currently own. Occasionally this type of survey also includes items relating to *future* purchases, but unless a follow-up verification survey is conducted, this type of forecast should be considered cautiously. There is some utility in a comparison of current brand ownership and self-reported future behaviors. This can be considered a rough measure of customer retention: respondents who indicate they currently have a given brand and intend to purchase it again in the future may be considered retained customers.

Market share estimates are sometimes calculated at a sales territory level and can entail significant data collection expenditures. For large, complex organizations that track key business metrics and customer satisfaction across a hundred or more sales territories, a market share intelligence-gathering program may involve tens of thousands of telephone interviews. For example, in order to achieve a quarterly 95% confidence interval of ±5% for each of 100 sales territories, roughly 400 completed interviews per territory must be completed every three months. On an annual basis, this type of program would entail 160,000 telephone interviews. Assuming an interviewing cost of $25 per hour and a completion rate of 2.0 interviews per hour, the total data collection budget for such a comprehensive program would be $2 million annually.

Market share clearly enjoys a unique role that spans customer retention and profitability. It is clearly dependent upon customer retention. Further, it is a very good indicator of profitability. Its relationship with profitability may well be curvilinear: as market share increases beyond an optimal point, customer satisfaction may drop. This could be attributed to the need to establish economies of scale in production to increase share and the consequent drift toward mass production where there is little room for customer-focused marketing activities. There is clear evidence to suggest that market share does not necessarily equal profitability. Heskett, Sasser, and Schlesinger (1997, 20) cited the case of Southwest Airlines, which has never been a strong market leader but nevertheless has been consistently rated alongside its most profitable competitors.

CUSTOMER SATISFACTION AND PROFITABILITY

Most companies express their business objectives in terms of profitability, market share, and growth. As an ultimate objective, profitability is a substantive goal. It may be expressed at the corporate level in absolute monetary terms, as a percentage of capital employed, or in terms of total assets, according to Jain (1990, 225). The objective may be set for the corporation as a whole, or differentiated goals may be set based on customer segment, business line, or specific geographic units such as sales regions. Optimally, profit goals are set at the same business unit level at which customer satisfaction data are collected.

A number of profitability ratios can be calculated at the strategic business unit level. It is worth briefly describing several of these measures, since the manner in which profitability is measured can affect the models we develop. This is particularly important given our interest in linking customer satisfaction—directly or indirectly through retention and market share—to profitability. Since profitability can be measured in a number of different ways, a review of these approaches seems warranted.

As noted, there are several different approaches to measuring profitability. These include profit margin on sales, rate of return on assets, and rate of return on common stock equity, according to Kieso and Weygandt (1977, 1026–28). The profit margin on sales is calculated by dividing net income by net sales for a given period, as shown in Figure 6.4.

Note that net income may be calculated in either of two ways. The capital maintenance approach to net income calculation, according to Kieso and Weygandt (1977, 113), "assumes that net income is measured by subtracting beginning net assets from ending net assets and adjusting for any additional investments during the period." In effect, this approach to net income measurement takes the net assets in period t_1 and measures income by the difference in capital values between period t_1 and t_2. Note that the capital maintenance approach to net income calculation can be implemented at the strategic business unit level and therefore can be supplied by, for example, sales region, state, or another operating unit, as depicted in Figure 6.5.

The preferred method of calculating net income is the transaction approach. This is an activity-based approach that provides substantially more detail than the capital maintenance technique. The transaction approach to net income calculation focuses on the activities that have occurred during a given accounting period. Rather than simply providing the net change over a period, this approach discloses the components that make up the change. These could include items such as cost of products sold or interest on long-term debt, as shown in Figure 6.6.

$$\text{Profit margin on sales} = \frac{\text{Net income}}{\text{Net sales}} = \frac{\$\ 300,000}{\$3,200,000} = 9.4\%$$

Figure 6.4 Profit margin on sales.

SuperTorque
Western Sales Division Net Income: 2001

Net assets as of December 31, 2001	$190,000
Net assets as of January 1, 2001	$100,000
	$ 90,000
Less:	
Year 2001 investments	$ 20,000
Net income for 2001	**$ 70,000**

Figure 6.5   Calculation of net income based on the capital maintenance approach.

SuperTorque
Western Sales Division Net Income: 2001

Revenues

Net sales	$190,000
Other revenue	$100,000
Total revenues	**$290,000**

Expenses

Cost of products sold	$120,000
Sales administration	$100,000
Interest on long-term debt	$ 30,000
Total expenses	**$250,000**
Income before taxes	$ 40,000
Income taxes	$ 12,000
Net income for 2001	**$ 28,000**
Profit margin on sales	14.7%

Figure 6.6   Calculation of net income based on the transaction approach.

When the profit margin on sales is combined with the asset turnover, we obtain the rate of return on total assets (Figure 6.7). The attractiveness of this measure is that it actually reflects how profitable a company was over a given period of time.

Total average assets is used to determine activity ratios and, when multiplied by the profit margin on sales, provides better insight into the profitability of a company. Total average assets is calculated as the average value of assets over an accounting period (such as a fiscal quarter). Banks typically calculate a daily average balance sheet. In particular, the resulting asset turnover ratio tells us how many times the assets turned over during a given period. As Kieso and Weygandt (1977, 1026) noted, some companies "have a small profit margin on sales and a high turnover (grocery and discount stores), whereas other enterprises have a relatively high profit margin but a low inventory turnover (jewelry and furniture stores)."

Instead of multiplying profit margin by asset turnover, the rate of return on assets can be calculated more simply by dividing net income by total average assets (Figure 6.8). There has been some debate regarding whether net income before taxes or after taxes should be used, according to Kieso and Weygandt (1977, 1029). For management purposes, a pretax measure may be used, as tax expense can fluctuate significantly from year to year due to unrelated tax-planning objectives.

Two additional reflections of corporate profitability are the rate of return on common stock equity and earnings per share. The former is the

$$\text{Rate of return on assets} = \text{Profit margin on sales} \times \text{Asset turnover}$$

$$\text{Rate of return on assets} = \frac{\text{Net income}}{\text{Net sales}} \times \frac{\text{Net sales}}{\text{Total average assets}}$$

Figure 6.7   Rate of return on assets.

$$\text{Rate of return on assets} = \frac{\text{Net income}}{\text{Total average assets}}$$

Figure 6.8   Rate of return on assets: alternate calculation.

ratio of net income after interest, taxes, and preferred dividends to the average common stockholder's equity, as shown in Figure 6.9.

Earnings per share (Figure 6.10), on the other hand, is one of the most familiar metrics used to evaluate a company's performance. There are a number of caveats associated with the earnings per share ratio as an objective measure. Kieso and Weygandt (1977, 1030), for example, warn that this measure can be increased simply by reducing the number of shares outstanding by purchasing treasury stock. This may happen if a company believes its stock is undervalued in the marketplace. Of more interest is the potential for earnings per share to increase over time. Kieso and Weygandt suggest that "earnings per share, all other factors being equal, will probably increase year after year if the stockholder reinvests earnings in the business because a larger earnings figure should be generated without a corresponding increase in the denominator, the number of shares outstanding."

The earnings per share and rate of return on common stock equity would be valuable in a meta-analysis that seeks to link customer satisfaction and financial performance across, for example, several hundred companies. Of course, this would assume that all of the participating companies used the same customer satisfaction measurements. Interestingly, this is exactly what the American Customer Satisfaction Index program described in chapter 4 has successfully done.

The preceding discussion has focused on measures of profitability that can be tracked at the corporate or strategic business unit level. When businesses have detailed information concerning their customers' purchasing behaviors, it is possible to calculate profitability at the individual customer

$$\text{Rate of return on common stock equity} = \frac{\text{Net income after preferred dividends}}{\text{Average common stockholder's equity}}$$

Figure 6.9   Rate of return on common stock equity.

$$\text{Earnings per share} = \frac{\text{Net income}}{\text{Number of shares outstanding}}$$

Figure 6.10   Earnings per share.

level. Financial services providers—banks, in particular—have been very successful over the past 10 years in their efforts to calculate profitability at the customer (household) level. Calculating profitability at the individual customer level requires input from a number of sources. The frequency with which profitability metrics are calculated is another matter. For example, a bank may choose to estimate profitability on a monthly basis, while a producer of sophisticated medical imaging devices might be more inclined to estimate net income associated with individual hospitals on an annual basis. Regardless of how frequently profitability is calculated, two inputs are necessary: the income from the customer and the cost of doing business with the customer.

First, the income associated with a given customer must be estimated. This estimate can be made on a yearly basis or more frequently, depending upon access to product usage data. Financial services providers face a complex task when assessing the profitability of individual households. Net income must be calculated based upon a household's product usage. Deposit and loan balances must be taken into account. Certain costs of capital assumptions must also be made to estimate the net income associated with loan and deposit products.

With respect to the costs associated with a given household, a bank must first estimate the transaction volume and the cost of each transaction type. For example, branch visits are quite expensive—so expensive, in fact, that in the 1990s some banks instituted a fee for branch banking. This was met with incredulity, and those banks that charged for branch banking visits no doubt lost some customers. Nonetheless, when a customer visits a branch, it costs the bank in terms of both personnel and the need to have a "bricks and mortar" channel for customers to use. If all customers used electronic banking, there would be little need for vast branch networks.

By implementing accounting procedures aimed at quantifying the customer value at the household level, banks are able to differentiate between profitable and unprofitable customers. The former group is of considerable importance because it is not uncommon for the top profit decile to support the remaining customer base. Indeed, members of the lowest profit decile may actually cost the bank money.

Not all organizations have the luxury of estimating profitability at the customer level. In a business-to-business environment, however, certain manufacturers are able to gauge the value of their customers. When large-scale, low-volume products are considered, the possibility of calculating the net profit associated with each sale is very good. A manufacturer of magnetic resonance imaging (MRI) equipment that is sold to hospitals is in a good position to calculate profitability at the customer (hospital) level. The key inputs are the costs of producing and marketing the equipment and, of course, the revenue its sale yields. Profitability is often enhanced by the revenue stream associated with a continuing technical support and maintenance relationship with the customer.

In many cases, the customer relationship is characterized by an initial purchase followed by years of maintenance or technical support. Home and business security systems, for example, start with an initial installation cost followed by continued monitoring costs. Certain computer software and hardware is also characterized by an initial purchase followed by an optional maintenance contract. In retailing, there has been a significant effort to lure consumers into multiyear maintenance contracts on a wide range of durable goods, including electronic equipment such as printers, stereos, televisions, and DVD players. To retailers, the allure of such a proposition is the revenue generated by the maintenance contract and the lengthening of the relationship with the consumer. Of course, the revenue associated with the maintenance contract may be offset by expenses related to repairing or maintaining the equipment. Still, this risk is manageable and has been accommodated in the price of the contract.

Clearly, the profitability of a customer relationship may continue long after the initial sale through maintenance, technical support, and consulting contracts. When this is the case, the profitability of a customer may be calculated by averaging the profitability across the useful life of the product. This helps avoid situations in which customers are highly profitable in the first year and contribute very little to the bottom line in subsequent years. Additionally, averaging the profitability of a customer over the life of the product facilitates comparisons of customers at any point in the product lifecycle. That is, without averaging profitability (or any other financial performance variable) across the product's life, customers who make the initial purchase will be very profitable while those in the maintenance phase may be less profitable. This type of comparison fails to take into consideration the *lifetime value* of a customer.

Heskett, Sasser, and Schlesinger (1997, 60–65) described the lifetime value of a customer as a highly encompassing measure that accommodates future purchase behavior. This measure further subsumes the value of word-of-mouth advertising—referrals. The authors cited the instance of Domino's Pizza, which calculated the lifetime value of a loyal pizza buyer to be $4,000 in revenue. A more dramatic example involved a Texas Cadillac dealership that estimated the lifetime value of a loyal customer to be $332,000 in new vehicles and service. Clearly, the lifetime value of a customer is simply the sum of the value (in terms of either revenue or profit) of the relationship over its lifetime.

A variety of approaches to modeling the relationships between customer satisfaction, employee satisfaction, and profitability are possible.

Companies without access to profitability measures at the customer level must strive to develop a longitudinal database that measures both customer satisfaction and profitability simultaneously on a monthly or quarterly basis. With a sufficient number of observations, these companies may attempt to relate the measures statistically using time series analysis. Other companies that do not have profitability data available at the customer level may be able to conduct cross-sectional analyses by measuring customer and employee satisfaction at the organization subunit (strategic business unit) level. Assuming there is a sufficient number of subunits, satisfaction—both internal and external—can be linked with financial performance variables. Finally, some organizations enjoy the ability to calculate measures of performance at the individual customer level. For these companies, there is typically a wealth of information that can be mined. For banks, this includes a variety of demographic and product ownership variables. Using one of these approaches, virtually any organization can attempt to link internal and external satisfaction with financial performance data.

7
Data Preparation

INTRODUCTION

We often wish to study the relationship between employee attitudes and customer loyalty. If we have data from two different studies, performing this analysis requires that we first merge the data from those two studies. This requires that we decide upon a "unit of analysis," as shown in Figure 7.1. That is, we must determine what will constitute a line in the data file that we build. Making this decision is more difficult than it may appear.

The unit of analysis decision is based on philosophical and operational considerations. The philosophical aspect involves deciding whether a given concept (such as employee satisfaction) is "at" the individual or the organizational unit level. If it is at the organizational level, at which level (for example, a store or a department within a store) within the organization is it? This is partly, but not wholly, a definitional issue. The operational aspect refers to determining which employees' data should be attached to which customer and how to actually accomplish that attachment.

We often also wish to study the relationship between customer loyalty and business outcomes. This entails the questions just discussed in addition to certain issues pertaining to the analysis itself. This chapter is necessarily broad in scope yet very detailed in some places. To assist the reader, the chapter has been divided into three sections: the relationship between employee attitudes and customer loyalty, the relationship between customer loyalty and business outcomes, and summary comments.

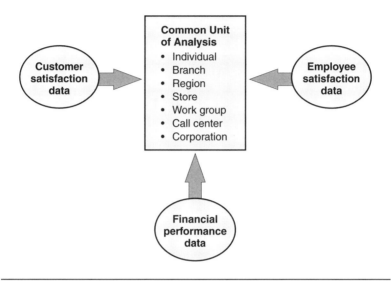

Figure 7.1   A common unit of analysis.

THE RELATIONSHIP BETWEEN EMPLOYEE ATTITUDES AND CUSTOMER LOYALTY

The Unit of Analysis

Any type of quantitative analysis requires a data file whose contents are interrelated in the form of a matrix. Each row is an object (usually a person in survey research, but not necessarily), and each column is a separate measurement. In the simplest case, one of those columns is employee overall satisfaction and the other is customer loyalty. But what does each row represent? A customer, an employee, a group of employees defined by company organization, or something else? The problem is that the employee and customer studies usually do not have a unit of analysis in common, and therefore one must be developed as illustrated in Figure 7.2.

Suppose that we make each employee a row in the data file. A difficulty with this strategy is that most analytical methods assume that the rows (or employees, in this instance) in the data file are "statistically independent" of each other. However, in our situation, the rows are not statistically independent of each other, as a given employee's overall satisfaction is correlated with the overall satisfaction of other employees in his or her organizational

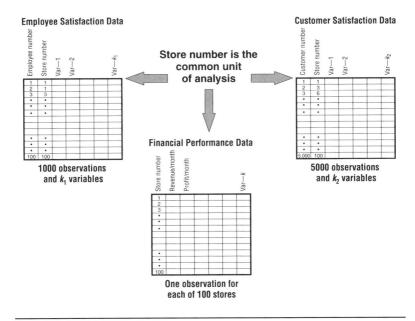

Figure 7.2   Customer satisfaction and employee satisfaction data structures.

unit. This improperly influences the results of significance testing in the analysis and may affect other results of the analysis.

Philosophical Issues

This evokes a larger philosophical issue: Should employee attitudes be measured at the individual or the organizational level? If the attitudes are measured at the organizational level, at which level within the organization should they be measured? In making this decision, we must distinguish among employee satisfaction, employee commitment, market orientation, and service climate.

It can be strongly argued that employee satisfaction and employee commitment are *by definition* employee-level phenomena and therefore that each row in the data file should represent an individual employee. But there are other considerations. One is that the satisfaction and commitment of an individual employee influences the satisfaction and commitment of other employees within the organizational unit. Furthermore, employees within a unit are functionally interdependent, and therefore the performance of one employee affects the performance of the organizational unit (generally and in terms of providing customer service).

In addition, the purpose of the research is to provide the client with guidance in managing employee satisfaction and commitment, and this management is performed at the organizational unit level. This partly explains why some of the questions in the employee questionnaire directly or implicitly reference an organizational unit, such as the employee's evaluation of his or her immediate manager and the employee's perceptions of the values of senior management.

Our decision is easier in the case of market orientation and service climate, as these are more clearly organizational unit phenomena. Admittedly, some researchers would disagree with this. The industrial/organizational psychology literature discusses this at length—interested readers should consult Glick (1988); Rousseau (1985); James, Joyce, and Slocum (1988); Ashkanasy, Wilderom, and Peterson (2000); and Schneider and Bowen (1985).

Operational Issues

Suppose that we continue to make each employee a row in the data file. How do we obtain the columns (variables) in the data file? Consider the simplest case, one with two columns representing employee overall satisfaction and customer loyalty. Typically, each employee has contact with multiple customers in the customer survey, and so we would obtain a customer loyalty score for each employee by taking the mean of the loyalty scores of the appropriate customers. But which customers are the appropriate ones? We will address this question for service and manufacturing companies separately.

Regarding service organizations, we know the organizational unit membership of each employee and can sometimes determine which particular organizational unit served a particular customer. Using a retail chain illustration, we know which store a given employee works in and we can probably determine which store a given customer visited by asking the appropriate questions in the customer interview. But information on which *particular* employee served which *particular* customer is usually unknown, as this information is seldom recorded, or even obtained, during the purchase process. (This is the case in business-to-consumer studies. On the other hand, this information is usually recorded in business-to-business interactions).

Making this association is much more problematic in the case of a product or manufacturing company. It is true that during the manufacturing process in many industries, identifying information is physically imprinted or attached to each unit of product or its packaging. This theoretically would enable us to determine which manufacturing plant produced the unit and perhaps even in which shift and which day or week the manufacturing process was completed. But this identifying information is seldom recorded by the retailer during the purchase process, and consequently we have no way to link a particular unit of product (and therefore a particular employee) with a particular customer. Theoretically, we could obtain this product-identifying information from the respondent, but this is also problematic. In some studies—but not many—the distribution system of the product is such that we can infer the manufacturing plant on the basis of the city in which the product was purchased. Another problem may arise if the product has components manufactured by different companies. Personal computers are an example, in that the hard disk, motherboard, and monitor are often manufactured by different companies. The respondent is not necessarily aware of how well or badly these components are functioning individually, and therefore we cannot ask him or her to evaluate them individually. Furthermore, the functioning of one component influences the functioning of other components.

Which Organizational Level Should We Use?

Let's assume that we have decided that each row in the data file will represent an organizational unit. We must now decide which level within the organization (for example, a store or a department within a store) will be represented. We must often make trade-offs in order to arrive at this decision. On one hand, the organizational level chosen needs to be such that within each organizational unit, the employees are as homogeneous as possible in terms of their attitudes. In most instances, this is the *lowest* organizational level (such as a department within a store). Homogeneity is desirable because it reduces the degree to which the effect of one employee "cancels out" the effect of another employee. This canceling-out effect can occur in three instances: (1) when the employee attitudinal scores are averaged to obtain a score for the organizational unit, (2) when the customer loyalty scores are averaged to obtain a score for the organizational unit, and (3) when a customer has contact with multiple employees.

On the other hand, the sampling variability of the mean *customer loyalty* score within the organizational units must be considered. A key issue here is that the number of organizational units is usually smaller at high organizational levels than at low organizational levels. For example, a company typically has fewer stores than it has departments within stores. Consequently, the number of customers interviewed within a given unit at lower organizational levels is often so small that sampling variability is unacceptably large, therefore requiring us to use a *higher* organizational unit.

We usually do not have to consider sampling variability of the mean *employee* scores within the organizational units, because we often do not draw a sample but rather attempt to interview all the employees. But measurement error is a consideration, and the reasoning in the preceding paragraph applies again here.

The number of organizational units is also a consideration in its own right. While the number of units required depends upon the analytical technique and the number of variables used, even simple analyses, with the exception of graphical ones, require at least 30 organizational units. However, this requirement can be decreased by obtaining measurements at multiple time periods (for example, quarterly) for each organizational unit. Not as many organizational units are needed if this is done, because each time period for each organizational unit is an observation in the analysis.

A Caveat

In even the most homogeneous organizational unit, employees and customers differ among themselves, and therefore individual persons will, to some degree, "cancel out" others when their scores are averaged. For example, a situation in which half the employees in a given organizational unit have high satisfaction scores while the other half have low satisfaction scores will yield the same mean score as one in which all of the employees are moderately satisfied.

This effect is usually very strong in product studies, because the number of employees in a manufacturing plant (or on a shift within a manufacturing plant) is typically much larger than the number of employees in an organizational unit in a service industry. The significance of this should be stressed: in our experience, attempts to analyze the relationship between employee attitudes in manufacturing companies and customer loyalty are seldom fruitful.

Empirical Guidance in Selecting Organizational Level

Support or disconfirmation of our decision on the organizational level can be obtained empirically as follows. Given our discussion of the reasons for attitudinal differences among employees, we can reasonably assert the following premise: *the "best" organizational level for our purposes is the one in which within-unit differences are as low as possible.* In assessing a given organizational level, we have found it useful to compare it with the total sample. The reasoning behind this is that, on average, the amount of variation (in employee attitudes and customer loyalty) within an organizational unit should be less than at the total sample level.

We can assess and compare amounts of variation by using certain concepts and statistics first used in classical analysis of variance (ANOVA) and later in cluster analysis. These concepts and statistics are as follows. In ANOVA, the total amount of variation in a variable is the sum of two values, the "within-group sum of squares" and the "between-group sum of squares." A "sum of squares" is calculated by subtracting the respective mean score from each respondent's score, squaring it (thereby obtaining the absolute value), and then summing across respondents.

In the case of the within-group sum of squares, the respective mean is the group mean. For example, in an ANOVA analysis in which state of residence is the independent variable and income (coded in dollar values) is the dependent variable, we would use the mean score of Texas respondents when using Texas residents in calculating the within-group sum of squares. Similarly, we would use the mean score of Wisconsin respondents when using Wisconsin residents in calculating the within-group sum of squares. Continuing the illustration, the between-group sum of squares is calculated by subtracting the grand mean (the mean using respondents from all states) from each state's mean score, squaring each score, and then summing across states. Some cluster analysis programs use these data to assess the statistical quality of a given cluster solution. This is done because most researchers believe that one of the desirable characteristics of a cluster solution is that respondents differ within their respective clusters less than respondents differ at the total sample level, in terms of the variables used to create the clusters.

For example, some cluster analysis programs calculate a "heterogeneity index" for each variable in the analysis, for each cluster by dividing the within-cluster sum of squares by the total sample sum of squares. A value of 1 on the heterogeneity index indicates that the members of the cluster are no more or less similar to each other (with respect to the variable under consideration) than respondents at the total sample level. A value of less than 1 indicates that the members of the cluster *are* more similar to each other than members of the total sample are similar to each other. Therefore, cluster solutions in which the clusters have heterogeneity indices of less than 1 are desirable.

A cluster whose heterogeneity index is greater than 1 is a cluster in which some members are "outliers"; that is, they are substantially different from the other members of the cluster. The reason that the computer program puts those respondents together is that the program "has to put them somewhere."

Returning to our situation, what we do is calculate heterogeneity indices treating each organizational unit (at the organizational level being considered) as a cluster. Note that a heterogeneity index is calculated for *each question* in the questionnaire for *each organizational unit*. These values need to be evaluated row-wise and columnwise. They should first be examined row-wise to identify organizational units whose members are so heterogeneous that they should be excluded from the analysis.

The heterogeneity indices should then be evaluated columnwise to identify questions in the questionnaire tending to have heterogeneity indices greater than 1; such questions may be more appropriately analyzed at a different organizational level. For example, suppose that we initially believe that we should use the store as the organizational level and that we therefore build a data file in which each store is a line in the data file. When we examine the heterogeneity indices as described above, we may find that most of the stores have heterogeneity indices less than 1 on most of the questions in the questionnaire but that there are some questions on which most stores have heterogeneity indices greater than 1. This may indicate that the latter questions should be analyzed at a different level, that is, using a data file in which each line is not a store but something else, such as a department within a store.

Of course, we can obtain guidance as to the appropriate level by considering the text of the question—does the question ask respondents to report the morale of their work group or to evaluate the store manager—and by considering the management structure of the company. On an operational note, the authors know of no publicly available software that can be used to calculate heterogeneity indices in our situation. However, custom software can be developed.

Further Discussion of Using the Appropriate Organizational Level

Standard analytical techniques used to perform driver analysis can use only one data file at a time. Consequently, they cannot, for example, simultaneously use one data file in which each store is a row and another data file in which each department within each store is a row. But it is well known that the results of driver analysis often differ depending upon the unit of analysis (Ostroff 1993). Consequently, *if standard analytical techniques are used in the driver analysis, the results may be incorrect if not all the questions in the questionnaire are measured at the same organizational level.*

The solution in this situation is to have multiple levels of analysis. One way to accomplish this is an analytical technique called hierarchical linear models (HLM), which is explicitly designed for analyses having multiple levels of unit of analysis. This technique is explained in Bryk and Raudenbush (1992) and Kreft and DeLeeuw (1998). However, HLM is more difficult to use than most techniques. It also complicates the sample design, as we need a sufficient number of respondents at multiple levels of analysis and a sufficient number at each level. Consequently, the practical applicability of this technique is limited.

An Interesting Finding

We often find that the correlations between employee satisfaction attributes and employee overall satisfaction are lower at the employee level than at the organizational level. This is consistent with our discussion that suggested that this relationship might be most appropriately analyzed at the organizational level. But there is another possible explanation for this finding, which has to do with measurement error. That is, the mean score of employees within an organizational unit may have less measurement error than any employee's individual score, on average. (Measurement error can attenuate the magnitude of correlations).

THE RELATIONSHIP BETWEEN CUSTOMER LOYALTY AND BUSINESS OUTCOMES

Business Outcomes

The relationship between customer loyalty and several business outcomes has been the focus of numerous investigations. The business outcomes studied include stock price, company market share, customer retention, purchase volume at the customer level (number of purchase occasions, number of units purchased, total dollar value of purchases, and share of wallet), and sales volume and profit margin at the organizational unit level, as shown in Figure 7.3.

In consumer markets, perhaps the most frequently studied business outcome is purchase volume at the customer level. This is partly because of

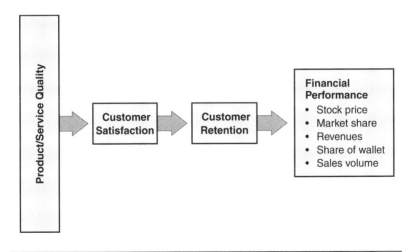

Figure 7.3 Financial performance as a result of customer retention.

the accessibility of this information, as it can be obtained in the customer loyalty survey interview (although its accuracy can be questioned in low-involvement product categories).

The Rows in the Data Matrix

As discussed in the employee–customer section, any type of quantitative analysis requires a data file the contents of which are interrelated in the form of a matrix in which each row is an object and each column is a separate measurement. In the simplest of studies, we would have two columns, one for customer loyalty and one for a business outcome. But what does each row represent? Fortunately, making this decision is not nearly as difficult here, largely because the philosophical aspects of the unit of analysis are less complex.

Philosophical Issues

As discussed earlier, there are several different business outcomes that can be studied. For each one, which level the business outcome is "at" is usually fairly obvious. For example, company stock price and company profit margin by definition are at the company level, store profit margin is at the store level, and so on.

Regarding customer loyalty, some of our discussion in the employee–customer section applies. Customer loyalty is at the customer level by definition, but there are other considerations. One is that the purpose of customer research is to provide the client with guidance in managing customer loyalty; because this management is performed at the organizational unit level, analysis at the organizational unit level may be appropriate.

Operational Issues

Matters get more difficult here. Suppose that the business outcome is at the individual level. Is business outcome information available for individual customers? In studies of most business-to-consumer situations, this is problematic. For example, consider fast food. As part of normal business operations, fast-food outlets do not obtain the customer's name or similar identifying information that would be necessary in merging customer survey information with business outcome information at the customer level.

Customer-level purchase behavior information can be obtained in the customer loyalty survey interview, although as mentioned earlier, its accuracy may be questioned in low-involvement product categories. In such instances, it may be more appropriate to conduct the analysis at the organizational unit level, that is, to make each organizational unit a row in the data file and to obtain customer loyalty and business outcome scores by calculating means across respondents within each organizational unit.

On the other hand, in some business-to-consumer situations (such as consumer banking) and in most business-to-business ones, customer-level purchase behavior information is collected and recorded as part of normal business operations. Conceivably, this could be merged with customer loyalty survey data and the analysis performed at the customer level.

Preparation and Reliability of Business Outcome Data

Even when the business outcome information is collected as part of normal business operations, certain data validity questions have to be addressed. Some of the more important ones are as follows: Does the business outcome data file contain all the respondents (customers) it should? If not, do the respondents who are missing differ systematically from those who are present, such as being disproportionately new customers or customers from certain organizational units? How many missing values does each field have? Do the respondents who are associated with missing data in a given field differ systematically from those who have supplied valid responses? How often is the information in the business outcome data file updated? In customer retention studies, if the client's data-processing system is such that customers who leave the company are removed from the business outcome data file, how do we know whether *all* of the respondents who are missing from the business outcome data file are missing because they have left the company?

There are dozens of other technical issues to be addressed. For example, in consumer banking, exactly how are *retained* and *left* defined? For example, if a person's balance drops below a certain level and has remained unchanged for a certain length of time, should that person still be classified as retained?

Other Issues

On average, the more frequently a product or service is purchased, the more likely it is that a relationship will be found between customer loyalty and business outcomes, especially if the analysis is performed at the individual level. The reason for this is the greater opportunity for the consumer's satisfaction to influence his or her purchase behavior. For example, a consumer who is dissatisfied with an automobile will nevertheless probably not purchase another automobile for several years because of the cost of replacement.

The *form* of the relationship between customer loyalty and business outcomes depends upon which business outcome is being studied. Specifically, this refers to retention or some measure of intensity of use. In our experience, the relationship between customer loyalty and retention is much stronger at the low end of the loyalty scale than at the high end. In contrast, the relationship between customer loyalty and intensity of use seldom has this shape.

In frequently purchased product categories, share of wallet is usually preferable to absolute measures of purchase volume. Share of wallet has the additional advantage of probably yielding less measurement error, especially in consumer studies. This is the case because a respondent can more likely accurately recall what percentage of all purchases were of a given brand value than accurately recall the absolute number of purchases of the brand.

Longitudinal versus Cross-Sectional Analysis

As a general rule, a longitudinal analysis is preferable to a cross-sectional one. Longitudinal analysis refers to data collected at intervals over time, whereas cross-sectional data are typically collected during one time period. For example, the following types of design are logitudinal:

- Relation of loyalty at t_1 to retention or intensity of use at t_2

- Relation of loyalty at t_1 to a change in retention or intensity of use between t_1 and t_2

- Relation of a change in loyalty between t_1 and t_2 to a change in retention or intensity of use between t_1 and t_2

As discussed earlier in the employee–customer relationship section, one advantage of the second and third types of longitudinal design is that they afford the researcher a greater ability to infer causation on the basis of the study's results. When a cross-sectional analysis is performed, the analysis should include factors that might influence customer loyalty and/or the business outcome under study, such as store or department size, population density of the area served by the store, and average income of residents in the area served by the store.

Another advantage of the second and third types of design is as follows. In a cross-sectional analysis, if there is a large amount of case-to-case variability in retention or intensity of use, an observed difference in retention or intensity of use that is actually due to differences in customer loyalty will probably be attributed to variation that normally occurs. Indeed, even large observed relationships between loyalty and intensity of use are often statistically insignificant.

A large amount of case-to-case variability in business outcome variables is frequently encountered in analyses at the organizational unit level, because of differences in store or department size, population density of the area served by the store, average income of the population in the area, and so on. High case-to-case variability is sometimes encountered at the customer level (in, for example, savings account balances).

This problem of great variation in intensity of use is largely sidestepped in the second and third longitudinal designs, because the analysis focuses on a *change* at the case level. This is relevant because there is usually much less case-to-case variation in a difference than there is case-to-case variation in the variables being used to create the difference. For example, stores differ more among themselves in terms of yearly sales than in terms of the change in sales from one year to the next.

The problem of case-to-case variability in business outcome variables can be completely avoided by studying the percentage change (calculated at the case level) instead of the absolute change. Continuing the earlier illustration, construct a variable equal to [(year 2 − year 1)/year 1] × 100. This is especially appropriate in studies in which share of wallet is an issue. However, a frequently encountered problem of the third longitudinal design is an insufficient number of customers (or stores) whose customer loyalty scores have changed. This is an issue because in order to examine the effect of a change in customer loyalty, customer loyalty must indeed change. An advantage possessed by all three designs is that they give the customer the opportunity for his or her satisfaction to influence behavior (assuming that we are able to study the customer over a sufficient length of time).

SUMMARY COMMENTS

It is well known among survey researchers that one part of a study design can affect other parts. This is the reasoning behind commonly heard statements such as "Don't begin data collection until you know how you will analyze the data." This is an overstatement with respect to any research study, and especially the type of study discussed here, because data analysis is performed in an iterative manner, with early analytical findings influencing plans for subsequent analyses.

But there is a lot of truth to such statements, especially in studies of this type. A critical instance of this truth is that the sample design greatly constrains our decision of analytical approach. Specifically, (a) a sufficient number of observations is needed at the level at which the analysis is performed, and (b) if the analysis is performed at the organizational unit level, we need enough employee interviews and enough customer interviews within *each* organizational unit.

For this reason, the decision on unit of analysis should be made early in the research design process. As explained earlier, this decision is based on philosophical and operational considerations. The philosophical aspect involves deciding the level of the concepts under study. This is not simply a definitional issue and should be guided by the experience and knowledge of the managerial structure of the company under study.

The operational aspect involves determining which employees' data should be attached to which customer and how to actually accomplish that attachment. Generally speaking, this is easier in business-to-business studies than in business-to-consumer studies; in consumer markets, it is easier when services (as opposed to products) are being studied.

8
Analysis Framework: Bivariate Relationships

INTRODUCTION

Linking customer and employee satisfaction to financial performance can be conducted on a number of levels. In the simplest scenario, we attempt to relate two univariate measures: customer or employee satisfaction and a financial performance metric. This chapter initially introduces a set of correlation measures and then turns to a case study involving the use of canonical correlation analysis, which is technically a multivariate procedure. It is used to quantify the level of association between two *sets* of variables. In the simplest case, we have available just two variables: a financial performance metric and either a customer satisfaction or employee satisfaction measure. From an analytical standpoint, our efforts will be aimed at establishing a relationship between the two variables. There is no explicit causality in correlation measures—two variables are simply shown to covary. Of course, there may be valid inferences concerning causality, particularly if there is a natural sequencing among the variables. Such could be the case when a customer (or employee) satisfaction measure is shown to covary with a financial performance measure. It seems reasonable to conclude that heightened customer or employee satisfaction is responsible for the change in financial performance. Of course, one could also argue the reverse ordering.

One of the simplest ways to relate customer or employee satisfaction to financial performance involves comparing two (or more) metrics at two points in time. This bivariate approach was recently implemented by a large North American bank. The project involved a total of 2000 customers and focused on relating their satisfaction at two points in time to key behavioral measures reflected in account activity and monthly profitability.

As shown in Figure 8.1, the project involved measuring satisfaction levels among a group of 2000 customers at two points in time. After the initial measurement in January 1999, we tracked the following key financial metrics for an entire year:

- Accounts opened or closed

- Deposit and loan balances

- Investment account balances

- Monthly household profit

The key to understanding this study involves the comparison of an individual customer's satisfaction level at the two measurement times. A 10-point scale was collapsed into three levels to facilitate comparisons across the two interview times. Specifically, the 10-point scale data were aggregated in the following manner:

1–6 = Low satisfaction

7–8 = Moderate satisfaction

9–10 = High satisfaction

By collapsing the distribution in this fashion, we simplified the t_1 versus t_2 comparisons. In effect, nine outcomes were possible when comparing individual satisfaction levels across the two time periods, as shown in Table 8.1.

A summary of the overall results is presented in Figure 8.2. The figure depicts a three-by-three matrix that reflects the nine change conditions described above. Note that the rows reflect t_1 satisfaction levels and the columns present t_2 satisfaction levels. The three cells that form the top-left-to-bottom-right diagonal indicate *no change* in satisfaction from t_1 to t_2.

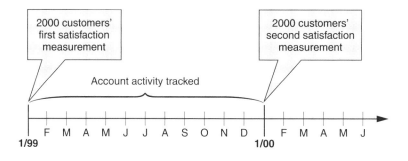

Figure 8.1   Project timeline.

Each cell in the matrix presented in Figure 8.2 reflects a change (or lack thereof) in profitability. The change in profitability is depicted by either an up arrow ($\uparrow$) or a down arrow ($\downarrow$) to represent an increase or a decrease, respectively. Modest changes are indicated with a single arrow, while more substantive increases or decreases are represented by multiple arrows.

Table 8.1 Possible changes in customer satisfaction across two study periods.

Time t_1	Time t_2	Difference
Low	Low	
Medium	Medium	No change in satisfaction
High	High	
Low	Medium	
Low	High	Increase in satisfaction
Medium	High	
Medium	Low	
High	Medium	Decrease in satisfaction
High	Low	

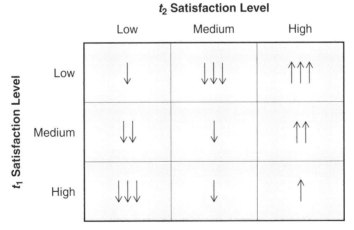

Figure 8.2 Summary of changes in key profitability indices.

As shown, there are substantive differences in the profitability index associated with significant increases and decreases in satisfaction. Of particular interest may be the substantive decrease in profitability associated with a drop from the high-satisfaction group in t_1 to low satisfaction in t_2. Conversely, moving from low satisfaction in t_1 to high satisfaction in t_2 yielded a large increase in profitability.

There also appeared to be implications associated with a lack of change in satisfaction across the two study periods. Of special interest were the findings that remaining at the low-satisfaction or high-satisfaction levels resulted in modest decreases and increases in profitability, respectively. Remaining at the medium level of satisfaction across the two time periods yielded a decrease in profitability. However, moving from the medium satisfaction level at t_1 to the high level of satisfaction at t_2 was associated with a substantial increase in profitability.

This study illustrates a relatively easy way to relate satisfaction to profitability at the customer level. Extensions of this design could aggregate individual household satisfaction levels at the bank branch level and add employee satisfaction to the mix. This added layer of complexity could be accommodated by the data matrix illustrated in Figure 8.3.

The design illustrated in Figure 8.3 will facilitate a bivariate analysis of the relative impact that changes in employee and customer satisfaction have on branch-level profitability. That is, one could ascertain the relative profit change associated with *row* versus *column* movement from t_1 to t_2.

The remainder of this chapter introduces a variety of bivariate measures of association. We initially review some standard measures of correlation and then turn to a technically multivariate measure of association (the canonical correlation coefficient) and present a case study in which this metric greatly simplifies the relationships among a series of sets of variables.

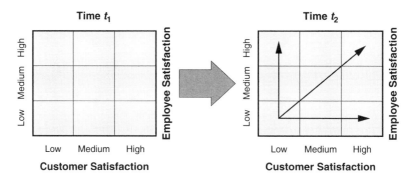

Figure 8.3 Branch-level time dependence of employee and customer satisfaction.

BIVARIATE MEASURES
OF ASSOCIATION

While the Pearson, Kendall, and Spearman correlation coefficients are most widely recognized, there are other less familiar coefficients intended to accommodate situations that do not involve two numeric variables. Phi and the point-biserial correlation coefficient are appropriate when both distributions are binary (phi) or when one is binary and the other continuous (point-biserial). The former case represents a nonparametric measure of association between *categorical* (nominal-level) variables. The biserial correlation accommodates another unique situation: when one variable is continuous and the remaining variable is recorded as binary but is characterized by underlying continuity and normality. Such may be the case when a continuous variable has been dichotomized. Other measures of association appropriate for categorical data include the Cramér coefficient V and the Spearman and Kendall rank-order correlation coefficients.

The correlation coefficient measures the extent to which two variables covary. There is no implied *causation,* per se. Rather, the correlation simply reveals that two variables tend to be related. The classic example involves intelligence and achievement. A high correlation exists between these two variables, and yet, despite the intuitive appeal of such a relationship, the strong correlation does not prove that intelligence *causes* achievement, only that the two are strongly related.

The most basic form of measuring the extent to which two variables are related—or are *dependent* upon one another—involves the correlation coefficient. This measure ranges from +1.00 to −1.00. A correlation coefficient of +1.00 indicates perfect agreement between two variables, while a coefficient of −1.00 suggests a perfect inverse relationship. When the value of a correlation is zero or very near zero, the implication is that there is no relationship whatsoever between the two variables. Figure 8.4 illustrates the types of bivariate relationships that can be summarized by the correlation coefficient.

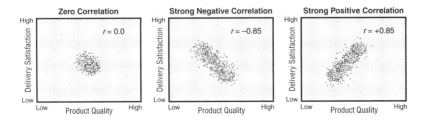

Figure 8.4   Illustration of correlation coefficients.

As implied above, the correlation coefficient represents the most basic form of dependence metric. This is because it measures the extent to which two variables covary. The analysis of more complex dependency relationships that are characterized by several predictor variables, such as those addressed by multiple regression, must take into account the simultaneous effects of all of the predictors. A significant strength of the simple correlation, however, is that only two variables are in question so that the impact of missing values is not as profound as it is in multivariate techniques. The simple correlation, while clearly limited, does permit us to make inferences involving variables that have high levels of missing data and would therefore be excluded from multivariate analyses.

A simple use of the correlation coefficient involves summarization of the relationship between customer satisfaction (x_1), employee satisfaction (x_2), and profitability (y). If the correlation (r_{x_1y}) between customer satisfaction and profitability is .40 and the correlation (r_{x_2y}) between employee satisfaction and profitability is .20, for example, we must compare these metrics cautiously. Concluding that the relationship between employee satisfaction and profitability $(r_{x_2y} = .20)$ is *half* as strong as the relationship between customer satisfaction and profitability $(r_{x_1y} = .40)$ would be erroneous. This is because correlation coefficients must be *squared* to be directly compared with one another. When squared, a correlation coefficient reflects the proportion of variance two variables have in common. It is this measure (r^2) that should be used for comparisons. In the present case, we should conclude that the relationship between customer satisfaction and profitability $(r^2_{x_1y} = .16)$ is considerably stronger than the relationship between employee satisfaction and profitability $(r^2_{x_2y} = .04)$. In fact, the customer satisfaction and profit measures share *four times* as much variance as the employee satisfaction and profit measures.

The unstandardized cousin of the correlation coefficient is the covariance measure. It is not scaled to 1.00 as the correlation coefficient is. Instead, it remains in the units of the phenomenon that is being measured. As a result, comparing the covariances of measures that use the same scale is acceptable. While customer and employee satisfaction are typically measured using a 5-point, 7-point, or 10-point scale, financial measures are typically captured in dollars. Thus, comparing the covariance between employee satisfaction and customer satisfaction with the covariance between employee satisfaction and financial performance would be meaningless.

Both the correlation matrix **R** and the covariance matrix **C** are routinely used as inputs to a variety of multivariate procedures. Principal components analysis, for example, involves the decomposition of either the correlation matrix or the covariance matrix. Similarly, multiple regression analysis can be conducted using only the correlation matrix. Latent and manifest variable path analyses are also based on a decomposition of either **R** or **C**. Table 8.2 summarizes the types of correlation coefficients available to analysts and notes the types of data each assumes.

Table 8.2 Summary of measures of bivariate association.

Correlation Type	Symbol	Calculation	Applications
Pearson	r_p	$$r_p = \frac{\sum_{i=1}^{n}(x_i - \bar{x})(y_i - \bar{y})}{\left[\sum_{i=1}^{n}(x_i - \bar{x})^2 \sum_{i=1}^{n}(y_i - \bar{y})^2\right]^{1/2}}$$	Technically referred to as the Pearson product moment correlation coefficient; assumes at least interval-level, normally distributed data.
Kendall's tau	τ	$$\tau = \frac{2S}{n(n-1)}$$	Rank-order correlation coefficient in which S is the sum of the number of pairs of ranks that are in their natural order on x_k when cases are ranked in ascending order on x_j. The number of pairs that are not in order is then subtracted from this.
Spearman rho	ρ_s	$$\rho = 1 - \frac{6\sum_{i=1}^{n}d_i^2}{n^3 - n}$$	Rank-order correlation coefficient in which the relationship between ordinal variables x_j and x_k is of interest.
Phi	ϕ	$$\phi = \frac{ad - bc}{\left[(a+b)(c+d)(a+c)(b+d)\right]^{1/2}}$$ or $\phi = \left(\frac{\chi^2}{n}\right)^{1/2}$	A measure of association between two variables that form a 2 × 2 contingency table. The coefficient ranges from 0 to 1, with the latter indicating perfect dependence.
Cramer's V	V	$$V = \left(\phi^2 / \min\left[(r-1)(c-1)\right]\right)^{1/2}$$	A measure of association similar to phi but applicable to tables larger than 2 × 2.
Point-biserial	r_{pb}	$$r_{pb} = \frac{\bar{y}_1 - \bar{y}_0}{S_y}\sqrt{pq}$$	Correlation coefficient that assumes that one variable is continuous (y) and the other is dichotomous (x). The calculation of r_{pb} assumes that $\bar{y}_1$ is the sample mean of y for observations where $x = 1$ and $\bar{y}_0$ is the mean of y for observations where $x = 0$, S_y is the standard deviation of y, and p is the percentage of observations where $x = 1$ and $q = 1 - p$.
Tetrachoric	r_t	See Kendall and Stewart (1958, 306)	Relates two binary variables x_j and x_k and estimates r_p if the binary variables are drawn from a normal distribution.

CASE STUDY: CANONICAL CORRELATION ANALYSIS

This case study focuses on an example of a manufacturer with very detailed customer and employee satisfaction data coupled with financial performance data. Unfortunately, this manufacturer had only 95 sales territories, which meant that sophisticated multivariate analysis was all but precluded. We also briefly discuss the role of multiple regression analysis in our effort to link customer and employee satisfaction to profitability. Finally, the bulk of this chapter focuses on causal modeling and how it can be used to test hypotheses that posit a causal sequencing among key variables.

Frequently, we encounter situations that are characterized by a very limited sample size. This was the case for a noted manufacturer with considerable employee and customer satisfaction data for each of its sales territories. In addition to the satisfaction data, the company also had very detailed financial performance data for each sales territory. Since the objective was to analyze the data at the sales territory level, the types of analysis that were feasible were constrained considerably. In effect, the small sample size precluded the use of multivariate techniques such as multiple regression and path analysis.

From an analytical standpoint, the project presented a challenge. Seven disparate data sets were the subject of the investigation; no single respondent was present in each. This reality precluded the traditional data analysis approach wherein the responses of *individuals* are analyzed and required to be present in each data set. The implication of this was that a higher level of analysis was necessary. Table 8.3 illustrates the nature of the data problem. As shown, the data sets were composed of varying numbers of records, and no respondent was present in all seven data sets simultaneously.

Four customer satisfaction surveys were included (CSS1–CSS4) and were associated with widely differing numbers of responses. Some of the

Table 8.3 Data set composition and size.

Data Set	Number of Records
CSS1—Transaction satisfaction (phone—12 items)	1,265
CSS2—Relationship satisfaction (phone—16 items)	24,790
CSS3—Problem resolution (mail—14 items)	188,767
CSS4—Sales experience (phone—14 items)	21,551
Employee satisfaction survey (mail—16 items)	11,909
District retention metric	95
District profitability metric	95

data sources were composed of sales-district-level data (namely, customer retention and profitability) and as such had only 95 physical records. In contrast, the CSS3 data included over 180,000 physical records. Clearly, a traditional analysis of the seven data sets was precluded unless they were concatenated based upon some common unit or level of analysis.

Our approach to the data analysis problem presented involved aggregating the data from each source to the district level. That is, each data set was *collapsed by sales district* into a much smaller matrix made up of 95 rows, each representing a sales district. The nature and number of variables in each data set were unaffected by this procedure. In effect, the procedure involved calculating the *mean* of each variable at the sales district level. Of course, this process was unnecessary for the data sets that were already composed of sales-district-level data (customer retention and profitability).

By collapsing the CSS1–CSS4 and employee satisfaction data by sales district, a common unit of analysis became available in each data set: the sales district. As a result, we were able to merge the seven data sets into one large matrix with 95 rows (one for each sales district). Figure 8.5 illustrates the combined data set, which has 95 rows and contains all of the variables from the seven input data sources. The key, however, is that the variables represent *means* at the sales district level.

Merging the data sets permitted traditional bivariate analytical techniques to be applied. As noted earlier, however, only 95 observations were

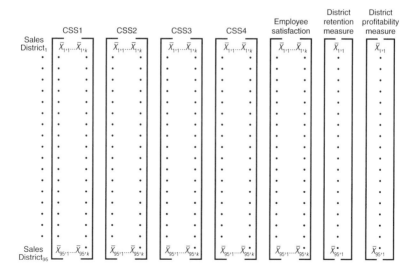

Figure 8.5 Collapsing seven data files by sales district.

available—one for each sales district. Each row of the combined data set contains a series of means—the average score on each variable for a given sales district. With so few observations ($n = 95$), a wide variety of multivariate techniques were not possible. We initially focused on *bivariate* relationships by examining correlations among all the variables in the combined data set.

To illustrate the size of the resultant (combined data) correlation matrix, consider a data set with 20 variables. If we examine every possible unique correlation among the variables in this data set, we must review about 200 individual coefficients. With 40 variables, the correlation matrix would contain over 500 unique correlations. The data set used in this analysis was composed of 95 rows and 74 columns. Clearly, a review of each correlation would be exhausting, and it would be difficult to isolate patterns of significant correlations by visually reviewing such a large matrix.

Figure 8.6 represents the substantial correlation matrix that was used for this analysis. Note that it is a *lower triangular matrix;* the top half is a mirror image of the bottom half and is therefore omitted.

The shaded diagonal of Figure 8.6 reflects correlations that are *within* a given data set. The shaded section labeled R_{11}, for example, represents the correlation matrix of all CSS1 variables with one another. This is of very limited use here since our interest involves relationships across studies. Thus, all of the relationships on the diagonal (R_{11} through R_{77}) involve

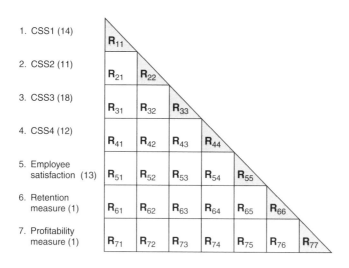

Figure 8.6   Illustration of lower triangular matrix for all survey and financial performance data.

the relationships *within* each of the seven data sets that make up the combined matrix. Note that the number of variables in each data set is included in parentheses.

In contrast to the relationships that exist on the diagonal, *off-diagonal* relationships are of considerable interest. They reveal the extent to which the variables in one data set are related to the variables in other studies. For example, R_{43} contains all the correlations between the CSS3 satisfaction variables and the CSS4 data. Similarly, R_{61} contains all the correlations between the retention measure and the 14 variables in the CSS1 data set. Of course, each of these cells comprises many individual correlations—too many to graphically depict in the figure. The exception to this is R_{76}, which comprises a single correlation coefficient that reflects the relationship between profitability and retention.

Our analytical approach *initially* involved assessing the patterns of correlations in each of the off-diagonal cells to determine the extent of the relationships between pairs of data sets. This rather subjective approach was used to determine whether any significant relationships between the studies existed. Given the limited sample size ($n = 95$), there was a very real possibility that this inspection would yield a complete absence of significant interstudy relationships. Once it was established that significant interstudy relationships were present, we used a technique known as *canonical correlation analysis* to summarize the extent to which key variables in one study were related to key variables in each of the others.

The canonical correlation coefficient is interpreted exactly as one would interpret a simple pairwise correlation. The key is that the canonical correlation measures the relationship between two *groups* of variables. This approach was very appealing in the present analysis since there were many different satisfaction items in each study. The canonical correlation coefficient lets us summarize the interstudy relationships with a *single* metric.

Typically, canonical correlation analysis considers one set of variables to be dependent upon the other. Of course, while this implies a causal relationship, no cause-and-effect sequence is established based on canonical correlation analysis. Interestingly, when there is only one dependent measure and a set of several predictor variables, the analysis framework reduces to multiple regression analysis. In fact, multiple regression analysis can be considered to be a special case of canonical correlation analysis. Canonical correlation analysis makes few assumptions regarding the distributions of the variables to be used. Variables can be measured at the ordinal or even nominal levels. However, as Dillon and Goldstein (1984, 339) warned, in order to test the statistical significance of the correlations, the data must be multivariate normal and be characterized by homogeneity of variance.

Statistical testing involving canonical correlation analysis was first outlined by Bartlett (1951). Testing the significance of canonical variates involves the use of Wilks' lambda likelihood–ratio criterion, defined as

$$\Lambda = \frac{\mathbf{W}}{\mathbf{W} + \mathbf{B}}$$

where $\mathbf{W}$ is the within-groups sum-of-squares matrix and $\mathbf{B}$ is the between-groups sum-of-squares matrix. As Dillon and Goldstein wrote (1984, 421), we reject H_0 that the p criterion variables are unrelated to the m predictor variables when values of Λ are small. When the null hypothesis can be rejected, the first canonical variate pair's contribution is removed from Λ and the same test for the remaining variate pairs is conducted.

It is important to note that the canonical correlation is a measure that only indirectly involves the original manifest variables. That is, canonical correlation analysis quantifies the relationships between composites of variables and not the original variables. As Dillon and Goldstein (1984, 337–38) suggested, canonical correlation analysis involves "two linear combinations, one for the predictor set and one for the criterion set, such that their ordinary product-moment correlation is as large as possible." While canonical correlation coefficients are analogous to ordinary bivariate measures of association such as the Pearson correlation coefficient, canonical correlations quantify the association between *canonical variates*, not the original variables. The canonical variates are computed using both sets of variables (criterion and predictor). A canonical variate is analogous to a component in principal components analysis. The primary difference, according to Dillon and Goldstein (1984, 338) "is that a variate consists of a maximally correlated predictor and criterion part. A maximum of M variates can be extracted where M is the number of variables in the smallest set. As in principal components analysis, the M variates are extracted so that they are independent of one another."

Interestingly, the canonical correlation coefficient is equivalent to the multiple correlation coefficient (R) in one case. That is, when one data set is comprised of a single measure and the other is characterized by multiple measures then we have a situation equivalent to multiple regression analysis. This can be easily demonstrated using any of the major statistical software packages. If we further reduce this scenario by limiting both data sets to one variable, the simple bivariate correlation coefficient is appropriate.

In the following discussion, we introduce a causal framework for understanding how the studies are related to one another. Two caveats must be introduced in this regard. First, this approach is intended to lend additional structure to the analysis and facilitate an understanding of the relationships.

We have not performed causal modeling or otherwise empirically established a causal sequence among the variables. Instead, we introduce a *theoretical framework* for understanding the relationships. The second caveat is related to the implied causal sequence and involves the *timing* of the individual studies. In particular, the data that were used in this study were derived over relatively long periods of time; the CSS4 data, for example, reflect interviews that were conducted over more than one year. This timing issue should be considered when reviewing the findings presented in this case study.

The matrix described in Figure 8.6 was initially reviewed in terms of the number of statistically significant correlations that emerged in each off-diagonal cell. Again, each off-diagonal cell is comprised of unique correlation coefficients that measure the relationship between the variables in two studies. Following this subjective review of the correlations, we used canonical correlation analysis to summarize the extent to which two groups of variables covaried.

Figure 8.7 provides a high-level summary of the extent to which the variables in one data source covaried with the variables in another. Recall that the covariation is measured across the 95 sales districts. The implication of strong covariation is that sales districts with high scores in one area (for example, CSS1) also have high scores in another (for example, CSS3).

Each cell in Figure 8.7 is shaded if the Wilks' lambda (Λ) is statistically significant at the 90% confidence level. As shown, there was considerable covariation across the survey data sets. Only the CSS1 data

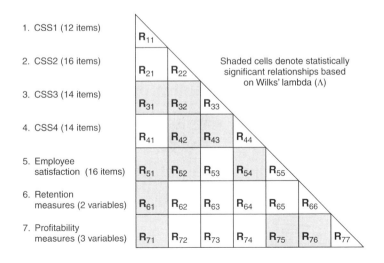

Figure 8.7 Summary of canonical correlations among data sources.

(transaction satisfaction) emerged as significantly related to both dependent variable sets. The employee satisfaction data were related to the profitability data. Finally, the two retention measures were significantly related to the three profitability variables.

CAUSAL FRAMEWORK

In an effort to structure the findings, we arranged the seven individual components of the analysis in a theoretical framework (Figure 8.8). This approach implicitly suggests that the components are causally linked. As noted earlier, however, there is no empirical evidence to support the causal framework; it is used principally to make the findings more understandable.

The studies are arranged in a causal sequence that flows from left to right. That is, employee satisfaction and the four customer satisfaction measures affect customer retention. Customer retention, in turn, is presumed to affect profitability.

We estimated the overall relationship between each pair of studies using the SAS Sytem's *canonical correlation* procedure. The results of the estimation process are presented in Figure 8.8, which translates the significant canonical correlation coefficients to paths for the purposes of this illustration. As shown, there are numerous strong relationships among the studies. Of key interest are the relationships between the first customer satisfaction study, the employee satisfaction study, and the profitability

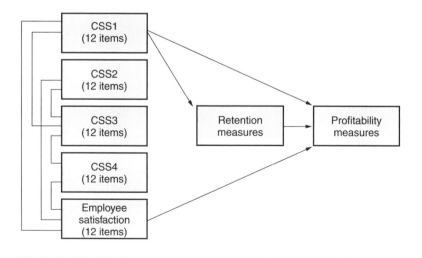

Figure 8.8   Theoretical framework.

measure. Note, too, that while none of the five predictor data sets was significantly linked to the retention measure, there was a significant relationship between the retention measure and profitability.

A number of points should be kept in mind when considering the results of this analysis. These are (1) sample size, (2) temporal ordering, (3) measuring association, and (4) causality. Perhaps the least ambiguous of these issues involves sample size. Clearly, 95 observations make a small sample upon which to base the general conclusions discussed in this analysis. The second limitation of this study involves when the data from each component were collected. In some cases (such as the event-based studies) a continuous sampling approach was used. In others (such as the retention and profitability metrics), a summary measure for the year was employed. The effect of this disparate ordering is unknown; it could affect the results presented here, however.

The final limitation of this research involves causality. By no means have we demonstrated a cause-and-effect relationship. We have, however, provided a *theoretical* framework for interpreting the relationships among the various studies. That no empirical evidence exists to support this framework cannot be overemphasized, however. In light of the preceding limitations, it was quite gratifying to uncover numerous significant relationships among the data sets. With so few observations it would have been reasonable to expect only modest—if any—relationships.

While technically a multivariate technique, canonical correlation analysis is analogous to its bivariate cousin. Canonical correlation analysis can play an important role when the analytical goal is to relate two (or more) sets of measurements. As an alternative to the approach described above one could generate a large correlation matrix relating all of the items in the multiple studies to one another. This, however, would have required a very large matrix that would have been difficult to interpret.

9
Analysis Framework: Regression Models

DEPENDENCE MODELING WITH MULTIPLE REGRESSION

In our attempts to understand the relationships between customer satisfaction, employee satisfaction, customer retention, and financial performance, there are a number of statistical techniques available to us. The most widely used technique in customer satisfaction research involves multiple regression analysis. It is used to demonstrate the simultaneous effects of a series of predictor variables upon a single dependent measure such as overall customer satisfaction. The model typically takes the form

$$y = \beta_0 + \beta_1 x_1 + \beta_2 x_2 + \ldots + \beta_k x_k + e$$

where y is a dependent measure such as overall satisfaction and the variables x_1 through x_k are predictor variables such as specific service and product quality issues. The influence of each predictor variable on the single outcome measure is determined by the magnitude of the beta (β) coefficient. We typically assume that larger values of the beta coefficient are associated with a stronger impact on the dependent variable. The error e is assumed to be a random variable with a mean of zero. Of course, this is a considerably simplified explanation of multiple regression analysis. Draper and Smith (1998) provide a comprehensive treatment of this technique.

In the present case, we are interested in how a series of predictor variables affects a single measure of financial performance. Multiple regression analysis lets us assess the impact of each predictor on the outcome variable.

As shown in Figure 9.1, a set of customer and employee satisfaction variables is used to predict a single financial performance outcome measure.

The magnitude of the *standardized* beta coefficient is used to assess the impact of a series of disparate predictor variables on the financial outcome measure. This is because often the types of scales used in employee satisfaction and customer satisfaction survey instruments rely upon different numbers of points. Employee satisfaction and customer satisfaction research programs are typically administered by different organizational units. Most often customer satisfaction programs are managed by marketing research or service quality departments, while employee satisfaction programs are run by human resource departments. It should come as no surprise that these programs frequently do not use the same measurement scales. As a result, we rely upon the standardized beta coefficient: it standardizes the effects of the predictor variables so that they can be reasonably compared.

One aspect of a multiple regression analysis that is almost always reported is the coefficient of determination R^2. This is the multivariate version of the simple bivariate correlation coefficient. The R^2 statistic is the squared multiple correlation coefficient. When R (the multiple correlation coefficient) is squared, the resulting summary statistic reflects the proportion of variance in y accounted for by the set of predictor variables. In customer and employee satisfaction studies in which the dependent measure is an overall summary judgment of satisfaction, we usually encounter R^2 values of greater than .75, which means that the set of predictor variables accounts for 75 percent of the variation in overall satisfaction. However, when the dependent measure is a financial performance metric, we rarely observe R^2 values in excess of .25. This should not be surprising, of course, because so many factors affect financial performance. These include macroeconomic

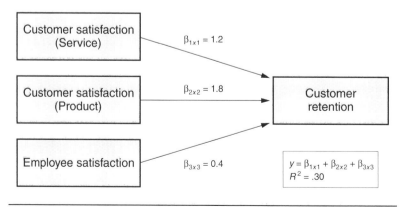

Figure 9.1 Illustration of multiple regression analysis.

variables reflecting consumer demand, accounting practices, and corporate finance decisions.

We frequently use the *adjusted R^2* measure to compare the efficacy of two regression models. This statistic takes into account the number of predictor variables that were entered into each model. The adjusted R^2 measure is desirable because the R^2 statistic can be artificially increased by adding predictor variables to the equation. Thus, when comparing two regression models, the adjusted R^2 should be used.

Another aspect of multiple regression models that is of interest involves the model development process. Because our predictor variables are nearly always correlated in customer and employee satisfaction research, it is difficult to ascertain which predictor variables are most strongly related to the dependent measure. Since they are all interrelated, it is challenging to determine which predictor variables make unique contributions with respect to our effort to account for variation in the dependent measure. The general problem of correlated predictor variables is referred to as collinearity or ill conditioning. When the correlations among predictor variables reach relatively high levels, the multiple regression equation can be harmed. Manifestations of severe collinearity include beta coefficients with the wrong signs and very large standard errors around the beta coefficients. In the former case, a model characterized by high levels of collinearity might suggest that decreasing satisfaction with product quality will increase financial performance. Clearly, such erroneous results should alert the researcher to the possibility that degrading levels of collinearity are present.

Several metrics are useful in diagnosing collinearity, which, incidentally, is always present at some level except when the predictor variables are orthogonal (perfectly uncorrelated). Two of the most frequently encountered conditioning diagnostics include variance infliction factors and the conditioning index. Both metrics are discussed in Dillon and Goldstein (1984, 271–78).

When the level of collinearity in a data set is so high that it adversely affects the regression model, a number of tacks are possible. One frequently employed technique is known as *ridge regression*. This method involves data manipulation based on a single parameter k. The ridge regression procedure was first treated by Hoerl and Kennard (1970, 55–67). The ridge regression technique simply augments the diagonal of the centered cross-product matrix for the predictor variables ($\mathbf{X}$) with k, as demonstrated:

$$\mathbf{b_r} = \left(\mathbf{X'X} + kI\right)^{-1}\mathbf{X'y}$$

When $k = 0$ there is no effect on the least squares solution, and any value $k > 0$ will change the estimates. In fact, as $k \to \infty$ (k approaches infinity), the estimates become smaller and smaller. There are a variety of ways to select an appropriate value of k, but most situations are characterized by values $0 \leq k \leq 1$. A plot called the *ridge trace* is frequently used to assess the effect of various values of k.

Ridge regression is controversial, primarily because the researcher must actually modify the original data set based on subjective estimates. Modifying a data set simply because it has properties (ill conditioning) that are mathematically inconvenient is considered by many critics to be a drastic step. On the other hand, ridge regression may be able to resolve a seemingly insurmountable problem of near linear dependency among predictor variables.

Another approach to highly collinear data is *principal components regression* (PCR), which is explained in much greater detail later in this chapter. This technique involves the use of principal components analysis to reduce the dimensionality of the predictor side (X) of the regression equation. By applying principal components analysis to the set of predictors, a subset of orthogonal component scores is derived. Since they are perfectly uncorrelated, the collinearity problem is moot. One problem with PCR, however, is that we essentially lose the original variables and have to turn to orthogonal linear combinations of them. Thus, it is somewhat more difficult to link specific variables to changes in financial performance. Instead, we must work with linear combinations of the original variables. Interpretation of the linear combinations is usually performed based on the "loadings" of the original variables on the principal components. In this fashion, the principal components are given labels such as "service quality," "product quality," "employee engagement," and so on.

Technically, PCR is the marriage of multiple regression and principal components analysis and can be represented in matrix form as:

$$\mathbf{b} = \mathbf{U}\left[\mathbf{U'X'XU}\right]^{-1}\mathbf{U'X'y}$$

(9-1)

where $\mathbf{b}$ is the vector of beta coefficients, $\mathbf{X}$ is the set of predictor variables, $\mathbf{y}$ is the vector of dependent variable values, and $\mathbf{U}$ is composed of the characteristic vectors derived through eigenanalysis.

Belsley, Kuh, and Welsch (1980, 193) suggested that one of the simplest approaches to conditioning problems involves adding new data. The addition of new data points, the authors suggested, may provide the additional variation necessary to reduce the level of linear dependence in the predictor variable data set. They conceded, however, that this tack may have limited utility to econometricians and other researchers who have limited data and resources for collecting more observations.

Belsley, Kuh, and Welsch (1980, 194–96) also introduced a series of three Bayesian-type techniques for circumventing the collinearity problem.

Bayesian approaches in statistics typically involve the introduction of probability values based upon prior knowledge with respect to the phenomenon in question. A full discussion of Bayes theory is beyond the scope of this book; Hartigan (1983) provides a comprehensive treatment of the subject. As Belsley, Kuh, and Welsch (1980, 194) suggested, the ill-conditioning problem "can in fact be dealt with if the investigator possesses (and is willing to use) subjective prior information on the parameters of the model." While Bayesian approaches are intuitively appealing, the authors cite several drawbacks associated with them. These include a lack of prior information, requirements for a rather precise estimate of the prior distribution, and reliance on statistical theory that is not widely understood.

Certain variable retention schemes are also used to remove variables in an effort to reduce harmful levels of collinearity. Of concern here is how many predictor variables should be retained in the final predictive model. A variety of model development procedures exist. Most frequently encountered are sequential selection procedures such as forward selection, backward selection, and stepwise selection. These mechanical procedures add predictor variables to or subtract them from the equation in an effort to obtain a subset of predictor variables that are all statistically significant. Dillon and Goldstein (1984, 235–42) provide a substantive treatment of selection procedures.

ALTERNATIVE REGRESSION MODELS

Multiple regression models based on ordinary least squares (OLS) are used so frequently that researchers often forget some of the fundamental assumptions underlying the technique. These assumptions involve the distribution of the residuals, correlations among the residuals, correlations between the X variables and the residual term, the distribution of the dependent variable, and the fact that there is no collinearity. Not infrequently, one or more of these assumptions is disregarded in the development of multiple regression models. We have introduced a number of approaches to multiple regression with highly collinear data. There are other occasions, however, when alternative regression models may be appropriate. Of special interest are the logistic regression model and the nonlinear regression model.

LOGISTIC REGRESSION ANALYSIS

The classic regression analysis framework is generally used in the following manner. A series of one or more *numeric* independent variables (such as satisfaction with service, billing, and product quality) are used to predict one *numeric* dependent variable (such as overall satisfaction). In the present case, the dependent variable is not numeric per se. It can take only two values. This might be the case when we want to differentiate between two groups, such as in determining whether a particular sales district posts financial performance scores that exceed the regional norm. In this case, the dependent variable is binary: either the sales district exceeds the regional norm or it does not.

When regression analysis employs a series of numeric independent variables to predict a single binary dependent variable, the classic OLS model tends to be inadequate (Hosmer and Lemeshow 1989, 5–7) based upon two important criteria. First, the conditional mean of *y* is constrained to take only two values—for example, 0 and 1. More technically, the conditional mean of the outcome variable $E(y \mid x)$ is limited and as it approaches its extremes (0 or 1) becomes increasingly curvilinear or S-shaped. The second difference between binary and interval- or ratio-level dependent variables cited by Hosmer and Lemeshow involves the distribution of the error term *e*. In short, the distribution of *e* under the conditions of a binary outcome variable violates the assumptions associated with OLS. Based upon these violations, researchers rely upon logistic regression analysis.

The logit link is nonlinear and has several advantages for classification purposes. In the binary dependent variable case, the logit $g_{(x)}$ is:

$$g_{(x)} = \ln \frac{\pi_{(x)}}{1 - \pi_{(x)}}$$

and

$$\pi_{(x)} = \frac{e^{g_{(x)}}}{1 + e^{g_{(x)}}}$$

where $\pi_{(x)}$ is equal to the *probability* of being a member of the highly (dis)satisfied group. The logit $g_{(x)}$ is calculated as one would if classical regression analysis were used:

$$g_{(x)} = \beta_0 + \beta_1 x_1 + \beta_2 x_2 + \ldots + \beta_k x_k + e$$

An example will facilitate an understanding of how the technique is applied. Consider the case of a hypothetical chemical company. Its 400 global sales districts vary considerably with respect to financial performance. Our interest focuses on which customer and employee satisfaction issues differentiate the top and bottom quartiles in terms of profitability.

Profitability was determined based on net income over net sales. This was then divided by the market potential of each sales district. Five specific satisfaction items were used to contrast the top and bottom quartiles of the profitability distribution:

- Overall customer satisfaction with problem resolution

- Overall customer satisfaction with service quality

- Overall employee satisfaction with engagement issues

- Overall employee satisfaction with management style

- Overall employee satisfaction with role definition

Note that issues beyond the control of the sales districts were not included. For example, while product quality is an important component of the corporate loyalty model, individual sales districts have little control over this issue. Similarly, employee compensation clearly drives overall employee satisfaction, but the individual districts must comply with corporate wage scales for the country in which they operate. The five satisfaction items included here, therefore, tend to involve issues that can be controlled by the individual sales districts. In each case, the average district score was used.

Our model takes the following form. First, we have a series of five predictor variables, all measured on a 10-point scale. Further, we have a single dependent measure that is binary in nature. It can take only two values, reflecting the top and bottom quartiles of the profitability distribution. It is a 1 when a sales district is in the bottom quartile of the profitability distribution and a 4 when a sales district is in the top quartile of the distribution. Sales districts in the second and third quartiles were removed from the analysis so that the reduced dataset contains only the two extremes. A sample of the data set is depicted in Table 9.1.

Table 9.1   Logistic regression data set using five predictor variables.

Sales District	Quartile	CSS1	CSS2	ESS1	ESS2	ESS3
001	1	8.9	8.5	8.6	8.9	9.0
002	1	8.7	8.3	8.3	8.5	8.9
003	4	9.1	9.1	9.0	8.9	8.8
004	1	8.8	9.1	8.7	8.9	9.1
005	4	8.7	9.3	9.4	9.1	8.9
:	:	:	:	:	:	:
400	4	9.1	9.0	8.7	8.6	9.1

Based upon the preceding, our model takes the following (somewhat) familiar form:

$$g_{(x)} = \beta_0 + \beta_1 x_1 + \beta_2 x_2 + \ldots + \beta_k x_k + e$$

Note that $g_{(x)}$ is the outcome variable—technically, the logit x. Calculation of $g_{(x)}$ employs maximum likelihood analysis. An explanation of this technique is well beyond the scope of this book. Interested readers may wish to refer to Hosmer and Lemeshow's (1989) exhaustive treatment of the logistic regression analysis technique.

For the purposes of this illustration, we have five predictor variables and one binary dependent variable. When we examine the average satisfaction scores between the two groups, it becomes clear that sales districts in the highest-profitability quartile enjoyed customer and employee satisfaction ratings that were higher than those of their colleagues in the lowest quartile. This is depicted in Figure 9.2.

When multiple logistic regression is used, the dependent variable can take on two values. In the present case, these were coded "1" and "4," indicating that the sales district was in the first (lowest) or fourth (highest) quartile, respectively. Table 9.2 suggests that problem resolution (x_1) has the greatest impact on the binary dependent variable. The logistic regression analysis confirms that the second best predictor of the dependent variable

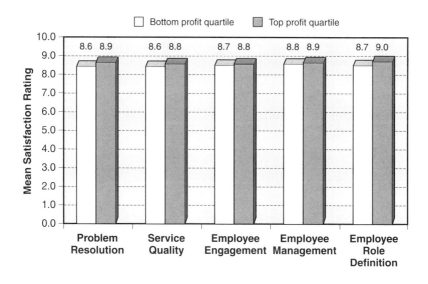

Figure 9.2   Differences across binary independent variables.

Table 9.2 Results of logistic regression.

Variable	Parameter Estimate	Standard Error	Chi-Square	Probability Chi-Square
Intercept	45.48	7.58	36.54	0.000
x_1. Problem resolution	−2.52	0.56	19.83	0.000
x_2. Service quality	−0.29	0.56	0.26	0.600
x_3. Empl. Engagemt.	0.31	0.70	0.20	0.650
x_4. Empl. managemt.	−1.03	0.66	2.42	0.119
x_5. Empl. role def.	−1.61	0.61	6.90	0.008

is employee role definition (x_5). These conclusions are based on the probability of the chi-square statistic associated with the parameter estimate.

Equations 9-2 and 9-3 represent the first steps in calculating the probability of group membership. The logit $g_{(x)}$ is calculated in a manner reminiscent of ordinary regression analysis. Thus, a sales district with an average score of 9.0 would have a $g_{(x)}$ value of −1.62, which by itself has little prima facie meaning. Interpreting $g_{(x)}$ requires us to return to the logit link shown in Equation 9-4.

$$g_{(x)} = 45.48 - 2.52_{(x_1)} - 0.29_{(x_2)} + 0.31_{(x3)} - 1.03_{(x4)} + 1.16_{(x5)} \qquad (9\text{-}2)$$

$$g_{(x)} = -45.48 - (2.52 \times 9.0) - (0.29 \times 9.0) + (0.31 \times 9.0)$$
$$- (1.03 \times 9.0) - (1.16 \times 9.0) \qquad (9\text{-}3)$$

$$\pi_{(x)} = \frac{e^{g_{(x)}}}{1 + e^{g_{(x)}}} \qquad (9\text{-}4)$$

If we now insert the value −0.78 for $g_{(x)}$, the value of $\pi_{(x)}$ becomes 0.458 divided by 1.458. Thus, the value of $\pi_{(x)}$ is approximately 0.31, or 31%. This means that a sales district with an average score of 9.0 on each of the five customer and employee satisfaction items has only a 31% chance of being in the lowest-profitability quartile. If we increase the average value of the predictor variables to 9.2, then $g_{(x)} = -1.79$ and $\pi_{(x)}$ becomes 0.167 divided by 1.167, or 0.14, which is equivalent to a 14% chance of being in the lowest-profitability quartile. Of course, these percentages can be inverted to reflect the probability of being in the highest-profitability quartile. A score average of 9.0 on each of the five satisfaction issues suggests a 79% probability of being in the upper quartile, while a score of 9.2 on each would yield an 86% chance of being in the top quartile.

Different statistical packages approach the interpretation of $\pi_{(x)}$ in varying ways. Most notably, SAS considers this the probability of being in the *lower-valued* binary code, which in this case is indicative of the "1" value. In contrast, SPSS produces the opposite output: the value of $\pi_{(x)}$ is considered the probability of membership in the *higher-valued* binary code. In the present case, the data suggest that a sales district with an average of 9.0 on each of the five satisfaction measures has a 79% chance of being in the top performing group. Thus, it is the nonlinear logit link presented in Equation 9-5 that permits inferences concerning the probability of group membership, purchase propensity, or any other binary states.

Logistic regression can accommodate other scenarios as well. For example, polychotomous or multinomial logistic regression is intended for dependent variables that take more than two states. Consider the case of a dependent variable with three possible values (0, 1, and 2). A conditional probability for each state must be considered, as shown in Equations 9-5 through 9-7.

$$P\left(Y=0|x\right)=\frac{1}{1+e^{g_1(x)}=e^{g_2(x)}} \tag{9-5}$$

$$P\left(Y=1|x\right)=\frac{e^{g_1(x)}}{1+e^{g_1(x)}+e^{g_2(x)}} \tag{9-6}$$

$$P\left(Y=2|x\right)=\frac{e^{g_2(x)}}{1+e^{g_1(x)}+e^{g_2(x)}} \tag{9-7}$$

This approach addresses the polychotomous logistic regression model for a nominal dependent variable that takes three values. Other models that accommodate ordinal level multinomial dependent variables are also available. A thorough review of all types is provided by McCullagh and Nelder (1983). Hosmer and Lemeshow (1989, 216–45) also provide discussions concerning polychotomous-model-building strategies.

PRINCIPAL COMPONENTS REGRESSION

The mechanics of least squares regression analysis have already been described. This section presents a technique that combines multiple regression analysis with principal components analysis (PCA). PCA is used in this context as a means for either reducing collinearity in the set of predictor variables or reducing the complexity (that is, the dimensionality) of a large set of predictor variables. In either case, the PCA technique is the same. A technical treatment of PCA is provided in the Appendix.

Technically, PCA is a multivariate data-reduction technique that seeks to transform an original data matrix into a smaller set of linear combinations that together account for most of the original matrix's total variance. The purpose is to explain as much of the data's total variation as possible with as *few* principal components as possible. As many components (m) as there are variables (p) can be extracted. Since $p = m$ is not a parsimonious reduction of the data, one must determine how many components (m) to retain. The first extracted component accounts for the most original data matrix variance. Subsequent extractions account for less and less variance until $p = m$. In short, PCA (and factor analysis) yield as many factors as there are variables. The objective is to develop a parsimonious reduction of the data matrix. This means we must account for as much of the original data variation as we can with as few components as possible.

$$PC_{(1)} = w_{(1)1}X_1 + w_{(1)2}X_2 + w_{(1)3}X_3 + \ldots + w_{(1)p}X_p$$
$$PC_{(2)} = w_{(2)1}X_1 + w_{(2)2}X_2 + w_{(2)3}X_3 + \ldots + w_{(2)p}X_p$$
$$PC_{(3)} = w_{(3)1}X_1 + w_{(3)2}X_2 + w_{(3)3}X_3 + \ldots + w_{(3)p}X_p$$
$$\vdots$$
$$PC_{(m)} = w_{(m)1}X_1 + w_{(m)2}X_2 + w_{(m)3}X_3 + \ldots + w_{(m)p}X_p \tag{9-8}$$

In equation 9-8 above, the first component $PC_{(1)}$ is the linear combination of the observed variables $X_j, j = 1, 2, \ldots, p$, where the weights $w_{(1)1}$, $w_{(1)2}, \ldots, w_{(1)p}$ are selected to maximize the ratio of the variance of the first component $PC_{(1)}$ to the *total* variation. The next component, $PC_{(2)}$, is the weighted linear combination of the original variables that is *uncorrelated* with the first. It also accounts for the maximum amount of the total remaining variation. As shown, it is possible to extract as many components as there are variables. However, the goal of PCA (and factor analysis) is to account for as much variance in the original data matrix as possible with as *few* components as possible. Determining how many components (or factors) to retain is discussed in detail below.

PCA and factor analysis decompose correlation matrices. In PCA, the diagonal of the correlation matrix is assumed to be made up of 1s, as shown in Table 9.3. The diagonal of 1s in the correlation matrix makes it easy to see its symmetry. The upper triangle is a mirror image of the lower triangle. In practice, only the lower triangle is depicted in reports; the upper triangle is shown here to illustrate the actual matrix and its symmetrical property.

Table 9.3 contains a hypothetical correlation matrix that has two clearly visible pockets of strong intercorrelations. The first involves the relationship between the employee satisfaction variables (ES1 through ES4) in the upper left portion of the correlation matrix. The second pocket of strong correlations appears in the lower right part of the matrix and involves the customer satisfaction variables CS1 through CS5. Note that outside of these two areas the matrix is characterized by relatively low correlations. It would be safe to assume that if it were subjected to PCA, this matrix would yield a two-component solution. That is, most of the variance in the correlation matrix could be accounted for with two principal components. Furthermore, since we know that PCA extracts components that account for less and less of the original data matrix variance, it would be reasonable to conclude that the first factor would involve variables CS1 through CS5, since they are characterized by the strongest intercorrelations. Figure 9.3 illustrates how components (or factors) are drawn. As shown, the first component is orthogonal to the second and accounts for

Table 9.3 Sample correlation matrix.

	ES1	ES2	ES3	ES4	CS1	CS2	CS3	CS4	CS5
ES1	**1.0**	.81	.79	.82	.24	.32	.31	.32	.21
ES2	.81	**1.0**	.89	.84	.34	.22	.31	.32	.21
ES3	.79	.89	**1.0**	.81	.42	.33	.32	.41	.28
ES4	.82	.84	.81	**1.0**	.34	.23	.42	.35	.29
CS1	.24	.34	.42	.34	**1.0**	.91	.84	.93	.88
CS2	.32	.22	.33	.23	.91	**1.0**	.92	.91	.89
CS3	.31	.31	.32	.42	.84	.92	**1.0**	.84	.88
CS4	.32	.32	.41	.35	.93	.91	.84	**1.0**	.87
CS5	.21	.21	.28	.29	.88	.89	.88	.87	**1.0**

Figure 9.3 Principal components of bivariate data.

the most *variation* in the data. The second component accounts for less variation. Had this figure been presented in three dimensions, a third line would have been drawn through the z axis of the data cluster.

That the diagonal of the correlation matrix in PCA is composed of 1s differentiates this technique from factor analysis. The total variance to be accounted for in a correlation matrix subjected to the PCA technique is equal to the sum of the diagonal elements, which all happen to be 1s. In the correlation matrix presented in Table 9.4, this equals nine, which is also the number of variables in the analysis since each contributes one unit of variance. The objective is to account for as much of this total matrix variance as possible with as few components as possible.

Technically, *principal components regression* (PCR) is the marriage of OLS multiple regression and PCA and can be represented in matrix form as shown in Equation 9-1. Rather than using a large set of predictor variables that might be beset with collinearity problems, PCR uses the subset of principal components as predictor variables. These are perfectly uncorrelated. Thus, PCR can solve two related problems simultaneously. First, it can help us make sense of a dizzying number of predictor variables by revealing the common dimensions underlying them. Second, PCR solves the collinearity problem by producing a smaller set of uncorrelated predictor variables.

An example of PCR illustrates how the technique can make a large set of predictor variables more manageable. Consider the case of Astro Loans, a consumer loan agency with retail operations in nearly 600 locations. This financial services organization conducted three different customer satisfaction studies and three short employee satisfaction studies over the course of one year. Following is a summary of the six survey efforts:

> CS1: 8-item customer satisfaction survey on service quality issues
>
> CS2: 10-item customer satisfaction survey on product quality issues
>
> CS3: 5-item customer satisfaction survey on problem resolution issues
>
> ES1: 3-item employee satisfaction survey on compensation issues
>
> ES2: 4-item employee satisfaction survey on management style issues
>
> ES3: 8-item employee satisfaction survey on working conditions

The intercorrelations among the 23 customer satisfaction variables and 15 employee satisfaction items are presented in Table 9.4. Correlations within a given survey are highlighted. Note that these are, in general, higher than the interstudy correlations. The last line in the table presents the correlations between the profit measure and the 38 employee and customer satisfaction items. As shown, this relationship is quite modest and rarely exceeds $r = .40$.

The Astro Loans data set comprises a single profit measure scaled to market potential and the 38 employee and customer satisfaction items for each of the nearly 600 retail operations. Of particular interest in this instance is the relationship between the 38 questionnaire items and the single financial performance outcome measure. Normally, we would use multiple regression analysis to assess the simultaneous impact of the 38 predictor variables on the single financial performance outcome variable. Calculation of the *condition index,* however, suggests that the predictor side of the equation suffers from degrading levels of collinearity. Belsley, Kuh, and Welsch (1980, 153) suggested "Condition indexes of 100 or more appear large indeed, causing substantial variance inflation and great potential harm to regression estimates." In the present case, the condition index slightly exceeds 100 and is sufficiently high to cause us to reevaluate our use of multiple regression. We could turn to one of numerous mechanical selection procedures such as stepwise, forward, or backward selection, but these exclude variables that have nontrivial relationships with the dependent variable.

The use of PCR in this case is a reasonable tack due to the high level of collinearity and the large number of variables involved. PCR will address both of these problematic conditions by reducing the number of variables that are orthogonal (perfectly uncorrelated). The variable-reduction task involves retaining only principal components that are meaningful inasmuch as they account for substantive proportions of variance in the predictor variable data matrix. This is an important step because PCA produces as many components as there are variables. Our charge is to retain only those dimensions that are meaningful.

In the present case, four factors were retained. The rotated factor pattern is presented in Table 9.5. The derivation of this matrix is described in the Appendix. As shown, the 38 variables each tend to load on one of the four principal components. The four components tend to parallel the survey structures quite well. Interestingly, most of the employee satisfaction items tend to load only modestly on the four components. The exception to this involves the four ES2 items, which involve management style issues. These emerged as a quite distinct dimension. The remaining employee satisfaction items were ambiguous in terms of their loadings. Clearly, PCR has

Table 9.4   Intercorrelations among customer satisfaction and employee satisfaction surveys.

	CS1a	CS1b	CS1c	CS1d	CS1e	CS1f	CS1g	CS1h	CS2a	CS2b	CS2c	CS2d	CS2e	CS2f	CS2g	CS2h	CS2i	CS2j	CS3a	CS3b	CS3c	CS3d	CS3e	ES1a	ES1b	ES1c	ES2a	ES2b	ES2c	ES2d	ES3a	ES3b	ES3c	ES3d	ES3e	ES3f	ES3g	ES3h	Profit
CS1a	1.0																																						
CS1b	0.6	1.0																																					
CS1c	0.6	0.6	1.0																																				
CS1d	0.7	0.7	0.7	1.0																																			
CS1e	0.5	0.6	0.6	0.6	1.0																																		
CS1f	0.6	0.6	0.6	0.7	0.6	1.0																																	
CS1g	0.6	0.6	0.6	0.6	0.5	0.5	1.0																																
CS1h	0.6	0.6	0.6	0.6	0.5	0.6	0.6	1.0																															
CS2a	0.5	0.4	0.5	0.5	0.4	0.5	0.5	0.5	1.0																														
CS2b	0.6	0.5	0.6	0.6	0.5	0.5	0.5	0.5	0.6	1.0																													
CS2c	0.6	0.5	0.6	0.6	0.5	0.6	0.6	0.5	0.5	0.7	1.0																												
CS2d	0.6	0.5	0.6	0.6	0.5	0.6	0.5	0.5	0.5	0.7	0.8	1.0																											
CS2e	0.6	0.5	0.5	0.6	0.5	0.6	0.5	0.5	0.5	0.6	0.7	0.8	1.0																										
CS2f	0.5	0.5	0.5	0.5	0.4	0.5	0.4	0.4	0.4	0.6	0.7	0.7	0.7	1.0																									
CS2g	0.5	0.5	0.5	0.5	0.5	0.6	0.5	0.5	0.4	0.6	0.7	0.7	0.7	0.7	1.0																								
CS2h	0.6	0.5	0.6	0.6	0.5	0.6	0.5	0.5	0.4	0.6	0.6	0.6	0.6	0.6	0.7	1.0																							
CS2i	0.6	0.5	0.6	0.6	0.5	0.6	0.5	0.5	0.4	0.6	0.6	0.6	0.5	0.6	0.6	0.9	1.0																						
CS2j	0.5	0.5	0.5	0.5	0.5	0.5	0.5	0.5	0.4	0.5	0.5	0.5	0.5	0.5	0.6	0.7	0.7	1.0																					
CS3a	0.6	0.5	0.6	0.6	0.6	0.6	0.5	0.6	0.5	0.6	0.5	0.5	0.5	0.5	0.5	0.6	0.6	0.5	1.0																				
CS3b	0.4	0.4	0.4	0.4	0.4	0.4	0.4	0.4	0.4	0.5	0.5	0.5	0.5	0.5	0.5	0.5	0.5	0.4	0.6	1.0																			
CS3c	0.4	0.4	0.4	0.5	0.4	0.5	0.4	0.4	0.4	0.5	0.5	0.5	0.5	0.4	0.5	0.4	0.4	0.4	0.5	0.6	1.0																		
CS3d	0.4	0.4	0.4	0.4	0.4	0.4	0.4	0.4	0.4	0.5	0.5	0.5	0.5	0.4	0.5	0.4	0.4	0.4	0.4	0.6	0.7	1.0																	
CS3e	0.5	0.4	0.5	0.5	0.4	0.5	0.4	0.5	0.5	0.5	0.5	0.5	0.5	0.5	0.5	0.5	0.5	0.5	0.6	0.6	0.6	0.6	1.0																
ES1a	0.5	0.5	0.5	0.6	0.5	0.6	0.5	0.5	0.5	0.6	0.6	0.6	0.6	0.6	0.6	0.6	0.6	0.6	0.6	0.5	0.5	0.5	0.6	1.0															
ES1b	0.6	0.5	0.6	0.6	0.5	0.6	0.6	0.6	0.6	0.6	0.6	0.6	0.6	0.6	0.6	0.6	0.7	0.6	0.6	0.5	0.5	0.5	0.6	0.8	1.0														
ES1c	0.4	0.4	0.4	0.4	0.4	0.4	0.4	0.4	0.4	0.4	0.3	0.4	0.4	0.4	0.4	0.4	0.4	0.4	0.5	0.5	0.6	0.5	0.6	0.5	0.6	1.0													
ES2a	0.4	0.4	0.4	0.4	0.4	0.4	0.4	0.4	0.4	0.4	0.4	0.4	0.4	0.4	0.4	0.4	0.4	0.4	0.5	0.5	0.6	0.5	0.5	0.5	0.6	0.6	1.0												
ES2b	0.4	0.4	0.4	0.4	0.4	0.5	0.4	0.4	0.4	0.4	0.4	0.4	0.4	0.4	0.5	0.4	0.4	0.4	0.5	0.6	0.5	0.5	0.6	0.6	0.6	0.6	0.7	1.0											
ES2c	0.4	0.4	0.5	0.5	0.4	0.5	0.5	0.5	0.4	0.5	0.5	0.5	0.5	0.4	0.5	0.4	0.4	0.5	0.6	0.5	0.5	0.5	0.5	0.6	0.6	0.5	0.6	0.6	1.0										
ES2d	0.5	0.5	0.5	0.5	0.5	0.6	0.5	0.5	0.4	0.6	0.6	0.6	0.6	0.5	0.6	0.5	0.5	0.5	0.6	0.5	0.5	0.5	0.5	0.6	0.6	0.5	0.6	0.6	0.7	1.0									
ES3a	0.5	0.5	0.5	0.6	0.5	0.6	0.5	0.5	0.5	0.6	0.6	0.6	0.6	0.6	0.6	0.6	0.6	0.6	0.6	0.6	0.5	0.6	0.6	0.6	0.7	0.5	0.6	0.6	0.6	0.7	1.0								
ES3b	0.5	0.5	0.5	0.6	0.5	0.6	0.5	0.5	0.5	0.6	0.6	0.6	0.6	0.6	0.6	0.6	0.6	0.6	0.6	0.6	0.5	0.6	0.6	0.6	0.7	0.5	0.6	0.6	0.6	0.7	0.8	1.0							
ES3c	0.5	0.5	0.5	0.5	0.5	0.6	0.5	0.5	0.5	0.6	0.6	0.6	0.6	0.5	0.6	0.5	0.5	0.6	0.6	0.5	0.5	0.5	0.5	0.6	0.6	0.5	0.6	0.6	0.6	0.7	0.7	0.7	1.0						
ES3d	0.5	0.5	0.5	0.5	0.5	0.6	0.5	0.5	0.5	0.6	0.6	0.6	0.6	0.5	0.6	0.5	0.5	0.6	0.6	0.5	0.5	0.5	0.6	0.6	0.7	0.5	0.6	0.6	0.6	0.7	0.8	0.8	0.8	1.0					
ES3e	0.4	0.4	0.5	0.5	0.5	0.5	0.5	0.5	0.4	0.5	0.5	0.5	0.5	0.5	0.5	0.5	0.5	0.5	0.6	0.5	0.5	0.5	0.6	0.5	0.5	0.5	0.5	0.5	0.6	0.6	0.7	0.7	0.8	0.8	1.0				
ES3f	0.4	0.4	0.5	0.5	0.5	0.5	0.5	0.5	0.4	0.5	0.5	0.5	0.5	0.5	0.5	0.5	0.5	0.5	0.5	0.5	0.5	0.5	0.6	0.5	0.5	0.5	0.5	0.5	0.5	0.6	0.7	0.7	0.7	0.8	0.7	1.0			
ES3g	0.4	0.4	0.5	0.5	0.5	0.6	0.5	0.5	0.4	0.6	0.6	0.6	0.6	0.5	0.6	0.5	0.5	0.5	0.5	0.5	0.5	0.5	0.6	0.5	0.5	0.5	0.5	0.5	0.5	0.6	0.7	0.7	0.7	0.8	0.7	0.7	1.0		
ES3h	0.5	0.5	0.5	0.6	0.5	0.6	0.5	0.5	0.5	0.6	0.6	0.6	0.6	0.6	0.6	0.6	0.6	0.6	0.6	0.6	0.5	0.6	0.6	0.6	0.7	0.5	0.6	0.6	0.6	0.7	0.8	0.8	0.7	0.8	0.7	0.7	0.7	1.0	
Profit	0.3	0.3	0.3	0.3	0.3	0.3	0.3	0.3	0.3	0.3	0.3	0.3	0.3	0.3	0.3	0.3	0.3	0.3	0.4	0.3	0.4	0.3	0.4	0.2	0.2	0.3	0.3	0.2	0.3	0.3	0.2	0.2	0.2	0.2	0.2	0.2	0.2	0.2	1.0

Table 9.5   Rotated factor pattern for Astro Loans data.

Variable Name	CSAT Problem Resolution	CSAT Product Quality	CSAT Service Quality	ESAT Management Style
CS3d	0.75821	0.32861	0.15147	0.16729
CS3c	0.73452	0.26834	0.17592	0.10675
CS3b	0.70483	0.30278	0.16176	0.12601
ES3g	0.70265	0.19973	0.20722	0.38758
ES3b	0.69292	0.29743	0.28320	0.38975
ES3f	0.68109	0.24098	0.22937	0.40648
CS3a	0.67474	0.28239	0.31732	0.14371
ES1a	0.66784	0.34088	0.30680	0.17400
CS3e	0.66778	0.23232	0.33957	0.23748
ES3d	0.65834	0.24643	0.27787	0.35209
ES3c	0.65516	0.26737	0.34925	0.38050
ES3e	0.60210	0.35464	0.32936	0.36948
ES3a	0.57452	0.37636	0.28529	0.41455
ES3h	0.56516	0.39243	0.31247	0.37258
ES1b	0.50813	0.48745	0.33472	0.04698
CS2e	0.32420	0.74188	0.32700	0.22516
CS2g	0.30377	0.70294	0.27035	0.21023
CS2h	0.27182	0.70005	0.42893	0.11308
CS2d	0.33187	0.69204	0.31694	0.25829
CS2i	0.34349	0.69082	0.40260	0.12673
CS2c	0.33187	0.68755	0.35122	0.26423
CS2a	0.32427	0.67196	0.25289	0.25488
CS2b	0.26507	0.66862	0.16916	0.24306
CS2f	0.36075	0.66840	0.22955	0.23597
CS2j	0.20871	0.60681	0.50291	0.06096
ES1c	0.45059	0.47318	0.42493	0.17274
CS1g	0.22597	0.17696	0.74244	0.19394
CS1b	0.26307	0.25344	0.74174	0.17398
CS1c	0.31178	0.28321	0.71912	0.15908
CS1d	0.17166	0.38886	0.70898	0.21868
CS1h	0.24172	0.24007	0.68351	0.14291
CS1a	0.21451	0.38677	0.67097	0.15133
CS1f	0.27296	0.29292	0.60431	0.29217
CS1e	0.28106	0.30801	0.58127	0.23470
ES2d	0.26877	0.24574	0.21833	0.75079
ES2c	0.30930	0.25446	0.16323	0.74869
ES2a	0.21594	0.18017	0.27204	0.66467
ES2b	0.45361	0.16029	0.20141	0.64007

simplified our task by reducing the number of variables we must deal with in a multiple regression model. Instead of having each respondent associated with 38 predictor variables, we now have to contend with only four. And, as an added benefit, the four new variables are perfectly uncorrelated.

Table 9.6 presents the results of a multiple regression analysis using the four principal components as predictor variables and the single financial performance outcome variable. As shown, the four components

Table 9.6   Multiple regression output for principal components regression.

Analysis of variance

Source	DF	Sum of Squares	Mean Square	*F* Value	*Pr* > *F*
Model	4	232391006	58097752	45.70	< .0001
Error	585	743727457	1271329		
Corrected total	589	976118463			
Root MSE	1127.53225	R-square	0.2381		
Dependent mean	4038.94068	Adj R-Sq	0.2329		
Coeff var	27.91653				

Parameter estimates

Variable	DF	Parameter Estimate	Standard Error	*t* Value	*Pr* > |*t*|
Intercept	1	4038.94068	46.41977	87.01	< .0001
F1: Prob res	1	422.20797	46.45916	9.09	< .0001
F2: Prod qual	1	283.85980	46.45916	6.11	< .0001
F3: Serv qual	1	250.48328	46.45916	5.39	< .0001
F4: Mgt style	1	270.13693	46.45916	5.81	< .0001

account for about 23% of the variance in the dependent measure. Of the four dimensions used to predict financial performance, the first has the strongest effect on the dependent variable. Note that the parameter estimates are in the same units as the dependent variable. Note, too, that the component scores used in the regression are standardized and sum to zero in addition to being perfectly uncorrelated with one another. The intercept value of about 4039 is measured in dollars and reflects the profitability of a retail operation when all four predictor variables are set to zero.

One drawback of PCR involves linking the original variables to the dependent measure. When we work with components or factors, there is no direct relationship between the individual variables that make up the factor and the dependent variable. The component or factor is itself a linear combination of all (38) variables across the six disparate survey systems. Still, the results depicted in Table 9.6 clearly suggest that satisfaction with problem resolution issues is the strongest driver of financial performance. To determine exactly which problem resolution items are most closely related to the first principal component requires us to refer to the rotated factor pattern in Table 9.5. The variables that load most strongly on the first principal component are CS3d and CS3c, according to the data in the table.

Note that in this analysis we were able to account for about 23% of the variance in the dependent financial performance measure. This is quite high based upon our experience. As noted elsewhere in this book, there are numerous phenomena that affect financial performance. These include economic conditions, regional differences, accounting procedures, cost of goods, and competitive forces. To account for 23% of the variance in the dependent measure, therefore, is laudable.

OTHER REGRESSION MODELS

To this point we have reviewed the three main types of dependence models used in efforts to link customer and employee satisfaction to financial performance: ordinary least squares regression, logistic regression, and principal components regression. There are other types of regression models that, although less frequently encountered, deserve mention. Nonlinear regression models are especially intriguing; however, they are virtually unheard of in applied settings. Many academicians have bemoaned the fact that in applied settings model development almost always assumes linear relationships. In fact, the relationships between many phenomena may not be linear at all. For example, the relationship between customer satisfaction and profitability may become nonlinear as customer satisfaction increases. That is, as customer satisfaction increases beyond an optimal level, there may be diminishing concomitant increases in profitability.

In nonlinear multiple regression, the regression parameters (beta coefficients) are nonlinear. This is quite different from the instance in multiple linear regression wherein a given *variable* is nonlinear, as would be the case if a particular variable were, for example, squared or cubed. In this case, while the variable's distribution may now be nonlinear, the beta coefficient is still linear.

Other regression models have been proposed for special purposes: in certain cases, the objective was to develop a regression model that was robust in the face of severe collinearity. Ridge regression, for example, which was originally developed by Hoerl (1962), represents an attempt to mathematically circumvent collinearity. Birkes and Dodge (1993, 173–88) provided an excellent overview of the technique.

Birkes and Dodge (1993) introduced and reviewed a variety of alternate regression models in their book. Of special interest may be least absolute deviations regression, M-regression, nonparametric regression, and Bayesian regression. A meaningful discussion of these techniques is beyond the scope of this book. We note them to underscore the fact that there are numerous approaches to the dependency model framework and that each has its own unique strengths and weaknesses. Without a doubt, OLS regression is used most frequently in applied efforts to link customer and employee satisfaction to financial performance measures. Marketing researchers have been criticized, in fact, for their sole reliance on OLS when in many cases other regression models may be more appropriate. In particular, nonlinear regression models are very powerful, but unfortunately they are more difficult to develop and convey to managers.

SUMMARY

Although it is a powerful tool, multiple regression analysis is constrained to quantifying the effects of a series of predictor variables on a *single* outcome measure. The effects of service and product quality, as we have seen in previous chapters, are exerted through a number of intermediate variables. Multiple regression analysis permits us to have only one dependent measure. Interested in depicting a sequence of variables and their effects, many researchers have turned to causal modeling as a way to test hypotheses concerning measurement situations characterized by *multiple* dependent variables. Chapter 10 focuses on causal modeling using a technique known as path analysis with manifest variables and then introduces a technique to relate a causal sequence of latent (unobservable) variables.

10
Analysis Framework: Causal Modeling

CAUSAL MODELING WITH PATH ANALYSIS

The bulk of this chapter reviews a statistical analysis technique known as *path analysis*. This family of techniques—typically referred to as structural equation modeling—is used to test hypotheses regarding a causal chain among a set of variables. It is particularly useful when we are attempting to model the development of corporate profitability, because it permits us to test relatively complex relationships among a series of variables that are presumably dependent upon one another.

We have endeavored to provide a nontechnical description of structural equation modeling. There are numerous resources noted throughout this chapter that provide detailed mathematical treatments of the subject. Our intent is to make these techniques understandable by demystifying what are otherwise considered to be very advanced statistical procedures. Two types of structural equation models are introduced in this chapter. The first involves *manifest* variables and the second accommodates *latent* variables. Manifest variables are directly observable, like items in a questionnaire. Age, sex, and income are all manifest variables. So are attitudinal items such as satisfaction with product or service quality. In contrast, latent variables are unobservable. An example of a latent variable is intelligence. Scores on an IQ test are presumed to be reflections of an underlying latent construct called intelligence.

Of the two types of causal models we introduce in this chapter, the manifest variable causal model is frequently referred to as path analysis. The latent variable causal model has been referred to as a LISREL model because of the software of that name. Both types of causal models can help us determine how customer and employee satisfaction affect profitability.

PATH ANALYSIS

Path analysis is by no means a recently introduced technique. In fact, it was first described in the early 1900s (Wright 1918, 1921). The contemporary interest in the application of this technique in customer satisfaction and loyalty research does not represent a noteworthy analytical advancement per se. Rather, the use of path analysis by researchers concerned with customer satisfaction and employee data represents a renewed fascination with a statistical technique that has been, at times, controversial. That this technique lends itself very well to depicting how key business metrics are affected by issues such as employee and customer satisfaction makes it of special interest here.

Path analysis and causal modeling techniques in general have been justly criticized. The primary criticism of causal modeling involves the use of cross-sectional data to draw *causal* inferences. There are three minimal criteria that must be met to establish causation, as shown in Figure 10.1.

These criteria must be met to establish a cause-and-effect relationship. Numerous authors concede that cross-sectional data do not meet these criteria. The consensus ranges from Schumacker and Lomax (1996, 28) to Asher (1983, 12). Perhaps the most cogent description of the causal inference problem is provided by Bollen (1989, 40–67). Bullock, Harlow, and Mulaik (1994) also offer specific presumptions with respect to causal inferences based on cross-sectional data.

The three criteria presented in Figure 10.1 involve temporal sequencing, concomitant variation, and the elimination of mitigating variables that might be responsible for observed causal relationships. The first involves the temporal ordering of the predictor and outcome variables. In short, the predictor must precede the outcome in time. Typically, cross-sectional

- Temporal sequencing

- Concomitant variation

- Elimination of mitigating variables

Figure 10.1 Minimal criteria for establishing causality.

data—especially customer and employee satisfaction data—fail this test. The second requirement for demonstrating causality involves concomitant variation: Does the outcome variable increase as the predictor variable(s) increase? For example, is there covariation between the predictor and outcome variables? The final aspect of establishing a causal relationship is more problematic. It involves the elimination of confounding factors that might influence the observed cause-and-effect relationship. While in theory this sounds simple enough, it is in reality a very difficult criterion to meet unequivocally, as Blalock (1964, 26) noted:

> No matter how elaborate the design, certain simplifying assumptions must always be made. In particular, we must at some point assume that the effects of confounding factors are negligible. Randomization helps to rule out some such variables, but the plausibility of this particular kind of simplifying assumption is always a question of degree.

That such a simplification may be necessary is inarguable in customer and employee satisfaction research. It is likely that in our effort to demonstrate robust, scientifically acceptable causality, we may *never* be able to meet the third criterion in customer satisfaction research. The most critical point to be made with respect to path analysis and causal modeling in general is that cross-sectional data will never meet all of the criteria required to demonstrate a true cause-and-effect relationship. Instead, we must make some concessions.

Cross-sectional customer satisfaction data preclude robust inferences concerning causality. This does not, however, mean that path analysis is unsuitable for customer and employee satisfaction research projects depicting the development of business performance metrics such as profitability or market share. Indeed, the technique can produce compelling results that are both mathematically sound and intuitively appealing.

The reader may still be in somewhat of a quandary with respect to path analysis technique. Consider the simple causal model presented in Figure 10.2. This two-variable model has one predictor variable and one outcome variable. The path coefficient (γ_{11}) is equivalent to the simple correlation (r_{x1y1}) between the two variables. This is not the case for the slightly more

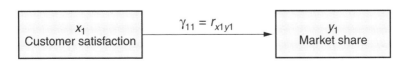

Figure 10.2 Simple causal relationship.

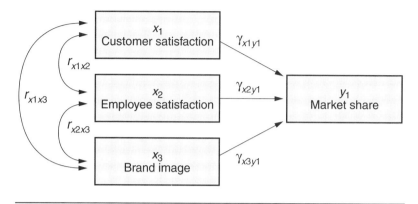

Figure 10.3   Multiple-predictor causal model.

complex case presented in Figure 10.3. Here, we encounter three predictor variables. Each has some level of covariance with the others. Interestingly, if the predictor variables were *orthogonal* (that is, perfectly uncorrelated), then the path coefficients would be equivalent to the simple correlations. Again, this would be the case only if the predictors were orthogonal, which is rarely so. A notable exception to this involves regressing an outcome variable on a series of factors or principal components that were extracted from the data in a manner that ensures orthogonality.

Path analysis permits us to assess the extent to which our data are consistent with the hypothesized causal structure. It does *not* establish true causal relation since, among other things, there is no temporal ordering among the variables that make up the causal sequence. Note, too, that path coefficients between exogenous and endogenous variables are depicted using gamma (γ), while the effect of one endogenous variable upon another is depicted using the more familiar beta (β) sign.

Figure 10.4 depicts a relatively simple path analysis model in which four predictor variables (x_1 through x_4) affect two outcome variables. The direction of causality is from left to right. Note that the first outcome variable (y_1) is also presumed to exert an effect on the second outcome variable (y_2). More interestingly, the four exogenous variables (x_1 through x_4) are unconstrained with respect to their ability to influence one or *both* of the outcome variables. Any of the predictor variables may exert an indirect effect on profitability (y_2) through customer retention (y_1). Thus, both direct and indirect effects are possible.

Other notable aspects of Figure 10.4 that are specific to path analysis include the covariance terms among all possible pairs of predictor variables and the *error terms* (e_1 and e_2) that affect y_1 and y_2. Finally, note that the

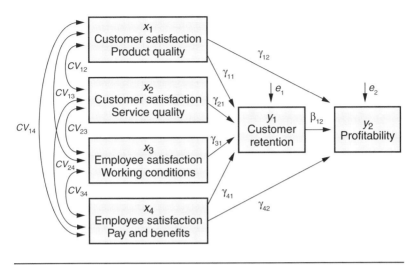

Figure 10.4   Path analysis model with two dependent variables.

straight lines represent path coefficients while the curved lines indicate covariances. For example, the term CV_{12} represents the covariation between x_1 and x_2. Unless there are empirical or theoretical justifications to the contrary, all variables are permitted to covary.

Of special interest in path analysis is the ability of any predictor variable to affect any or all of the endogenous (y) variables. As shown in Figure 10.4, an exogenous variable is permitted to *simultaneously* affect one, two, or even more outcome variables. This is a critical difference between regression analysis and path analysis. Nonetheless, path coefficients can be regarded as beta coefficients from regression analysis and, when compared numerically, are often very similar.

One of the primary differences between path analysis and regression analysis is that the former is a confirmatory technique. Regression analysis is considered to be an exploratory technique. Path analysis is confirmatory because we first specify the hypothesized model and then test it. The model is then rejected or accepted. In contrast, regression analysis typically involves the specification of a model and then examination of the significance level of all the predictor variables. Significant predictors are noted, while the remainder are typically given little attention.

Figure 10.5 suggests that in most applied situations path analysis is a quasi-confirmatory technique. That is, when the hypothesized model is not supported by the data, researchers rarely terminate their efforts. Rather, they modify the model based upon theoretical or empirical grounds and start the process again. In the example shown in Figure 10.5, the hypothesized model

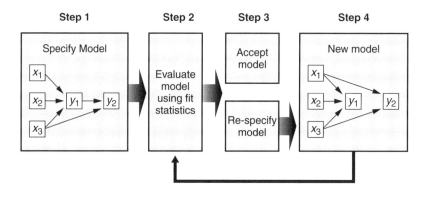

Figure 10.5 Quasi-confirmatory model-building approach.

is rejected because it does not represent a good "fit" with the data. It is respecified in step 4. A path is added between x_1 and y_2 and the model is then reevaluated. If the model fit is below certain statistical thresholds, the model is accepted as consistent with the relationships in the data. The notion of model fit will be discussed in greater detail below.

ASSESSING MODEL FIT

Model fit simply refers to the extent to which the hypothesized model replicates the input variance–covariance matrix. Suppose, for example, that the model hypothesized in Figure 10.4 failed to recognize that service quality satisfaction (x_2) exerted a *strong* effect on customer retention (y_1). By not specifying this path, we would be implicitly constraining the relationship between x_2 and y_1 to be zero despite the fact that it is actually quite substantial. This omission would lead to "poor fit" and the regrettable conclusion that the hypothesized model must be rejected as invalid.

Fit is measured through a variety of statistics, a detailed discussion of which is beyond the scope of this book. Excellent treatments of fit statistics and model evaluations are given by Hu and Bentler (1995, 76–99), Schumacker and Lomax (1996, 119–37), and Bollen (1989, 256–87). We will focus on the metric that is typically presented; knowledge of this will arm the reader with sufficient information to critically evaluate the fit of a causal model. The best-known fit statistic is chi-square (χ^2). Typically, researchers are most interested when this value is sufficiently *high* that it reaches statistical significance at the 95% confidence level. In structural equation modeling, we are interested in the exact opposite. In effect, chi-square measures *lack of fit.* Thus, high levels that are statistically significant indicate poor fit. Chi-square levels that do not reach statistical significance reflect hypothesized models that do not substantively depart from the relationships in the data. In short, a model is accepted if the chi-square value is *not* significant.

Fortunately, while the purist may elect to discard his or her data and embrace a new hypothesized causal flow if the data do not support the model, this is seldom actually the case in practice. As shown in Figure 10.5, the model-developing process—although ostensibly confirmatory—is frequently quasi-exploratory and is characterized by researchers who employ an iterative approach to model development.

CASE STUDY: PITSTOP EMPLOYEE SATISFACTION, CUSTOMER SATISFACTION, AND PROFITABILITY

This case study utilizes a reduced survey instrument for the purposes of illustration. The employee satisfaction measurement program of PitStop convenience stores employed a postcard survey on an annual basis. Employees in 700 stores were surveyed. As shown in Figure 10.6, the questionnaire comprises several items. Of these, six (x_1–x_6) will be considered exogenous. The last three questions (y_1–y_3) are clearly endogenous. The first of the three dependent measures (y_1) measures overall job satisfaction, whereas the remaining two are intended to provide a measure of employee loyalty. Notice that the store number is coded on every questionnaire and that the annual baseline entails roughly 8 to 10 completed employee interviews for each of the 700 retail outlets. In total, between 5600 and 7000 employee interviews are conducted each year.

Figure 10.7 presents the abbreviated PitStop customer satisfaction questionnaire. The annual PitStop customer satisfaction survey is administered to a total of approximately 100 customers per retail outlet. Roughly 70,000 customer satisfaction surveys are conducted annually using the mail questionnaire. As shown in Figure 10.7, the survey instrument contains nine items; six of these can be considered exogenous from a model development perspective. The first dependent measure involves overall customer satisfaction, while the remaining two are presumed to reflect customer loyalty.

Note that in this case the employee satisfaction and customer satisfaction surveys are quite similar. That is, they use the same number of scale points and identical anchors. This is not always the case. Since customer satisfaction and employee satisfaction programs are frequently administered by different departments in an organization, there is often little effort

---

PitStop Convenience Stores, Inc.

Employee Satisfaction Survey

Store Number: 982

Dear Valued Employee:

At PitStop, we try to continuously monitor and improve our employees' satisfaction. You have been randomly selected to participate in our study. Please spend a few minutes filling out the brief survey below. Note that the postcard is already stamped and addressed so all you have to do upon completion is drop it in the mail.

For the questions below, please use the 7-point scale to indicate your satisfaction. The scale ranges from 1 (very dissatisfied) to 7 (very satisfied).

	Very Dissatisfied						Very Satisfied
1. Coworkers	1□	2□	3□	4□	5□	6□	7□
2. Supervisors	1□	2□	3□	4□	5□	6□	7□
3. Hourly pay	1□	2□	3□	4□	5□	6□	7□
4. Vacation and holidays	1□	2□	3□	4□	5□	6□	7□
5. Convenience to home	1□	2□	3□	4□	5□	6□	7□
6. Arrangements for your personal safety	1□	2□	3□	4□	5□	6□	7□
7. Considering all these aspects of your job at PitStop, how satisfied are you with your job?	1□	2□	3□	4□	5□	6□	7□

How much do you agree with the following two statements? Please use the 7-point scale to indicate your level of agreement.

	Strongly Disagree						Strongly Agree
8. I would recommend working at PitStop to a friend.	1□	2□	3□	4□	5□	6□	7□
9. I like working at PitStop.	1□	2□	3□	4□	5□	6□	7□

~ Thank You ~

Figure 10.6   PitStop convenience stores employee satisfaction instrument.

PitStop Convenience Stores, Inc.

Customer Satisfaction Survey

Store Number: 982

Dear Valued Customer:

At PitStop, we try to continuously monitor and improve our customers' satisfaction. You have been randomly selected to participate in our study based on your participation in our recent sweepstakes offer. Please spend a few minutes filling out the brief survey below. Note that the postcard is already stamped and addressed so all you have to do upon completion is drop it in the mail.

For the questions below, please use the 7-point scale to indicate your satisfaction. The scale ranges from 1 (very dissatisfied) to 7 (very satisfied).

<table>
<tr><td></td><td align="center">Very
Dissatisfied</td><td align="center">Very
Satisfied</td></tr>
<tr><td>1. Clerk's courtesy</td><td colspan="2" align="center">₁☐ ₂☐ ₃☐ ₄☐ ₅☐ ₆☐ ₇☐</td></tr>
<tr><td>2. Store hours</td><td colspan="2" align="center">₁☐ ₂☐ ₃☐ ₄☐ ₅☐ ₆☐ ₇☐</td></tr>
<tr><td>3. Product quality</td><td colspan="2" align="center">₁☐ ₂☐ ₃☐ ₄☐ ₅☐ ₆☐ ₇☐</td></tr>
<tr><td>4. Parking</td><td colspan="2" align="center">₁☐ ₂☐ ₃☐ ₄☐ ₅☐ ₆☐ ₇☐</td></tr>
<tr><td>5. Convenience to home</td><td colspan="2" align="center">₁☐ ₂☐ ₃☐ ₄☐ ₅☐ ₆☐ ₇☐</td></tr>
<tr><td>6. Product variety</td><td colspan="2" align="center">₁☐ ₂☐ ₃☐ ₄☐ ₅☐ ₆☐ ₇☐</td></tr>
<tr><td>7. Considering all these aspects of your last visit to a PitStop, how satisfied are you with us?</td><td colspan="2" align="center">₁☐ ₂☐ ₃☐ ₄☐ ₅☐ ₆☐ ₇☐</td></tr>
</table>

How much do you agree with the following two statements? Please use the 7-point scale to indicate your level of agreement.

<table>
<tr><td></td><td align="center">Strongly
Disagree</td><td align="center">Strongly
Agree</td></tr>
<tr><td>8. I would recommend PitStop to a friend.</td><td colspan="2" align="center">₁☐ ₂☐ ₃☐ ₄☐ ₅☐ ₆☐ ₇☐</td></tr>
<tr><td>9. I will keep shopping at PitStop in the future.</td><td colspan="2" align="center">₁☐ ₂☐ ₃☐ ₄☐ ₅☐ ₆☐ ₇☐</td></tr>
</table>

~ Thank You ~

Figure 10.7   PitStop convenience stores customer satisfaction instrument.

expended to ensure that the two programs are parallel from a measurement perspective. It is not uncommon, for example, to encounter in one organization a customer satisfaction survey that uses a 7-point scale and an employee satisfaction survey that relies upon a 5-point scale. When disparate scales are used in regression analysis, path analysis, and other dependence models, it is important to consider the *standardized* beta scores, as they take into consideration the different ranges of the two sets of variables. Of course, comparing univariate statistics across disparate scales is considerably more problematic.

Financial performance data at the store level included a variety of financial measures. Of particular interest was the net profitability variable. While other financial performance metrics were available, they did not yield particularly attractive models. In particular, variables such as revenues and annual change in revenues yielded models with little explanatory power. Table 10.1 summarizes the data available for each PitStop store. As shown, each store is associated with nine customer satisfaction scores and nine employee satisfaction scores. Each score is an average and subsumes the responses of multiple customers and employees, respectively. In the case of the nine customer satisfaction scores, each average reflects the responses of up to 100 customers per store. Similarly, the employee satisfaction scores are the average responses provided by between 8 and 10 employees per store.

Figure 10.8 presents a model based upon the data set summarized in Table 10.1. As shown, the six employee satisfaction items (questions 1–6) are presumed to affect a single dependent measure (question 7). In a similar vein, the six customer satisfaction items (questions 1–6) are believed to affect the dependent measure (question 7) in the survey instrument. Each of the two dependent measures, in turn, are presumed to affect the single financial performance variable (profitability).

Table 10.1 PitStop employee satisfaction, customer satisfaction, and profitability data.

Store Number	Employee Satisfaction Measures (avg.)	Customer Satisfaction Measures (avg.)	Net Profit*
0001	4.3 5.2 4.2 3.1 4.1 5.9 6.2 5.2 6.7	4.2 5.1 6.7 5.5 6.4 6.3 5.4 6.4 6.3	$25.4
0002	5.3 6.5 5.5 6.4 4.5 5.6 4.3 4.9 6.3	4.6 5.4 6.2 5.7 6.2 6.1 5.2 6.2 6.1	$22.6
⋮	⋮ ⋮ ⋮ ⋮ ⋮ ⋮ ⋮ ⋮ ⋮	⋮ ⋮ ⋮ ⋮ ⋮ ⋮ ⋮ ⋮ ⋮	⋮
0700	4.5 6.2 5.9 6.7 4.3 4.4 4.5 4.8 6.1	4.8 5.3 5.9 4.9 6.1 6.0 5.9 5.9 6.4	$21.8

*Net profit is in thousands of dollars.

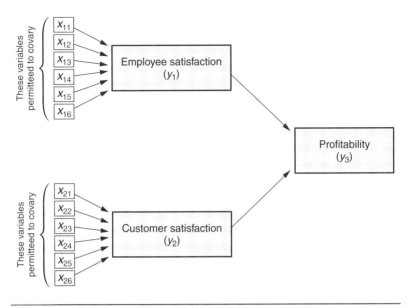

Figure 10.8 PitStop path analysis relating employee and customer satisfaction and profitability.

Notice that in Figure 10.8 none of the paths are labeled with a beta (β) or gamma (γ) coefficient yet. This is because the model shown in the figure represents the *hypothesized structure*. We will test whether the hypothesized causal sequence is consistent with the relationships in the data in the model assessment stage. This involves a single test—either the model "fits" the data or it doesn't. There is no compromise; the model is either rejected or accepted based upon the extent to which the hypothesized relationships are consistent with the covariance structures encountered in the data set.

Another feature of the model depicted in Figure 10.8 that should be noted involves the covariance among the six customer satisfaction items and the six employee satisfaction items. As shown, the six customer satisfaction measures are presumed to covary, and the six employee satisfaction items are also permitted to covary. However, none of the six employee satisfaction variables covaries with any of the six customer satisfaction variables. This means that we are explicitly assuming that there are very low correlations between the two sets of items. Whether or not this is true will be revealed when the model is tested. If there are actually very strong correlations between the employee satisfaction and customer satisfaction items, then the model will not fit the data well.

Figure 10.9 presents the finalized model with beta coefficients for each path. All of the paths that are shown are statistically significant ($t > 1.96$) at the 95% confidence level. As shown in the figure, the six employee satisfaction variables affect the overall measure (question 7 in the employee satisfaction survey instrument). Similarly, the six customer satisfaction variables all affect the overall customer satisfaction measure. The two intermediate variables—overall customer and employee satisfaction—affect the third and final dependent variable: profitability.

The model depicted in Figure 10.9 reflects the types of results we have encountered in this sort of project. In particular, we find the R^2 statistics related to the employee satisfaction and customer satisfaction relationships to be quite high. Accounting for up to 85% of the variance in the dependent measure (overall employee or customer satisfaction) is not at all uncommon. In contrast, the two intermediate variables (y_1 and y_2) usually account for less than 25% of the variance in the financial performance variable. The reason for this may be that a wide variety of circumstances affect financial performance measures such as profitability. Some of these may be as arbitrary, for example, as competitive activity, the labor market, or the type of accounting procedures that are used to quantify the cost of materials.

The fit of the model depicted in Figure 10.9 was evaluated using the chi-square statistic. The hypothesized model was rejected based upon this

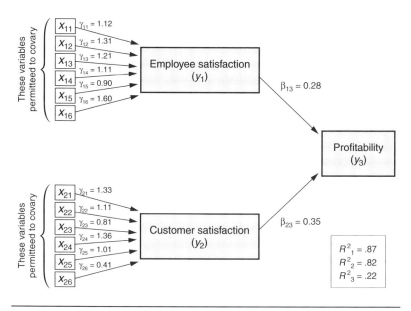

Figure 10.9 Final PitStop path analysis model.

assessment. The model as specified in Figure 10.9 was too restrictive. In particular, we had to relax the restriction that prohibited covariances between the two sets of variables. That is, it was necessary to permit the six employee satisfaction variables to covary with the six customer satisfaction variables. This was because there were substantive intercorrelations among the two sets of variables—an intuitively appealing finding. When the respecified model was evaluated, its fit was acceptable, and the model was used as a tool to guide service quality and employee satisfaction programs.

LATENT VARIABLE PATH ANALYSIS

One of the greatest sources of confusion surrounding structural equation modeling (SEM) involves the computer program known as LISREL. It has been common for researchers to refer to the SEM *technique* as LISREL, which is clearly erroneous. LISREL, like EQS, AMOS, the SAS CALIS procedure, and other software packages, is an application designed to conduct SEM. Rigdon (1998, 266–68) provides a brief but thorough review of additional SEM software packages.

Few statistical techniques incorporate as many Greek symbols and as much matrix algebra as latent variable SEM. It is our intent to present an *understandable* treatment of all of the techniques used in customer satisfaction research. This is especially true in the case of latent variable SEM—to the extent possible, *conceptual treatments* rather than *mathematical treatments* will be presented for these models. Readers who wish to delve into the underlying matrix algebra and theoretical statistics will have no difficulty finding books that meet their requirements.

The latent variable structural equation model is best understood when decomposed into its two main components: the *measurement model* and the *structural model*. The measurement model represents the confirmatory factor analytic component. In effect, the measurement model formally explicates the relationships between manifest (observed) variables and unobservable latent constructs such as intelligence or motivation. The structural portion of the latent variable SEM model specifies the causal linkages among the latent variables. That the construct *intelligence* causes *motivation*, for example, represents the structural (or causal) relation between two latent variables.

It is easy to see how latent variable SEM represents the marriage of confirmatory factor analysis and manifest variable path analysis. Its utility for researchers interested in customer satisfaction and loyalty research cannot be overstated. A relatively contemporary technique, the latent variable SEM approach was introduced by Jöreskog and Sörbom in the early 1970s and thus predates the development of intense interest in service quality research by, at best, a decade. Still, the conceptual development of this approach occurred in the 1960s and involved sociologists such as Blalock, according to Bollen (1989, 7). He and other sociologists considered the need for a comprehensive analytical platform that would permit the integration of Wright's (1918) path analysis and confirmatory factor analysis. While other techniques were developed in the late 1960s and early 1970s, the popularity of Jöreskog and Sörbom's LISREL software led many to conclude erroneously that the technique had eponymous software . . . or vice versa. This confusion remains today; many researchers still refer to structural equation models as LISREL models. The terms *SEM* and *path analysis* are routinely interchanged; however, *SEM* seems to be favored by authors today.

Latent variable SEM is a simple extension of the variant described above. That is, the two variants of path analysis can be differentiated based upon the types of variables included. Earlier, we reviewed manifest variable path analysis. Each variable could be traced directly to a specific question in the survey instrument. In contrast, latent variable path analysis involves variables that are actually *factors*. Examples of factors include elusive concepts such as intelligence, motivation, and empathy. Latent variable SEM involves mapping the relationships among a series of factors. We might propose, for example, that intelligence and motivation affect job satisfaction, which in turn affects physical health.

We now turn our attention to the structural equations with latent variables model. Figure 10.10 introduces a model with three latent exogenous variables (product quality satisfaction, service quality satisfaction, and employee satisfaction) and two latent endogenous variables (loyalty and corporate health). The data in this hypothetical example were collapsed to the bank branch level in order to achieve a common unit of analysis. As in the previous case study, customer satisfaction data were recorded as averages at the branch level. Employee satisfaction data were treated in a similar fashion.

Again, the model presented in Figure 10.10 posits that three latent exogenous variables (product quality satisfaction, service quality satisfaction, and employee satisfaction) affect customer and employee loyalty. These, in turn, are presumed to affect corporate health as defined by three variables: profitability (y_6), market share (y_7), and annual revenue change (y_8). Note that financial performance is treated as a latent variable: corporate health. Table 10.2 summarizes the symbols and their implications. This form of representing latent variable path modeling is standard regardless of the SEM software one selects. Note that latent variables are depicted in circles and manifest variables are represented by squares. Similarly, paths from one latent variable to another are represented by straight arrows, while curved arrows indicate covariation between two (latent) variables.

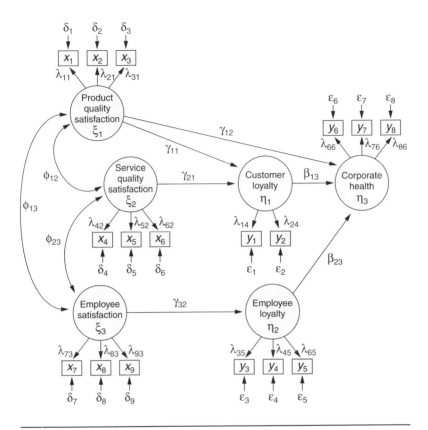

Figure 10.10 Seven Peaks National Bank latent variable SEM.

Table 10.2 Summary of SEM path diagram elements.

Symbol	Description
◯	Latent variable (endogenous or exogenous); factor.
▢	Manifest variable (endogenous or exogenous), such as a specific item in a questionnaire.
▢◀—◯ ◯—▶▢	Relationship between latent and manifest variable. The Greek letter λ (lambda) is used to denote this path, which can be interpreted as a factor loading.
◯—▶◯ ◯◀—◯	Causal relationship between two latent variables. If the path is between an exogenous and endogenous variable, the symbol γ_{ij} is used. If the path leads from one endogenous latent variable to another, the symbol β_{ij} is used.
◯ ◯	Covariance between two latent variables.

Table 10.3 provides a summary of the Greek letters used in latent variable path modeling. Two very important variables in any latent variable path model are η (eta) and ξ (xi), which represent the latent dependent and independent variables, respectively. The relationships between independent and dependent latent variables are denoted using the path coefficients γ and β. When one dependent variable affects another, the β coefficient is used. In contrast, γ is used to depict the impact of an exogenous variable on one of the two dependent variables.

Another important relationship involves the latent variables (such as service quality satisfaction) and their manifest indicators. Note that the arrow points *from the latent variable to the manifest variable*. The implication of this is that the manifest variable is caused by the underlying latent variable. This is the core of the factor analytic component of the latent variable path model. That is, a complete factor analysis is subsumed by the relationships denoted by the λ_x coefficients.

For an illustration of the relationship between Figure 10.10 and an actual survey instrument, refer to the questionnaires presented in Figures 10.11 and 10.12. Each item in the causal model is identified by a unique survey question number.

Table 10.3 Summary of SEM matrix nomenclature.

Symbol	Name	Element	Description
Structural Model			
η	Eta	η	Vector of endogenous latent variables
ξ	Xi	ξ	Vector of exogenous latent variables
Γ	Gamma	γ	Matrix of regression coefficients corresponding to effects of latent exogenous variables on latent endogenous variables
B	Beta	β	Matrix of regression coefficients corresponding to effects of latent endogenous variables on one another
Φ	Phi	φ	Matrix of variance–covariance ξ
Ψ	Psi	ψ	Matrix covariance of ζ
Measurement Model			
Λ_x	Lambda-x	λ_x	Matrix of regression coefficients corresponding to factor loading on exogenous latent variables
Λ_y	Lambda-y	λ_y	Matrix of regression coefficients corresponding to factor loading on endogenous latent variables

Seven Peaks National Bank

Customer Satisfaction Survey

Mt. Vinson Branch

Dear Customer:

We value your business, and in our continuing effort to offer you the best service and products, we periodically survey a sample of our customers. Please take the time to complete the brief survey below. We appreciate your participation.

Please tell us how satisfied you are with each of the following services and products. Indicate your satisfaction with each item by using the 7-point scale, on which 1 means "very dissatisfied" and 7 means "very satisfied."

A. Products	Very Dissatisfied						Very Satisfied
1. Seven Peaks Value CD	₁☐	₂☐	₃☐	₄☐	₅☐	₆☐	₇☐
2. Seven Peaks Passbook Savings	₁☐	₂☐	₃☐	₄☐	₅☐	₆☐	₇☐
3. Seven Peaks Auto Loans	₁☐	₂☐	₃☐	₄☐	₅☐	₆☐	₇☐

B. Service

4. Hours of operation	₁☐	₂☐	₃☐	₄☐	₅☐	₆☐	₇☐
5. Teller courtesy	₁☐	₂☐	₃☐	₄☐	₅☐	₆☐	₇☐
6. Parking	₁☐	₂☐	₃☐	₄☐	₅☐	₆☐	₇☐

C. Overall Impression of Seven Peaks National Bank

To what extent do you agree with the following two statements? Please use the 7-point scale to express your level of agreement.

	Strongly Disagree						Strongly Agree
7. I would recommend Seven Peaks to a friend.	₁☐	₂☐	₃☐	₄☐	₅☐	₆☐	₇☐
8. Overall I am satisfied with Seven Peaks as my bank.	₁☐	₂☐	₃☐	₄☐	₅☐	₆☐	₇☐

Thanks for participating in this customer survey. At Seven Peaks National Bank, we do everything possible to satisfy our customers. We care about you and hope to continue providing you with quality financial services support.

Figure 10.11 Seven Peaks National Bank customer satisfaction instrument.

Seven Peaks National Bank
Annual Employee Satisfaction Survey
Mt. Elbrus Branch

Dear Valued Employee:

Each year we survey our employees to help us provide you with the most rewarding work environment. Please take a moment to complete the questionnaire below. Your answers will be kept completely confidential. Thank you in advance for your participation in this study.

Please tell us how satisfied you are with each of the following aspects of your job. Indicate your satisfaction with each item by using the 7-point scale, on which 1 means "very dissatisfied" and 7 means "very satisfied."

	Very Dissatisfied		Very Satisfied
A. Benefits			
1. Vacation and holidays	₁☐ ₂☐ ₃☐ ₄☐ ₅☐ ₆☐ ₇☐		
2. Retirement planning	₁☐ ₂☐ ₃☐ ₄☐ ₅☐ ₆☐ ₇☐		
3. Insurance programs	₁☐ ₂☐ ₃☐ ₄☐ ₅☐ ₆☐ ₇☐		
4. Overall satisfaction with benefits	₁☐ ₂☐ ₃☐ ₄☐ ₅☐ ₆☐ ₇☐		
B. Working Conditions			
1. Coworkers	₁☐ ₂☐ ₃☐ ₄☐ ₅☐ ₆☐ ₇☐		
2. Managers	₁☐ ₂☐ ₃☐ ₄☐ ₅☐ ₆☐ ₇☐		
3. Policies and procedures	₁☐ ₂☐ ₃☐ ₄☐ ₅☐ ₆☐ ₇☐		
4. Overall satisfaction with working conditions	₁☐ ₂☐ ₃☐ ₄☐ ₅☐ ₆☐ ₇☐		
C. Career Opportunities			
1. Training classes	₁☐ ₂☐ ₃☐ ₄☐ ₅☐ ₆☐ ₇☐		
2. Tuition reimbursement	₁☐ ₂☐ ₃☐ ₄☐ ₅☐ ₆☐ ₇☐		
3. Advancement opportunities	₁☐ ₂☐ ₃☐ ₄☐ ₅☐ ₆☐ ₇☐		
4. Overall satisfaction with career opportunities	₁☐ ₂☐ ₃☐ ₄☐ ₅☐ ₆☐ ₇☐		

To what extent do you agree with the following two statements? Please use the 7-point scale to express your level of agreement.

	Strongly Disagree		Strongly Agree
D. Overall Impression			
1. I would recommend working at Seven Peaks to friends.	₁☐ ₂☐ ₃☐ ₄☐ ₅☐ ₆☐ ₇☐		
2. I would rather work at Seven Peaks than any other bank.	₁☐ ₂☐ ₃☐ ₄☐ ₅☐ ₆☐ ₇☐		
3. Overall, I'm very content working for Seven Peaks.	₁☐ ₂☐ ₃☐ ₄☐ ₅☐ ₆☐ ₇☐		

Thank you for participating in the annual employee survey. Your confidential responses will help us make your job as enriching and challenging as possible.

Figure 10.12   Seven Peaks National Bank employee satisfaction instrument.

The convention in SEM with latent variables is to depict manifest variables in squares and latent variables in circles. Each of the labeled squares in Figure 10.10 corresponds to an actual question in the survey instrument shown in Figure 10.11. Thus, the three variables (x_1–x_3) that reflect the latent construct labeled product quality satisfaction (ξ_1) involve satisfaction with three specific products (survey questions 1, 2, and 3). Similarly, the second latent variable (ξ_2) involves service quality satisfaction (x_4–x_6) and is also associated with three questions (4, 5, and 6) from the survey. These three manifest variables relate to hours of operation, teller courtesy, and parking.

Figure 10.12 presents the bank's employee satisfaction questionnaire. Three variables (A4, B4, and C4) were used in the latent variable relating to employee satisfaction. These corresponded to satisfaction with benefits, working conditions, and advancement opportunities and are represented as variables x_7–x_9 in the model depicted in Figure 10.10. Again, for the purposes of this analysis, the data were collapsed at the branch level to yield a common unit of analysis.

On the right-hand side of the model presented in Figure 10.10 are three latent endogenous variables (η_1, η_2, and η_3) that reflect customer loyalty, employee loyalty, and corporate health measures, respectively. The first latent endogenous variable (η_1) represents customer loyalty and is associated with two manifest variables. A review of the questionnaire confirms that these items request summary judgments concerning overall satisfaction and likelihood to recommend. The second latent endogenous variable (η_2) involves employee loyalty. Three manifest variables (y_3–y_5) are related to this construct. The third latent endogenous variable (η_3) is associated with three manifest variables. These are recorded at the branch level and involve overall profitability (y_6), market share estimate (y_7), and change in revenue (y_8). Combined, these three questions are presumed to reflect a latent construct called corporate health (η_3).

INTERPRETATION

The model depicted in Figure 10.13 is composed of two parts: a structural component and a measurement component. The measurement component of the figure relates the manifest questionnaire variables (x_1–x_9 and y_1–y_8) to the latent constructs, or factors. There are three exogenous latent variables (product quality satisfaction, service quality satisfaction, and employee satisfaction), each of which is associated with three manifest variables. Notice that in each case one of the factor loadings has been set to 1. This convention scales the remaining two loadings to unity. There are also three latent endogenous variables. Customer loyalty is associated with two manifest variables (y_1 and y_2). Three manifest variables (y_3-y_5) reflect employee loyalty (η_2). The ultimate latent endogenous variable (corporate health) is presumed to be reflected in a set of three manifest corporate financial performance variables (y_6-y_8).

The structural component of the final model presented in Figure 10.13 relates the latent variables defined in the measurement component described above. The results suggest that the first exogenous latent variable (product quality satisfaction) directly affects two endogenous latent variables: customer loyalty and corporate health. Product quality satisfaction, therefore, exerts both a direct and an indirect effect on corporate health. Service quality satisfaction exerts an indirect influence on corporate health. Finally, employee satisfaction emerges as strongly predictive of employee

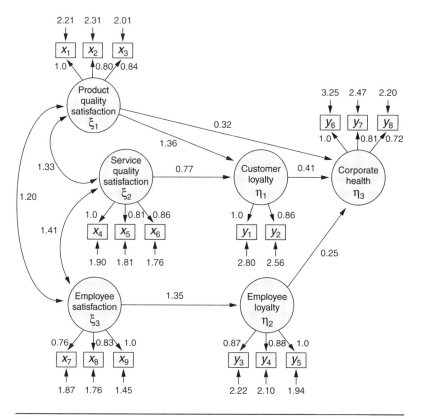

Figure 10.13 Seven Peaks National Bank latent variable SEM results.

loyalty, which affects corporate health. Both service quality satisfaction and employee satisfaction, therefore, exert indirect effects on corporate health.

The causal structure posited in Figure 10.13 is consistent with the cross-sectional covariance structures encountered in the data. As a result, the "fit" of this model is acceptable. Of course, we have not proven causality with this model. One of the most crucial criteria for demonstrating causality—temporal sequencing—was clearly not met. Nonetheless, the causal sequence and measurement model depicted in Figure 10.13 seems intuitively palatable.

ASSESSING THE MODEL

Assessing the hypothesized latent variable model depicted in Figure 10.10 requires the use of SEM software such as LISREL, EQS, AMOS, SAS, or SPSS. It is important to keep in mind that the posited causal model is never unequivocally *proven*. We test to see whether the relationships (both structural and measurement) hypothesized in the model are consistent with the relationships actually present in the data. To evaluate a model, its "goodness of fit" with the data is assessed. The chi-square statistic is the oldest of the fit measures. It is used as a means of evaluating confirmatory factor analysis models. Interpreting the chi-square measure as it relates to the goodness of fit of a given model is counterintuitive. Under ordinary circumstances (such as in exploratory analyses), a statistically significant value of chi-square is generally a desirable finding. It suggests that there is a significant relationship between two variables. In confirmatory analyses, however, the chi-square statistic reflects the extent to which the hypothesized model is consistent with the data. As the two become more and more disparate, the chi-square statistic increases and its statistical significance is more likely. Thus, we interpret the chi-square statistic and its significance level as indicators of whether our hypothesized model *significantly* departs from the relationships present in the data. In confirmatory analyses, we accept the hypothesized model if the chi-square statistic is *not* statistically significant. Unfortunately, the chi-square statistic is very sensitive to sample sizes: as the sample increases, chi-square is more likely to be statistically significant. In the case of SEM, this is not desirable as it may lead to erroneous rejection of a model that actually fits the data quite well (Hu and Bentler 1995, 77–81).

There are many goodness-of-fit measures that are not as sensitive to sample size as chi-square. Among these are the root mean square error of approximation (RMSEA), which was developed by Steiger (1990) and is advocated by Jöreskog and Sörbom (1993, 124). Of course, many, many other fit indices exist. Among the more popular choices are the GFI and AGFI, Bentler's Comparative Fit Index, and Bollen's Indices.

Exhaustive reviews of fit statistics abound. Marsh, Balla, and Hau (1996) provide an excellent discussion of fit indices, as do Hu and Bentler (1995). A comprehensive discussion of fit is beyond the scope of this book. The most important aspect of goodness of fit is that it is the single measure that leads us to accept or reject a hypothesized causal model. In SEM, a model is either accepted or rejected; there is no "in between" as one would encounter in exploratory analyses.

11

The Future of Linkage Research

INTRODUCTION

This chapter discusses some of the trends and recent innovations in customer loyalty research and the effort to link customer and employee satisfaction to financial performance. These include perspectives on the drivers of customer loyalty, data collection, the use of customer loyalty survey data in decision-support tools for managers, and comparison of satisfaction and loyalty scores across countries. We conclude the chapter with a summary of how the effort to link customer and employee satisfaction to financial performance may be affected by developments in data collection, analysis, and reporting.

SIMULATION SYSTEMS: SATNAV

The SatNav system was developed as an answer to increasing demands for simulation software that would manage increasingly complex customer satisfaction data sets. The globalization of corporate America led to the need to compare data across countries. More important, the vast amounts of customer-related data some companies were capturing needed to be managed more efficiently. This was exacerbated by the recognition that critical multivariate analyses such as multiple regression analysis should be conducted at the lowest possible organizational unit. In many cases, the organizational unit corresponds to a specific geographic unit. For example, one bank in Florida tracks its branch performance at the county level. Other superregional organizations track performance at the state level, while global conglomerates often track performance at the country or even the continent level. In each case, performance metrics and key driver analyses are tracked at the lowest geographic unit and are frequently rolled up into higher-level geographic units such as states, regions, countries, or even continents. Of course, there are many organizations with structures that do not parallel geographic boundaries. The advantage to working with organizations whose structures parallel known geographies is that mapping software can be leveraged to enhance the meaning and clarity of the results.

In a nutshell, the SatNav system performs a separate key driver analysis for each organizational subunit corresponding to a specific geographic unit such as a county, state, country, or continent. These models are executed dynamically and permit the user to pose questions like the following ones:

- "If I increased satisfaction with technical support by 10%, in which counties would I enjoy the greatest concomitant increases in customer loyalty?"

- "Which countries would be associated with the highest increases in overall customer satisfaction if we increased satisfaction with product quality by two points?"

- "Which continent would yield the greatest increase in customer loyalty if satisfaction with technical support were increased by 10% and satisfaction with customer service were increased by 15%?"

Figure 11.1 presents an actual screen from the program that illustrates the types of geographic units that can be mapped using the simulation software. As shown, counties, states, regions, and countries can be used to depict the effects of manipulating different service and product quality satisfaction levels. Again, users may pick any outcome variable available in the data set, including measures of overall satisfaction, loyalty, profitability, and share of wallet. The dependent variable is limited only by the availability of data.

Figure 11.2 illustrates the output of one simulation trial. The map depicts the effect of increasing satisfaction with call center courtesy by 20%. Color coding is used to depict the effect of this manipulation on overall satisfaction. The color codes reflect the integration of both performance and importance data. Each region falls into one of four strategic categories. When overall satisfaction is driven strongly by call center courtesy, satisfaction and overall satisfaction ratings are higher than average and the region is depicted in green. In contrast, if call center courtesy is a strong driver of overall satisfaction in a given region and the performance level is

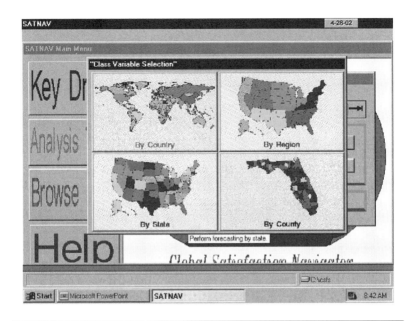

Figure 11.1   SatNav simulation introductory screen illustrating map types.

Adapted from SatNav application © Market Probe, Inc. Milwaukee, WI, 2002.

Figure 11.2   SatNav output with color-coded output at regional level.

Adapted from SatNav application © Market Probe, Inc. Milwaukee, WI, 2002.

lower than average, the region is depicted in red. If, for a given region, call center courtesy is not a key driver of overall satisfaction and performance levels for that variable are lower than average, then the region is depicted in yellow. Finally, when call center courtesy is not a key driver of overall satisfaction and the performance levels for this variable are higher than average, the region is shown in blue.

Note that within each region of the map in Figure 11.2 are counties. We can obtain customer satisfaction, employee satisfaction, and financial performance data for each county. With this type of data set, we can map the effects of manipulating specific customer satisfaction and employee satisfaction data on financial performance at the county level. As a result, we can establish guidelines for implementing changes to key employee satisfaction and customer satisfaction variables across the network. For example, the simulation could show us which 10 counties would yield the greatest increase in profitability based on a 5% increase in satisfaction with technical support and a 10% increase in employee satisfaction with promotional opportunities.

Figure 11.3 also presents the output of a simulation trial. In this case, the results of the simulation are presented by state. The effects of increases

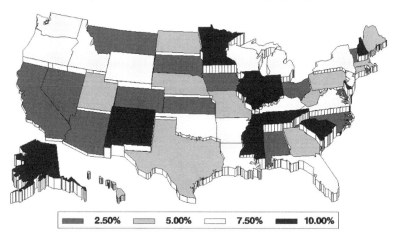

Figure 11.3   SatNav output with three-dimensional mapping feature.
Adapted from SatNav application © Market Probe, Inc. Milwaukee, WI, 2002.

in two variables ("work performed correctly the first time" and "bill consistent with the estimate") are presented across the states. Again, a separate key driver equation is developed dynamically for each state. When the two predictor variables are manipulated, this results in differential effects across the states. The benefit of this approach is that we can isolate those states that will yield the greatest increase in overall satisfaction, loyalty, or even profitability and implement programs only in those states.

The SatNav system and programs like it permit simulations that would otherwise take many hours of programming to perform. In short order, the user can perform hundreds of regression analyses, manipulate key predictor variables, and present the forecasts in the form of easily interpretable maps. This type of system is limited only by the availability of data. When profitability, customer satisfaction, and employee satisfaction data are all available, it is a relatively simple matter to link them quantitatively and forecast results based upon endless "what if?" scenarios.

MANAGEMENT DECISION TOOLS: LOYALTY Rx

One of the main purposes of customer loyalty research is to help address strategic management decisions, including resource allocation. The attribute importance values produced by regression analysis are just one of the factors that should be considered in this regard. We also need to consider the company's current level of performance on the attributes, in light of the following:

- The current level of performance on an attribute determines the amount of improved performance that is logically possible on that attribute. For example, little improvement is possible if you already have a mean of 9.5 on a 10-point rating scale.

- In many product categories, moving a person from 9 to 10 requires greater *actual* performance improvement than moving him or her from 5 to 6.

- There is a "tough cases" issue. That is, every company's customer base contains some customers that are more difficult to satisfy on some attributes than other customers. If your average performance on those attributes is already high, you must either get new customers or satisfy an increased number of difficult customers in order to improve your average performance.

The extent to which the attributes differ in terms of the proportion of the customer base affected should be considered as well. For example, the proportion of the customer base may differ from one customer contact point or distribution channel to another. The financial cost of improved performance on an attribute should also be considered.

Graphical methods have been developed to enable the user to simultaneously consider attribute importance and the company's current performance on the attributes. One of the more common of these methods is the "quadrant map." A quadrant map is primarily a scatter plot in which importance is depicted on one axis, performance is shown on the other axis, and the attributes are plotted as points. In addition, two lines are drawn on the quadrant map, one across the map vertically and the other horizontally, thereby dividing the map's area into four parts and prioritizing them for management action. Each of the four parts is labeled to reflect its priority; one of the many labeling schemes used in the industry is shown below.

- Concentrate here (high importance and low performance)

- Keep up the good work (high importance and high performance)

- Possible overkill (low importance and high performance)

- Low priority (low importance and low performance)

However, quadrant maps have several deficiencies. The prioritization is imprecise in that the map reflects only four levels of priority; the attributes are not prioritized within those levels. In addition, each of the two lines drawn across the map is drawn at the mean or median value of the respective axis. Recognize that, in the case of the performance axis, doing this in effect establishes that point as the needed or target level of performance. But there is no managerial justification for this. Related to the above weakness is the following: By dividing each axis into two parts, we necessarily form four quadrants. Consequently, even when performance is very high in absolute terms on all the attributes, some of the attributes usually fall in the high-priority quadrant. Further, the proportion of the customer base affected is usually not considered. Actually, this can be easily done by adjusting the importance values before the graphic is constructed. That is, attribute by attribute, one may multiply importance by the proportion of the customer base affected.

The obstacle is that most computer software for driver analysis cannot handle a situation in which a question is asked of only a portion of the respondents, and so researchers typically exclude those questions from the driver analysis. Some computer programs, though, are able to handle such questions (for example, the "Logistic" procedure in SAS). Finally, the financial cost of improved performance is not considered.

A number of researchers have responded to some of these criticisms by developing nongraphical approaches. In particular, some have proposed a "priority-for-improvement score" for each attribute. The attributes are then sorted high to low according to this score. At a broad conceptual level, most of these approaches are alike in that the priority-for-improvement score is calculated by multiplying a performance deficit value by importance, attribute by attribute. Most researchers define the performance deficit as the difference between the mean score on the respective attribute and the mean score across all attributes.

These approaches have some of the same deficiencies as the graphical approaches. Some of these involve treating the mean score across attributes as a target level of performance. Another deficiency is that the cost of improvement is not considered. This is a serious limitation because the attributes typically differ greatly in terms of the financial cost of a given amount of improved performance.

Some researchers have developed approaches for calculating priority-for-improvement scores that address these criticisms. Most of these methods are proprietary, and so their details are not publicly available. We can, however, describe one of them in broad conceptual terms.

The approach begins by recognizing that *the client's business question is essentially a resource allocation question.* The approach operationalizes this question as follows:

> Given an overall performance improvement objective, how can I optimize my resource allocation across multiple service or quality enhancement projects?

For example, if you can improve your performance on the attributes by a total of 25 points across all attributes, how much of the 25 points should be on the first attribute, how much should be on the second attribute, and so on? This is answered by taking a total amount of improved performance and dividing it *in proportion to* the four factors discussed earlier (importance, amount of improved performance that is possible, proportion of the customer base affected, and cost). For example, if the attributes are equal to each other on the other three factors, the algorithm would execute as follows: If an attribute is twice as important as another, we should improve performance on it twice as much as on the other attribute. If the cost of a one-unit increase in performance on an attribute is one-third what it is on another attribute, we should improve performance on it three times as much as on the other attribute. Each of these four factors is given equal weight in this allocation decision.

One of the key issues to be addressed has to do with the metric that is used to express the importance scores when the priority-for-improvement scores are calculated. Some of these approaches, regardless of the statistical technique used to produce the importance scores, are scaled to sum to

100 across the attributes. That is, the coefficients from the driver analysis are summed, and then each coefficient is divided by that sum. When importance scores scaled in this way are used in the calculation of the priority-for-improvement scores, an assumption, perhaps a bold one, is being made: the amount of improvement in loyalty will be in proportion to these scaled importance scores. The problem is that even if none of the attributes has a strong influence on loyalty in absolute terms, the scaled importance scores will sum to 100.

Another issue involves recognizing that companies often set customer loyalty goals for their managers to achieve. In this circumstance, managers need more focused guidance than we have discussed. Managers need to know how much performance improvement is needed on each attribute in order to achieve the loyalty goal. Determining this requires that we calculate the priority-for-improvement scores and then make inferences regarding the required levels of performance on the attributes. Some researchers have developed methods for accommodating this need. Figure 11.4 presents a variant of the priority-for-improvement score approach.

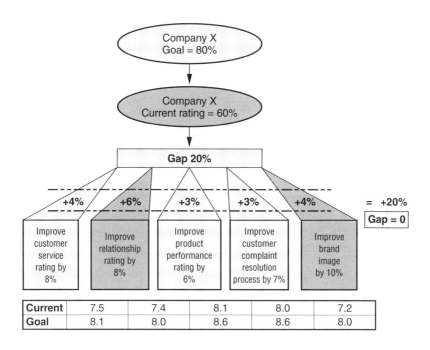

Figure 11.4 Loyalty Rx.

In this example, the company's loyalty goal is 80%. Their current score is 60%, representing a performance gap of 20 percentage points.

The company's *current* mean performance ratings on the attributes are shown in the row labeled "current." The mean levels of performance on the attributes *that are estimated to be necessary* to increase loyalty by 20 points are shown in the row labeled "goal." The percentages in the row of boxes (8, 8, 6, 7, and 10) are these same values expressed in percentage change terms (from the current level of performance on the respective attributes).

The percentages in the top row (4, 6, 3, 3, and 4) are estimated loyalty "payoff" values. For example, if the company were to improve its performance on customer service by 8%—that is, to go from its current level of performance of 7.5 to 8.1—its loyalty score would theoretically rise by four percentage points.

These calculations do not require cost information in absolute terms; relative terms are sufficient. This information can be obtained by asking a manager to judgmentally rank the attributes from high to low in terms of the financial cost of a one-unit improvement in performance (on the satisfaction scale used in the questionnaire). Then, starting with the second attribute from the bottom, have the manager estimate how much more expensive that attribute is than the preceding attribute in percentage terms (for example, 5% more expensive).

Given a set of importance scores on the attributes, there are thousands of alternative combinations of performance levels on the attributes that would theoretically produce an increase of a given number of points in loyalty. But as described above, the values in the combination developed by this type of approach have been "optimized" with respect to the factors (importance, and so on) being considered.

The dependent variable that is used in the driver analysis should be expressed in the same metric as the goals set by management. For example, if the management-set goal is stated in terms of a percentage, the statistical technique used in the driver analysis should be one designed for analysis of percentages (as opposed to means).

The findings of these types of analysis should be used with caution, of course. In particular, a great deal of caution should be exercised in treating the priority-for-improvement score as a forecast. One consideration involves whether the driver analysis was based on cross-sectional data or longitudinal data. We did not follow customers over time to identify those who changed their scores on a given attribute and then see whether their loyalty scores changed. Consequently, in calculating the priority-for-improvement score, we made a key assumption: if the people currently giving a rating on an attribute were to increase their ratings to a certain point, their loyalty scores would rise to that of the respondents at that second point. That is, if the respondents currently giving "4" ratings on an attribute were to increase their ratings to "5," their loyalty scores would rise to the level of the people currently giving "5" responses on that attribute. We are also assuming that "everything else stays as it was at the time of the interview"; that is, among other things, that the competition does not change its performance on the attributes and that brand positioning does not change.

THE GLOBAL PERSPECTIVE

Throughout this book we have stressed the importance of reporting both performance metrics (such as the top-two-box satisfaction score) and key driver analysis at the lowest possible organizational subunit. This involves conducting analysis at the lowest meaningful strategic business unit, such as the sales district, county, or region. In certain cases where customer groups transcend business unit definitions, reporting may be conducted at the customer segment level.

Typically, we have assumed that there are no substantive cultural differences across strategic business units that would affect the measurement of customer or employee satisfaction. This is primarily because our interest has focused on domestic programs. Increasingly, however, multinational corporations are requiring customer satisfaction programs to be conducted at a global level. In this case, the strategic business unit is assumed to be a country or, in some cases, a region within a country.

Cross-cultural differences can potentially affect both sides of the reduced model

$$FP = (ESAT_{EP} - ESAT_{PP}) + (CSAT_{EP} - CSAT_{PP})$$

where FP = Financial performance

$ESAT_{EP}$ = Employee satisfaction (expected performance)

$ESAT_{PP}$ = Employee satisfaction (perceived performance)

$CSAT_{EP}$ = Customer satisfaction (expected performance)

$CSAT_{PP}$ = Customer satisfaction (perceived performance)

That is, measurements on the independent variable portion of the model (for both employee satisfaction and customer satisfaction) are susceptible to cultural differences across respondents. On the other hand, the dependent measure may be more robust when it comes to cultural differences. The measurement of profitability at the individual country level within a multinational corporation is typically standardized; the idiosyncratic financial accounting practices of individual countries would generally not be permitted to affect the calculation of financial performance variables. The need for standardized accounting across countries would typically ensure that cultural differences have a minimal effect on financial performance metrics.

It is likely that there are subtle cultural differences across the United States that affect customer satisfaction scoring. For example, we have encountered significant differences between rural and urban customers with respect to their overall satisfaction with banks. That regional cultural differences may also exist is a distinct possibility, despite the general assumption that the United States is a culturally homogeneous "melting pot."

There is also a good chance that employee satisfaction differs regionally within the United States. It is likely that this is an artifact of urban versus rural demographic categories. For example, the northeastern portion of the United States is considerably more urban than the Southwest. Whether city dwellers are generally more or less satisfied with their jobs than their rural peers is unclear.

While it is debatable whether cultural differences within the United States affect customer or employee satisfaction results, there is a great deal of evidence to suggest that there are differences across countries. For multinationals interested in comparing performance levels across a global network of operations, cultural differences may make measuring and comparing customer satisfaction across countries somewhat problematic.

When a multinational corporation is interested in comparing how operations in different countries perform with respect to both customer and employee satisfaction, some interesting questions arise. In particular, it is unclear whether differences in performance across countries are attributable to cultural variations or to real differences in the extent to which managers in each country have satisfied their customers.

Note that cultural differences may affect customer and employee satisfaction statistics in a variety of ways. In the simplest case, the summary reporting metric may be affected. For example, respondents from certain cultures may be more inclined to give positive satisfaction scores because it is less acceptable (or less polite) to express dissatisfaction. Of course, not only mean or percentage scores can be affected by cultural differences. The distribution of scores may also be affected. In a culture that tends to provide positive scores because of the social desirability of doing so, the distribution may be even more skewed than normal. There may also be a concomitant decrease in variance around the mean score.

It is also possible for cultural differences to affect key driver analyses. This requires us to consider the possibility that covariance structures may be affected by cultural differences across respondent groups. Focusing exclusively on the predictor side of the equation, we must consider the possibility that the correlation matrices of customer and employee satisfaction items differ substantively across two or more countries. For example, with respect to the customer satisfaction items, the null hypothesis would be that the correlation matrix in one country is equivalent to that in all of the others. Covariance structure analysis provides a platform for conducting this type of test.

A more interesting question involves the extent to which cultural differences may affect multiple regression analyses in terms of the R^2 and magnitude of the beta coefficients. The former is simply the multivariate extension of the bivariate correlation coefficient. That two sets of predictor variables (employee and customer satisfaction measures) could account for differing proportions of variance in the dependent financial performance measure is quite possible. There are tests to determine whether two parallel beta coefficients are significantly different from one another. In each model, the dependent measure (FP) is a reflection of profitability at the country level.

$$FP_1 = \beta_{11}CS_1 + \beta_{21}CS_2 + \beta_{31}ES_1 + \beta_{41}ES_2$$

$$FP_2 = \beta_{12}CS_1 + \beta_{22}CS_2 + \beta_{32}ES_1 + \beta_{42}ES_2$$

In effect, our test could include any or all of the beta coefficients from the two parallel multiple regression equations. In the case of the effect of CS_1 on FP, we would test the difference between β_{11} and β_{12}, which are the beta coefficients for the first customer satisfaction variable. Differences between these two beta coefficients would suggest that the role of CS_1 is different in the two countries. In the case when the difference between β_{11} and β_{12} is statistically significant, the implication is that, in one case, there is a strong relationship between CS_1 and financial performance. The question at hand, of course, is whether this difference is due to cultural differences or to actual differences in terms of service or product quality variance.

Determining whether covariance structures are affected by cultural differences across respondent groups has not received a great deal of attention in applied settings. That cultural differences could affect covariance structures is a somewhat difficult concept to grasp. Unlike a mean or percentage score, which may be affected by, for example, a particular culture's tendency to provide positive feedback regardless of the level of perceived quality, it is difficult to imagine how covariance structures could be affected by cultural differences. If respondents in a given country tend to give high scores for all customer and employee satisfaction attributes, there will be less variance across the scores within that country. As a result, it is possible that within a country, financial performance models (developed at the customer level) would tend to have low R^2 values because customer satisfaction scores would tend not to vary with financial performance. Thus, if a culture is associated with a tendency to use only the top or top two scores on a service or product quality measurement scale, there will be less variance to leverage in our efforts to model outcomes such as financial performance.

Most researchers interested in how cultural differences affect customer and employee satisfaction measurement programs have focused on how to modify simple reporting metrics such as the mean or top-two-box score to reflect these differences. Research and interesting theoretical perspectives are offered by Van de Vijver and Poortinga (1982), England and Harpaz (1983), McCauley and Colberg (1983), and Bhalla and Lin (1987). Several approaches to developing cultural bias adjustments are possible. Two relatively unsophisticated approaches involve regional comparisons and normative indexing.

The regional comparison approach to the problem of cultural differences involves simply constraining reporting to a given geographic region. Thus, Denmark might be compared only with other Scandinavian countries, and Saudi Arabia only with other Middle Eeastern countries. The most substantive potential problem with this approach is that there may also be cultural differences among the countries in a given region.

Another approach to adjusting for bias attributable to cultural differences involves normative indexing. This approach can take two forms. First, a corporate norm can be established for a given country. Performance scores can then be expressed as values relative to the country or regional norm. While this helps managers compare their performance levels with the country standard, it does little to facilitate intercountry comparisons. Another approach to the normative indexing technique is to assess performance relative to another multinational's performance. For example, Coca-Cola could gauge its performance in terms of distribution, access, price, and other variables against its main competitor—Pepsi. Similarly, an auto manufacturer in Europe might choose to use the performance of Mercedes-Benz as a benchmark.

A more sophisticated approach to assessing cultural bias was developed by Crosby (1992). Crosby's approach presumed that there was a fixed cultural bias error term for every country. This could be used to adjust scores for each country in the following manner:

$$PQ_o = f(PP - EXP) + RB_j + e$$

where PQ_o = Observed rating

PP – EXP = Perceived performance minus expected performance

RB_j = Response bias common to a specific country

e = Random error

While this seems straightforward enough, the method used to determine RB_j is more complicated. The adjustment factor is developed using a standard set of questions that represent different levels of performance in a variety of settings. These range from a theater performance to airline travel delays:

There is one awkward pause in a professional theater performance as an actor tries to recall his lines.

An astronomer in your country discovers a star.

Your arrival by air on a one-hour flight is delayed by 15 minutes.

A supplier averages 10 minutes late for most meetings.

Responses to a set of 30 day-to-day occurrence items like these are used to develop a unique adjustment factor for every country in a study. The adjustment factors are calculated using the grand mean across all 30 questions for each country. A global mean is then calculated using the responses for all the countries combined. Next, one country is chosen as a benchmark against which all the other countries will be compared. For a U.S. multinational, the United States would typically be selected as the benchmark. Following the selection of the benchmark, each country's mean is then subtracted from the global mean to calculate the individual country adjustment factors. These are then applied to the actual performance scores.

Crosby's approach to developing cultural bias adjustment factors is based upon certain fundamental assumptions. Among these are that respondents in a country are likely to use multipoint scales in the same way as people in other countries. Perhaps more important is the assumption that the 30 items in the day-to-day occurrence battery are answered in a manner that is transportable to the specific case in which product or service quality is being evaluated. Crosby does not specifically address employee satisfaction, but we can assume that the same adjustment factors could be applied to this type of data.

As globalization escalates, there will be an increasingly compelling call for customer and employee satisfaction programs that include comparisons across countries. The development of techniques such as those introduced here will be important cornerstones for multinational service and product quality programs. The possibility that covariance structures are also affected by cultural bias is worth additional focus.

REFINING OUR UNDERSTANDING OF LOYALTY

Researchers disagree on the appropriate definition of customer loyalty, but they do agree that the concept of customer loyalty is multifaceted and consequently is best measured using a combination of (metrics) questions. The questions most commonly used involve the following factors:

- Overall satisfaction

- Overall quality

- Intent to repurchase

- Intent to purchase other products or services

- Willingness to recommend

- Willingness to "go out of one's way for"

- Identification with the company or brand

Typically, some combination of two or three of these questions is used. Researchers usually use a combination whose questions differ systematically. For example, it is common to select one question that is cognitive/rational, one that is affective, and one that relates to readiness to act.

Researchers sometimes sum the responses to the questions and treat the sum as a metric variable in the analysis. A disadvantage of this practice is that it assumes that a given distance on the variable represents the same amount of loyalty from one area of the scale to another. For example, the distance between 7 and 8 is assumed to represent the same amount of loyalty as the distance between 14 and 15. But empirical analysis suggests otherwise. For illustration purposes, suppose that we define loyalty as the sum of overall satisfaction, intent to repurchase, and willingness to recommend and that each of these questions is measured on a 5-point scale. The sum of the responses to these questions will therefore range from 3 to 15. Empirical analyses have shown a tendency for respondents having scores of "14" to *differ more* (in satisfaction and purchase behavior) from respondents having scores of "15" than respondents with scores of "13" differ from respondents having scores of "14." Consequently, when sample size permits, researchers usually treat loyalty as a categorical variable, not a metric one. It is usually defined as having three or four (ordinal) categories.

A related measurement advance involves the definition of customer and employee *commitment*. Larger batteries of items are being used to measure these constructs. The additional questions address the importance of the product category to the customer, the attractiveness of competing products, and the stated propensity to switch to a competitor. The key is that these measures of commitment are believed to be better predictors of desirable behaviors than measures of customer and employee satisfaction. That is, customer commitment measures have been shown to covary more strongly with corporate financial performance. Similarly, employee commitment is currently believed to be a better predictor of critical behaviors such as absenteeism and turnover.

The new customer commitment batteries go beyond simple measures of repurchase intent or propensity to recommend. They often include items that quantify the importance of the product *category* to the customer. It is believed that a consumer will be less likely to give a strong repurchase intent rating if the product category is relatively unimportant to him. Other items used in customer commitment batteries relate to competitive context. That is, customer commitment measures often entail comparisons with competing products. Another item frequently encountered in customer commitment indices involves a value assessment as defined by the ratio of price to quality. It should be clear that there is a trend to make customer commitment indices much more encompassing. Traditional loyalty items such as repurchase intent and willingness to recommend are more encompassing than a single measure such as customer satisfaction.

With respect to employee commitment, this measure is expanded well beyond simple job satisfaction. Commitment batteries include items relating to engagement, interpersonal relations, personal growth, reciprocity, and equity. Together these items are believed to provide a construct that is more robust and a better predictor of important employee behaviors. These employee behaviors, in turn, can be linked directly to corporate financial performance.

Our purpose in defining employee and customer commitment is to obtain a better understanding of, and to better predict, *behaviors*. Many applied studies have validated definitions of commitment that use these new batteries of questions, but little information on their findings has been made public because the data were considered proprietary. However, the information that is available indicates that these new definitions of loyalty or commitment are more predictive of—more strongly associated with—desirable behavioral outcomes that yield enhanced financial performance.

INTANGIBLE DRIVERS OF CUSTOMER LOYALTY

Historically, customer loyalty studies have focused almost entirely on tangible benefits of the product or service under study (such as its quality, reliability, durability, and design). Over the past few years, some efforts have been made to include intangible benefits (Schneider and Bowen 1999). The strategy behind this work has been to begin by identifying fundamental human needs, such as the need to nurture, the desire to feel connected to others, the desire for social acceptance, and the need for self-esteem. Each fundamental need is then studied, and an effort is made to identify ways in which the product or service under study could satisfy the respective need. Questions corresponding to these needs are then included in the questionnaire.

As of this time, not enough of this type of work has been done to allow us to predict its future. We can say that, based on theory, we would expect these efforts to be most successful in high-involvement product categories in which the products and services are differentiated largely on the basis of brand image, such as automobiles, clothing, jewelry, and cosmetics. However, there have been limited successes to date in other product categories. Another approach has been to try to capture the "brand power" of the brand by including statements such as "I like what the X name stands for" and "My X product reflects my values and interests/lifestyle."

CONCLUDING REMARKS

Customer satisfaction and loyalty analysis generally and the effort to link these constructs to financial performance specifically can be considered in the framework depicted in Figure 11.5. As shown in the figure, the linkage process is composed of four key elements. Each presents unique opportunities with respect to future advancements. For example, measurement issues involving both attitudes and business performance metrics may emerge as fruitful areas for future research. Efforts to establish customer profitability are being undertaken by more companies each year. It is also likely that the advent of Internet surveys will revive some long-forgotten attitude measurement scales. Web surveys will make possible, for example, sliding measurement scales with true interval-level properties.

Forces operating in the broader survey research industry are also operating in the customer satisfaction and loyalty research industry. For example, administering questionnaires by telephone in consumer studies

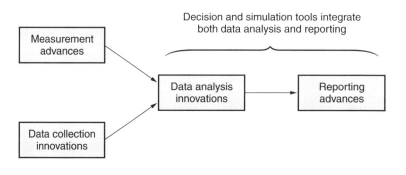

Figure 11.5   Key phases in the linkage research process.

is becoming more problematic because of decreased access to respondents. This decreased access is due to telephone answering machines, voice-mail systems, current options such as Privacy Manager in respondents' homes, and increased competition for respondents' time (especially from telemarketers).

This is motivating researchers to identify other modes of questionnaire administration. One that is sometimes used is a type of two-stage process in which the consumer is asked, perhaps during the checkout process in a retail store, to call a particular phone number for a prerecorded interview. The latter is called IVR (interactive voice response). A benefit of this is that it sidesteps the often-troublesome task of obtaining consumers' phone numbers.

There have also been an increased number of studies in which interviews are administered over the Internet or by e-mail. But we recommend caution in doing this in consumer (as opposed to business-to-business) studies at this time. Until recently, a substantial portion of the population did not have access to Internet or e-mail, and they may have differed in relevant ways from those that did have access. Within the past few years, research firms have devoted enormous internal resources to Web surveys to determine the advantages and disadvantages of this methodology in different areas. Much progress has been made, but the verdict will likely remain unknown for several years to come as to which types of studies among which types of groups of people work the best.

Advances in data analysis are virtually certain over the next decade. Marketing research and quality analysis have borrowed analytical techniques from a wide variety of fields. It is likely that this trend will continue. Fields such as social psychology, educational psychology, and sociology have provided fertile grounds from which to borrow statistical techniques and research methodologies.

With respect to advances in reporting, it is likely that the Internet will continue to play a critical role. The dissemination of results via Web sites will further hasten the obsolescence of paper reports. Web-based reports will also be dynamic, offering users the ability to "drill down" and seek increasingly detailed information. Similarly, dynamic Web-based reports may offer users the ability to perform ad hoc analyses and share data with other IT systems. This could facilitate analyses that link customer and employee satisfaction to other data sources involving distribution systems, manufacturing, and marketing.

Several of the simulation tools described earlier in this chapter span both the data analysis and reporting components depicted in Figure 11.5. These tools permit users to conduct analyses and provide increasingly sophisticated data visualization interfaces. Three-dimensional plots that can be rotated are now commonplace graphic options. The ability to perform profit forecasts based on increases in service or product quality satisfaction was illustrated with the SatNav software described earlier in the chapter.

This book has attempted to synthesize a considerable amount of theoretical and technical information relating to the relationships between customer and employee satisfaction and corporate financial performance. We have provided an analytical framework for establishing an empirical linkage between these variables. Using any of these techniques, readers may experiment with a variety of analytical approaches. These range from bivariate techniques to sophisticated latent variable modeling.

It should be clear at this point that we have advocated an approach that yields a consistent unit of analysis. This involves collapsing customer satisfaction, employee satisfaction, and business performance data to the strategic business unit level. Such an approach is applicable only when an organization can be defined in terms of a set of mutually exclusive subunits. Often these are tied to specific geographic units, but not always. When meaningful subgroups cannot be established, the linkage process is more problematic. Empirically, relating financial performance to employee and customer satisfaction requires either cross-sectional or longitudinal data. If cross-sectional data cannot be generated using the procedures described in this book, it may be necessary to develop a longitudinal data set. The latter case may entail, at best, retrieving historical data or, at worst, developing a prospective program that could yield viable time series data after several years.

Clearly, the availability of data at the appropriate level of analysis represents a challenge for some organizations. This may be the main hurdle for companies that mass-produce low-involvement consumer packaged goods or have very infrequent interactions with their customers. It could be argued that the types of empirical linkages discussed in this book are simply not appropriate in the former case. Indeed, consumer packaged-goods marketers are typically more concerned with brand awareness and brand equity than customer satisfaction.

There appears to be theoretical and empirical evidence to support the relationship between customer and employee satisfaction and corporate financial performance. We hope that this book facilitates additional investigation and stimulates discussion among theoreticians and applied researchers.

Appendix
Matrix Algebra in Statistics

Matrix algebra represents a very useful shorthand for statistical data analysis. There are numerous texts that provide excellent treatments of the subject. Some of the better books on matrix algebra are Searle (1982), Steinberg (1974), and Eves (1966). A more technical treatment is provided by Perlis (1991). The use of matrix algebra to convey statistical analysis is now commonplace in both books and journals. This appendix provides a brief overview of matrix algebra and its role in the statistical analyses used in customer satisfaction research.

The three objects manipulated in matrix algebra are scalars, vectors, and matrices. Scalars are simply numbers such as 1, 32, and ⅕. On the other hand, vectors, and matrices are sets of numbers. In both cases, the size of a given matrix or vector is referred to in terms of its dimensions. The dimensions of a matrix or vector are given by its *rows* and *columns*.

$$\mathbf{a} = \begin{bmatrix} 3 \\ 6 \\ 2 \end{bmatrix} \qquad \mathbf{b} = \begin{bmatrix} 6 & 1 & 4 & 8 \end{bmatrix}$$

For example, the column vector $\mathbf{a}_{3\times1}$ is a 3×1 vector; it has three rows and one column. In contrast, the row vector $\mathbf{b}_{1\times4}$ has one row and four columns.

Vectors are actually a special form of matrix. The matrix $\mathbf{C}_{3\times4}$ shown below has three rows and four columns. Note that we differentiate matrices and vectors with uppercase versus lowercase letters, respectively.

$$\mathbf{C}_{3\times4} = \begin{bmatrix} 1 & 3 & 6 & 2 \\ 2 & 1 & 4 & 8 \\ 3 & 8 & 1 & 6 \end{bmatrix}$$

Any single element of C can be identified based on its coordinates. For example, the element in the third row and second column is 8. The elements of C can be uniquely identified by their row and column addresses. Thus, the value of c_{32} is 8.

$$C = \begin{bmatrix} c_{11} & c_{12} & c_{13} & c_{14} \\ c_{21} & c_{22} & c_{23} & c_{24} \\ c_{31} & c_{32} & c_{33} & c_{34} \end{bmatrix}$$

A matrix that has as many rows as columns is referred to as a square matrix. For example, the matrix D is square because it has two rows and two columns. Note that in most texts and journal articles, matrices are denoted with bold capital letters and their elements are assigned lower-case equivalents.

$$D = \begin{bmatrix} d_{11} & d_{12} \\ d_{21} & d_{22} \end{bmatrix}$$

MATRIX AND VECTOR OPERATIONS

Matrices and vectors can be added and subtracted from one another if their dimensions are exactly the same.

$$a = \begin{bmatrix} 3 \\ 2 \\ 1 \end{bmatrix} \qquad b = \begin{bmatrix} 1 \\ 1 \\ 2 \end{bmatrix}$$

$$a - b = c \qquad c = \begin{bmatrix} 2 \\ 1 \\ -1 \end{bmatrix}$$

The column vector b can be subtracted from a because they both have three rows and one column. Similarly, the matrices F and G may be added to produce a new matrix (H) of the same dimension.

$$F = \begin{bmatrix} 1 & 2 & 3 \\ 2 & 3 & 1 \end{bmatrix} \qquad G = \begin{bmatrix} 6 & 1 & 4 \\ 2 & 8 & 3 \end{bmatrix}$$

$$H = F + G \qquad H = \begin{bmatrix} 7 & 3 & 7 \\ 4 & 11 & 4 \end{bmatrix}$$

Each element of **H** equals the sum of the corresponding elements in **F** and **G**. For example, $h_{12} = 3$, which is the sum of $f_{12} = 2$ and $g_{12} = 1$. The matrix **H**, therefore, is simply the sum of the matrices **F** and **G**.

$$\begin{bmatrix} f_{11}+g_{11} & f_{12}+g_{12} & f_{13}+g_{13} \\ f_{21}+g_{21} & f_{22}+g_{22} & f_{23}+g_{23} \\ f_{31}+g_{31} & f_{32}+g_{32} & f_{33}+g_{33} \end{bmatrix}$$

A scalar can be added to a matrix of any size. Doing so involves adding the scalar value to every element of the matrix. This operation can be performed regardless of the dimensions of a given matrix or vector.

$$a = 6 \quad \mathbf{B} = \begin{bmatrix} 2 & 3 \\ 4 & 8 \end{bmatrix} \quad a + \mathbf{B} = \begin{bmatrix} 8 & 9 \\ 10 & 14 \end{bmatrix}$$

$$a + \mathbf{B} = \begin{bmatrix} b_{11}+6 & b_{12}+6 \\ b_{21}+6 & b_{22}+6 \end{bmatrix}$$

$$\mathbf{C} = \begin{bmatrix} 3 \\ 1 \\ 3 \\ 1 \end{bmatrix} \quad a + \mathbf{C} = \begin{bmatrix} c_{11}+6 \\ c_{21}+6 \\ c_{31}+6 \\ c_{41}+6 \end{bmatrix}$$

MATRIX MULTIPLICATION

Of the operations performed in matrix algebra, matrix multiplication is one of the most powerful. Matrix multiplication requires that the matrices be compatible. In order to multiply two matrices, the number of *columns* in the first must be the same as the number of *rows* in the second.

Dimension of new matrix

$$\mathbf{R}_{2\times3}\mathbf{S}_{3\times2} = \mathbf{T}_{2\times2}$$

Must be identical

$$\mathbf{R}_{2\times3} = \begin{bmatrix} 1 & 2 & 3 \\ 4 & 2 & 1 \end{bmatrix} \quad \mathbf{S}_{3\times2} = \begin{bmatrix} 6 & 1 \\ 4 & 2 \\ 1 & 3 \end{bmatrix}$$

$$\mathbf{RS} = \begin{bmatrix} (r_{11}s_{11})+(r_{12}s_{21})+(r_{13}s_{31}) & (r_{11}s_{12})+(r_{12}s_{22})+(r_{13}s_{32}) \\ (r_{21}s_{11})+(r_{22}s_{21})+(r_{23}s_{31}) & (r_{21}s_{12})+(r_{22}s_{22})+(r_{23}s_{32}) \end{bmatrix}$$

While **RS** yields a new 2×2 matrix **T**, we cannot assume that **SR** will also equal **T**. Indeed, unlike scalar mathematics in which 2×3 is the equivalent of 3×2, such is not the case in matrix algebra. While the product of **RS** was $\mathbf{T}_{2\times2}$, product **SR** may not even exist. In the present case, however, we can find the product of **SR**.

$$\mathbf{SR} = \mathbf{V}_{3\times3}$$

$$\mathbf{V}_{3\times3} = \begin{bmatrix} (s_{11}r_{11}) + (s_{11}r_{21}) & (s_{11}r_{12}) + (s_{12}r_{22}) & (s_{11}r_{13}) + (s_{12}r_{23}) \\ (s_{21}r_{11}) + (s_{22}r_{21}) & (s_{21}r_{12}) + (s_{22}r_{22}) & (s_{21}r_{13}) + (s_{22}r_{23}) \\ (s_{31}r_{11}) + (s_{32}r_{21}) & (s_{31}r_{12}) + (s_{32}r_{22}) & (s_{31}r_{13}) + (s_{32}r_{23}) \end{bmatrix}$$

$$\mathbf{V}_{3\times3} = \begin{bmatrix} 10 & 14 & 10 \\ 12 & 12 & 14 \\ 13 & 8 & 6 \end{bmatrix}$$

Clearly, **SR** yields a very different matrix from **RS**. To differentiate between these two matrix products, we use the terms *premultiply* and *postmultiply*. Matrix $\mathbf{V}_{3\times3}$ is the result of premultiplying **S** with **R**. Conversely, matrix $\mathbf{T}_{2\times2}$ is the result of postmultiplying **S** with **R**.

Vectors present a unique opportunity in matrix algebra. Consider the two vectors **a** and **b**. Note that **a** is a row vector and **b** is a column vector. We can calculate **ab** because the number of rows in **a** equals the number of columns in **b**. This operation (**ab**) will yield a scalar equal to the sum of the products of the elements in the matrices.

$$\mathbf{a}_{1\times4} = \begin{bmatrix} 3 & 2 & 5 & 6 \end{bmatrix} \qquad \mathbf{b}_{4\times1} = \begin{bmatrix} 2 \\ 2 \\ 1 \\ 1 \end{bmatrix}$$

$$\mathbf{ab} = \begin{bmatrix} 21 \end{bmatrix}$$

In contrast, the matrix **BA** has a total of 16 elements.

$$\mathbf{BA} = \begin{bmatrix} 6 & 6 & 3 & 3 \\ 4 & 4 & 2 & 2 \\ 10 & 10 & 5 & 5 \\ 12 & 12 & 6 & 6 \end{bmatrix}$$

The transpose of a matrix **A** is denoted as **A′**. The transpose operation simply involves exchanging the rows and columns in a matrix. For example, the matrix **A** and its transpose **A′** illustrate the effects of transposing a matrix.

$$\mathbf{A}_{3\times 2} = \begin{bmatrix} 2 & 1 \\ 3 & 3 \\ 4 & 6 \end{bmatrix} \qquad \mathbf{A'}_{2\times 3} = \begin{bmatrix} 2 & 3 & 4 \\ 1 & 3 & 6 \end{bmatrix}$$

Assume that the matrix **A** is composed of three observations and two variables. When we calculate a new matrix **A′A**, it has some interesting properties.

$$\mathbf{A'A} = \begin{bmatrix} 29 & 35 \\ 35 & 46 \end{bmatrix}$$

The matrix **A′A** is referred to as the uncorrected sums of squares and cross-products (SSCP). In the case of **A′A**, we know that the diagonal elements are equal to the sum of squared values for the first of our two hypothetical variables. That is, $29 = (2^2) + (3^2) + (4^2)$. Similarly, $46 = (1^2) + (3^2) + (6^2)$. The off-diagonal elements of **A′A** are equal to the sum of cross-products between the two hypothetical variables. Note that the upper-right and lower-left entries are equal; both are 35, which is the sum of cross-products for our two variables. So, $35 = (2 \times 1) + (3 \times 3) + (4 \times 6)$ is the sum of cross-products. In general, the SSCP matrix takes the following form.

$$\mathbf{X'X} = \begin{bmatrix} \sum_{i=1}^{N} x_{i1}^2 & \sum_{i=1}^{N} x_{i1}x_{i2} & \cdots & \sum_{i=1}^{N} x_{i1}x_{ik} \\ \sum_{i=1}^{N} x_{i1}x_{i2} & \sum_{i=1}^{N} x_{i2}^2 & \cdots & \sum_{i=1}^{N} x_{i2}x_{ik} \\ \vdots & \vdots & & \vdots \\ \sum_{i=1}^{N} x_{i1}x_{ik} & \sum_{i=1}^{N} x_{i2}x_{ik} & \cdots & \sum_{i=1}^{N} x_{ik}^2 \end{bmatrix}$$

Note that the diagonal elements of **X′X** are the sums of squares for each variable. The off-diagonal elements are the sums of cross-products for each variable pairing. Finally, notice that **X′X** is symmetric. That is, **A′A** = (**A′A**)′, which underscores the fact that the top-right element is the same as the bottom-left element.

The SSCP matrix has little intrinsic value. It is not standardized; it reflects raw measurement units and is difficult to interpret. The SSCP matrix must be centered in order to produce the mean corrected sum of squares and cross-products matrix **S**. The mean corrected sum of squares and cross products is the basis for developing the covariance matrix **C** and correlation matrix **R**.

In order to produce **S**, we must find the mean for each variable in **A**. Since our data matrix is so small, it is a simple matter to calculate that $\bar{x}_1 = 3$ and $\bar{x}_2 = 3.33$. In matrix algebra we can use a row vector of ones (1´) and the sample size (N) to begin the centering process.

$$\mathbf{A}_{3 \times 2} = \begin{bmatrix} 2 & 1 \\ 3 & 3 \\ 4 & 6 \end{bmatrix}$$

$$\overline{\mathbf{A}} = \frac{1}{N} \mathbf{1}' \mathbf{A}$$

$$\overline{\mathbf{a}} = \frac{1}{3} \begin{bmatrix} 1 & 1 & 1 \end{bmatrix} \begin{bmatrix} 2 & 1 \\ 3 & 3 \\ 4 & 6 \end{bmatrix}$$

$$\overline{\mathbf{a}} = \frac{1}{3} \begin{bmatrix} 9 & 10 \end{bmatrix}$$

$$\overline{\mathbf{a}} = \begin{bmatrix} 3 & 3.33 \end{bmatrix}$$

The next step in the centering process is to generate a new matrix with elements that are centered with respect to the matrix $\overline{\mathbf{a}}$. This entails finding the matrix **S**.

$$\mathbf{S} = \mathbf{A}'\mathbf{A} - \frac{1}{n}(\mathbf{A}'\mathbf{1})(\mathbf{1}'\mathbf{A})$$

For the two-variable situation, **S** is calculated in the following fashion.

$$\mathbf{S} = \begin{bmatrix} 2 & 3 & 4 \\ 1 & 3 & 6 \end{bmatrix} \begin{bmatrix} 2 & 1 \\ 3 & 3 \\ 4 & 6 \end{bmatrix} - \frac{1}{3}\left(\begin{bmatrix} 2 & 3 & 4 \\ 1 & 3 & 6 \end{bmatrix} \begin{bmatrix} 1 \\ 1 \\ 1 \end{bmatrix} \right)\left(\begin{bmatrix} 1 & 1 & 1 \end{bmatrix} \begin{bmatrix} 2 & 1 \\ 3 & 3 \\ 4 & 6 \end{bmatrix} \right)$$

$$\mathbf{S} = \begin{bmatrix} 29 & 35 \\ 35 & 46 \end{bmatrix} - \frac{1}{3}\left(\begin{bmatrix} 9 \\ 10 \end{bmatrix} \begin{bmatrix} 9 & 10 \end{bmatrix} \right)$$

$$\mathbf{S} = \begin{bmatrix} 29 & 35 \\ 35 & 46 \end{bmatrix} - \frac{1}{3}\begin{bmatrix} 81 & 90 \\ 90 & 100 \end{bmatrix}$$

$$\mathbf{S} = \begin{bmatrix} 29 & 35 \\ 35 & 46 \end{bmatrix} - \begin{bmatrix} 27 & 30 \\ 30 & 33.33 \end{bmatrix}$$

$$\mathbf{S} = \begin{bmatrix} 2 & 5 \\ 5 & 12.66 \end{bmatrix}$$

With the mean corrected SSCP matrix, the calculation of a covariance matrix $\mathbf{C}$ is a simple matter. Note that $\mathbf{C}$ contains variances on the diagonal and covariances on the off-diagonal. $\mathbf{C}$ is a symmetric matrix in that it equals its transpose: $\mathbf{C} = \mathbf{C}'$.

$$\mathbf{C} = \frac{1}{n-1}\mathbf{S}$$

$$\mathbf{C} = \frac{1}{2}\begin{bmatrix} 2 & 5 \\ 5 & 12.66 \end{bmatrix}$$

$$\mathbf{C} = \begin{bmatrix} 1 & 2.50 \\ 2.50 & 6.33 \end{bmatrix}$$

The correlation matrix $\mathbf{R}$ can be calculated using either the covariance matrix $\mathbf{C}$ or the mean corrected SSCP matrix. $\mathbf{C}$ contains valuable information concerning the dispersion of the two variables. The diagonal is especially useful since it is composed of variances. This can be verified using a calculator.

If we define a new matrix $\mathbf{V}^{-1/2}$ consisting of the reciprocal square roots of the variances for x_1 and x_2 and use it to pre- and postmultiply the covariance matrix $\mathbf{C}$, we find the correlation matrix $\mathbf{R}$.

$$\mathbf{V}^{-\frac{1}{2}} = \begin{bmatrix} \dfrac{1}{\sqrt{\mathbf{S}_1^2}} & 0 \\ 0 & \dfrac{1}{\sqrt{\mathbf{S}_2^2}} \end{bmatrix}$$

$$\mathbf{V}^{-\frac{1}{2}} = \begin{bmatrix} 1 & 0 \\ 0 & .397 \end{bmatrix}$$

$$\mathbf{R} = \mathbf{V}^{-\frac{1}{2}}\mathbf{C}\mathbf{V}^{-\frac{1}{2}}$$

$$\mathbf{R} = \begin{bmatrix} 1.0 & .993 \\ .993 & 1.0 \end{bmatrix}$$

This analysis reveals a very strong level of linear dependence between x_1 and x_2. Of course, $\mathbf{R}$ was based upon only three observations for the purposes of illustration. Larger data matrices can be subjected to the same analysis. However, it would be advisable to use software capable of manipulating matrices. For example, SAS IML and MATLAB both permit the types of matrix operations demonstrated above.

LEAST SQUARES REGRESSION

Matrix algebra notation greatly simplifies how we convey ordinary least squares regression. Performing regression analysis using matrix algebra requires the introduction of an additional operation: the matrix inverse. The inverse of a matrix is analogous to the reciprocal in scalar mathematics. For example, while $10 \times \frac{1}{10} = 1$, $\mathbf{AA}^{-1} = \mathbf{I}$. $\mathbf{I}$ is the symbol for the identity matrix; it has many of the characteristics that the number 1 has in scalar mathematics. Any matrix pre- or postmultiplied by the identity matrix equals itself.

$$\mathbf{I}_{4\times 4} = \begin{bmatrix} 1 & 0 & 0 & 0 \\ 0 & 1 & 0 & 0 \\ 0 & 0 & 1 & 0 \\ 0 & 0 & 0 & 1 \end{bmatrix}$$

$$\mathbf{AI} = \mathbf{A}$$

$$\mathbf{IA} = \mathbf{A}$$

The example below confirms that just as 1×10 equals 10, so too do $\mathbf{IA}$ and $\mathbf{AI}$ equal $\mathbf{A}$.

$$\mathbf{A} = \begin{bmatrix} 4 & 3 \\ 2 & 1 \end{bmatrix} \qquad \mathbf{I} = \begin{bmatrix} 1 & 0 \\ 0 & 1 \end{bmatrix}$$

$$\mathbf{AI} = \begin{bmatrix} (4\times 1)+(3\times 0) & (4\times 0)+(3\times 1) \\ (2\times 1)+(1\times 0) & (2\times 0)+(1\times 1) \end{bmatrix}$$

The inverse of $\mathbf{A}$ is $\mathbf{A}^{-1}$. The inverse of a matrix also has a scalar analogue: the reciprocal. Just as $10 \times \frac{1}{10} = 1$ in scalar mathematics, a matrix pre- or postmultiplied by its inverse is equal to the identity matrix $\mathbf{I}$, which is composed of ones on the diagonal and zeros on the off-diagonal.

$$\mathbf{AA}^{-1} = \mathbf{I}$$
$$\mathbf{A}^{-1}\mathbf{A} = \mathbf{I}$$

$$\mathbf{A} = \begin{bmatrix} 3 & 2 & 3 \\ 1 & 4 & 6 \\ 8 & 2 & 4 \end{bmatrix} \qquad \mathbf{A}^{-1} = \begin{bmatrix} 0.4 & -0.2 & 0.0 \\ 4.4 & -1.2 & -1.5 \\ -3.0 & 1.0 & 1.0 \end{bmatrix}$$

$$\mathbf{A}^{-1}\mathbf{A} = \begin{bmatrix} (3\times 0.4)+(2\times 4.4)+(3\times -3.0) & (3\times -0.2)+(2\times -1.2)+(3\times 1.0) & (3\times 0)+(2\times -1.5)+(3\times 1.0) \\ (1\times 0.4)+(4\times 4.4)+(6\times -3.0) & (1\times -0.2)+(4\times -1.2)+(6\times 1.0) & (1\times 0)+(4\times -1.5)+(6\times 1.0) \\ (8\times 0.4)+(2\times 4.4)+(4\times -3.0) & (8\times -0.2)+(2\times -1.2)+(4\times 1.0) & (8\times 0)+(2\times -1.5)+(4\times 1.0) \end{bmatrix}$$

$$\mathbf{A}^{-1}\mathbf{A} = \begin{bmatrix} 1 & 0 & 0 \\ 0 & 1 & 0 \\ 0 & 0 & 1 \end{bmatrix} = \mathbf{I}$$

A matrix term that is closely related to the inverse operation is the determinant of a matrix. The determinant indicates whether an inverse exists for a given matrix. When an exact linear dependency exists between two variables, the determinant is zero, which indicates that an inverse does not exist.

The inverse of $\mathbf{X}'\mathbf{X}$ plays a pivotal role in regression analysis. If it does not exist (that is, if there is an exact linear dependency involving two or more predictor variables), the regression analysis cannot be conducted. Of course, this represents the most egregious case. All too often we encounter instances in which the determinant of $\mathbf{X}'\mathbf{X}$ *approaches* zero. This indicates potentially harmful levels of collinearity.

Least squares regression analysis in matrix algebra involves the following system of linear equations.

$$\mathbf{b} = \left(\mathbf{X}'\mathbf{X}\right)^{-1}\mathbf{X}'\mathbf{y}$$

This simply indicates that a vector $\mathbf{b}$ of beta coefficients is equal to the inverse of $\mathbf{X}'\mathbf{X}$ times $\mathbf{X}'\mathbf{y}$ where $\mathbf{y}$ is a vector of dependent variable values.

Consider the following example involving three predictor variables in $\mathbf{X}$ and a single dependent measure $\mathbf{y}$. The three predictor variables reflect responses to a brief questionnaire that subsumes three service quality issues: responsiveness, courtesy, and timeliness. The single outcome measure depicted in $\mathbf{y}$ reflects the respondents' overall satisfaction. To find the three beta coefficients that correspond to the predictor variables, we solve $\mathbf{b} = (\mathbf{X}'\mathbf{X})^{-1}\mathbf{X}'\mathbf{y}$.

$$
\mathbf{X} =
\begin{array}{c}
\begin{array}{ccc} x_1 & x_2 & x_3 \end{array} \\
\begin{bmatrix}
4 & 1 & 5 \\
5 & 1 & 3 \\
4 & 2 & 5 \\
4 & 1 & 4 \\
6 & 3 & 6 \\
1 & 2 & 3 \\
1 & 6 & 1 \\
2 & 3 & 6 \\
5 & 2 & 5 \\
6 & 3 & 6
\end{bmatrix}
\end{array}
\qquad
\mathbf{y} =
\begin{bmatrix}
6 \\
5 \\
6 \\
4 \\
6 \\
3 \\
3 \\
1 \\
5 \\
6
\end{bmatrix}
$$

$$
\mathbf{X}'\mathbf{X} =
\begin{bmatrix}
176 & 81 & 184 \\
81 & 78 & 98 \\
184 & 98 & 218
\end{bmatrix}
$$

$$(\mathbf{X'X})^{-1} = \begin{bmatrix} 0.048 & 0.002 & -0.042 \\ 0.002 & 0.029 & -0.015 \\ -0.042 & -0.015 & 0.047 \end{bmatrix}$$

$$\mathbf{X'y} = \begin{bmatrix} 194 \\ 100 \\ 206 \end{bmatrix}$$

$$\mathbf{X'X}^{-1}\mathbf{X'y} = \begin{bmatrix} 0.99 \\ 0.26 \\ -0.01 \end{bmatrix} = \mathbf{b}$$

$$\hat{\mathbf{y}} = .99_{x1} + .26_{x2} - .01_{x3}$$

Of the three predictor variables, responsiveness appears to have the strongest effect on overall satisfaction. Note that had we wanted an intercept term ($\mathbf{B}_0$), a vector of ones would have been placed on the far left of the data matrix $\mathbf{X}$.

Inverting the matrix $\mathbf{X'X}$ is a critical step in regression analysis. The determinant of a matrix $\mathbf{X}$ is denoted $|\mathbf{X}|$. If the determinant of a matrix is zero, no inverse for the matrix exists.

Linear dependencies within a data set are responsible for small or even zero determinants. Collinearity is discussed in chapter 9 of this book. The linear dependencies associated with collinearity are integrally linked to the inversion of $\mathbf{X'X}$.

The matrix $\mathbf{X}$ below is a 2 × 2 matrix characterized by an exact linear dependency. That is, the first column can be used to predict exactly the second column. In this case $x_2 = 2_{x1}$. Calculating a determinant by hand is an easy matter for a 2 × 2 matrix, but a computer is needed for larger-order matrices.

$$\mathbf{X} = \begin{bmatrix} 2 & 4 \\ 4 & 8 \end{bmatrix}$$

To find the determinant of $\mathbf{X}_{2\times2}$ requires that

$$|\mathbf{X}| = \begin{bmatrix} x_{11} & x_{12} \\ x_{21} & x_{22} \end{bmatrix} = x_{11}x_{22} - x_{12}x_{21}$$

The determinant of **X** is zero:

$$\mathbf{X} = \begin{bmatrix} 2 & 4 \\ 4 & 8 \end{bmatrix}$$

$$|\mathbf{X}| = (2 \times 8) - (4 \times 4)$$

$$|\mathbf{X}| = 0$$

which means no inverse for **X** exists. It is a rare instance in applied customer satisfaction research that we encounter an exact linear dependency. More frequently we encounter a situation similar to that in matrix **A**.

$$\mathbf{A} = \begin{bmatrix} 3 & 3 \\ 4 & 5 \end{bmatrix}$$

$$|\mathbf{A}| = (3 \times 5) - (3 \times 4)$$

$$|\mathbf{A}| = 3$$

An examination of the determinant of a matrix is an excellent shortcut to understanding the level of collinearity present in the data. As the determinant approaches zero, which is indicative of an exact linear dependency, regression models become increasingly unstable.

PRINCIPAL COMPONENTS ANALYSIS

Principal components analysis (PCA) is frequently used in analyses that involve customer and employee satisfaction data and their relationship with financial performance data. PCA applications typically involve circumventing collinearity problems or reducing the dimensionality of X when there are too many predictor variables. In the latter case, the objective is to reveal a small set of dimensions that are linear combinations of the original variables. In PCA these are called principal components, and in common factor analysis they are referred to as factors.

A simple example illustrates how PCA works. This example uses a very small data set: it has only two variables: x_1 = customer satisfaction, and x_2 = employee satisfaction. Despite the limited number of variables, the illustration demonstrates that as many components p as there are variables k are extracted. First, assume the following matrices and vectors:

$$\mathbf{X} = \begin{bmatrix} 9.9 & 10.8 \\ 10.4 & 9.8 \\ 9.8 & 9.6 \\ 9.8 & 9.6 \\ 9.6 & 9.7 \\ 8.6 & 8.7 \\ 8.8 & 8.9 \\ 9.5 & 9.3 \\ 9.7 & 9.4 \\ 9.6 & 9.5 \\ 8.7 & 8.6 \\ 9.2 & 9.0 \\ 8.3 & 8.5 \\ 9.7 & 9.8 \\ 8.5 & 9.2 \end{bmatrix}$$

$$\bar{x} = \begin{bmatrix} \bar{x}_1 \\ \bar{x}_2 \end{bmatrix} \qquad \bar{x} = \begin{bmatrix} 8.873 \\ 8.833 \end{bmatrix}$$

$$\mathbf{S} \begin{bmatrix} s_1^2 & s_{12} \\ s_{12} & s_2^2 \end{bmatrix} = \begin{bmatrix} 0.108 & 0.080 \\ 0.080 & 0.101 \end{bmatrix}$$

Note that $\bar{x}$ is the vector of means on variables x_1 and x_2 and $\mathbf{S}$ is the variance covariance matrix associated with these two variables. In this example, $n = 15$ and

$$s_{ij} = \frac{n\Sigma x_{ik} x_{ik} - \Sigma x_{ik} \Sigma_{jk}}{[n(n-1)]}$$

Of further interest is the correlation between the customer and employee satisfaction measures:

$$r_{ij} = 0.769$$
$$(P = 0.0008)$$

PCA is based on an eigenanalysis of either the correlation matrix $\mathbf{R}$ or covariance matrix $\mathbf{S}$. One would choose to use $\mathbf{R}$ if the data were measured in different units (if, for example, different scales were used). Another reason for using $\mathbf{R}$ involves the variances of the variables. If these vary widely, undue weight may be given to some variables. Of considerable importance is the fact that eigenanalysis of the same data based on **R** and **S** will yield different results. As Jackson (1991, 65) notes, large variations in the variables' variances will result in more divergent results.

An eigenanalysis is based on the fundamental notion that the covariance matrix **S** (or any symmetric, nonsingular matrix such as **R**) may be reduced to a diagonal matrix **L** by the following operation:

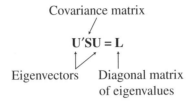

Covariance matrix

$$\mathbf{U'SU = L}$$

Eigenvectors   Diagonal matrix
of eigenvalues

The elements of **L** (ℓ_1, ℓ_2, ..., ℓ_p) are referred to as the eigenvalues of **S** (or **R**). The eigenvalues may also be referred to as latent roots or characteristic vectors of **S**. The eigenvalues of **S** are derived in the following manner:

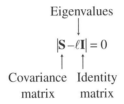

Eigenvalues

$$|\mathbf{S} - \ell\mathbf{I}| = 0$$

Covariance   Identity
matrix   matrix

This is referred to as the characteristic equation where **S** is the covariance matrix, ℓ is the vector of eigenvalues, and **I** is an identity matrix of order k.

$$|\mathbf{S} - \ell\mathbf{I}| = \begin{bmatrix} 0.108 - \ell_1 & 0.080 \\ 0.080 & 0.101 - \ell_2 \end{bmatrix} = 0$$

The values $\ell_1 = 0.184$ and $\ell_2 = 0.024$ satisfy this equation and are derived by the pth degree polynomial for ℓ. Using these values as the characteristic vectors we first note that:

$$[\mathbf{S} - \ell\mathbf{I}] = 0 \qquad \mathbf{L} = \begin{bmatrix} 0.184 & 0 \\ 0 & 0.024 \end{bmatrix}$$

and the *i*th eigenvector

$$\mathbf{u}_i = \frac{\mathbf{t}_i}{\sqrt{\mathbf{t}'_i \mathbf{t}_i}}$$

where *i* ranges from 1 to *p* where *p* equals the number of variables or, more technically, the order of the symmetric, nonsingular matrix **S** (or **R**). For *i* = 1:

$$[\mathbf{S} - \ell_1 \mathbf{I}]\, \mathbf{t}_1 = \begin{bmatrix} 0.108 - 0.184 & 0.080 \\ 0.080 & 0.101 - 0.184 \end{bmatrix} \begin{bmatrix} \mathbf{t}_{11} \\ \mathbf{t}_{21} \end{bmatrix} = \begin{bmatrix} 0 \\ 0 \end{bmatrix}$$

This expression is equivalent to two homogeneous linear equations in two unknowns. To solve this, we let $\mathbf{t}_{11} = 1$ and use the first equation:

$$-0.076 + 0.080\, \mathbf{t}_{21} = 0$$
$$0.080\, \mathbf{t}_{21} = 0.076$$
$$\mathbf{t}_{21} = 0.950$$

The two values of $\mathbf{t}_1$ are now known:

$$\mathbf{t}_1 = \begin{bmatrix} 1.000 \\ 0.950 \end{bmatrix}$$

At this point we return to the normalizing equation to obtain the first eigenvector:

$$\mathbf{u}_i = \frac{\mathbf{t}_i}{\sqrt{\mathbf{t}'_i \mathbf{t}_i}}$$

$$\mathbf{u}_i = \frac{\mathbf{t}_i}{\sqrt{\mathbf{t}'_i \mathbf{t}_i}} = \frac{1}{1.380} \begin{bmatrix} 1.000 \\ 0.950 \end{bmatrix} = \begin{bmatrix} 0.724 \\ 0.688 \end{bmatrix}$$

The second eigenvector is derived in a similar fashion:

$$[\mathbf{S} - \ell_2 \mathbf{I}]\, \mathbf{t}_2 = \begin{bmatrix} 0.108 - 0.024 & 0.080 \\ 0.080 & 0.101 - 0.024 \end{bmatrix} \begin{bmatrix} \mathbf{t}_{12} \\ \mathbf{t}_{22} \end{bmatrix} = 0$$

Again, this is equivalent to two homogeneous linear equations in two unknowns. To solve, we let $\mathbf{t}_{22} = 1$ and focus on the first equation:

$$0.084 + 0.080 \, \mathbf{t}_{12} = 0$$

$$0.080 \, \mathbf{t}_{12} = -0.084$$

$$\mathbf{t}_{12} = -1.050$$

$$\mathbf{t}_2 = \begin{bmatrix} -1.050 \\ 1.000 \end{bmatrix}$$

$$\mathbf{u}_2 = \frac{\mathbf{t}_1}{\sqrt{\mathbf{t}'_i \mathbf{t}_2}} = \frac{1}{1.450} \begin{bmatrix} -1.050 \\ 1.000 \end{bmatrix} = \begin{bmatrix} -0.689 \\ 0.724 \end{bmatrix}$$

The vectors $\mathbf{u}_1$ and $\mathbf{u}_2$ together make up the eigenvector matrix $\mathbf{U}$.

$$\mathbf{U} = \begin{bmatrix} \mathbf{u}_1 : \mathbf{u}_2 \end{bmatrix} = \begin{bmatrix} 0.724 & \vdots & -0.689 \\ 0.689 & \vdots & 0.724 \end{bmatrix}$$

Further, $\mathbf{U}$ is orthonormal, meaning

$$\mathbf{u}'_1 \mathbf{u}_1 = 1 \qquad \mathbf{u}'_2 \mathbf{u}_2 = 1 \qquad \mathbf{u}'_1 \mathbf{u}_2 = 0$$

Finally, we can demonstrate that when the covariance matrix $\mathbf{S}$ is pre- and postmultiplied by the eigenvector matrix $\mathbf{U}$, the result is the diagonal matrix $\mathbf{L}$ containing the eigenvalues $\ell_1, \ell_2, \ldots, \ell_p$.

$$\mathbf{U}'\mathbf{S}\mathbf{U} = \begin{bmatrix} 0.724 & 0.689 \\ -0.689 & 0.724 \end{bmatrix} \begin{bmatrix} 0.108 & 0.080 \\ 0.080 & 0.101 \end{bmatrix} \begin{bmatrix} 0.724 & -0.689 \\ 0.689 & 0.724 \end{bmatrix} = \begin{bmatrix} 0.184 & 0 \\ 0 & 0.024 \end{bmatrix}$$

EIGENVECTOR SCALING

As described in the preceding, the $\mathbf{U}$ matrix is desirable because it is scaled to ± 1.00 regardless of the scaling of the original variables. Two alternate scalings are possible: $\mathbf{W}$ and $\mathbf{V}$.

$$\mathbf{v}_i = \sqrt{\ell_i \mathbf{u}_i} \quad \text{or} \quad \mathbf{V} = \mathbf{U}\mathbf{L}^{1/2}$$

$$\mathbf{w}_i = \frac{\mathbf{u}_i}{\sqrt{\ell_i}} \quad \text{or} \quad \mathbf{W} = \mathbf{U}\mathbf{L}^{-1/2}$$

Given the matrix $\mathbf{U}$ of eigenvectors related to our data set of employee and customer satisfaction scores, the characteristic vectors in $\mathbf{U}$ can be rescaled to $\mathbf{V}$ and $\mathbf{W}$ as shown:

$$\mathbf{L} = \begin{bmatrix} 0.184 & 0.000 \\ 0.000 & 0.024 \end{bmatrix}$$

$$\mathbf{U} = \begin{bmatrix} 0.724 & -0.689 \\ 0.689 & 0.724 \end{bmatrix}$$

$$\mathbf{V} = \begin{bmatrix} 0.310 & -0.106 \\ 0.295 & 0.112 \end{bmatrix}$$

$$\mathbf{W} = \begin{bmatrix} 1.687 & -1.750 \\ 1.606 & 1.839 \end{bmatrix}$$

The $\mathbf{V}$ vectors are interesting because $\mathbf{VV'} = \mathbf{S}$, but these scores are not commonly used in PCA. They have some appeal, however, because while they are still orthogonal, they are scaled to their roots and the variances are equal to the squares of the eigenvalues. The $\mathbf{V}$ vectors are frequently referred to as factor loadings.

The correlation between the original variables x_1 and x_2 with the principal components is derived by

$$r_{zx} = \frac{\mathbf{u}_{ji}\sqrt{\ell_i}}{s_j}$$

Using this, we can produce a matrix containing the correlations between each variable and the two principal components. When the SAS factor procedure is used and the principal components extraction method (default) with the COV option is used, this matrix is equivalent to the "factor pattern" matrix. This same factor pattern matrix is given by the $\mathbf{V}$ vectors when a correlation matrix ($\mathbf{R}$) is decomposed using eigenanalysis.

The correlations between the two variables and the principal components is shown below, again it is equivalent to $\mathbf{V}$ when $\mathbf{R}$ is used rather than $\mathbf{U}$.

$$\begin{array}{cc} & \begin{array}{cc} \mathbf{PC}_1 & \mathbf{PC}_2 \end{array} \\ \mathbf{x}_1 & \begin{bmatrix} 0.945 & -3.25 \\ 0.932 & 0.353 \end{bmatrix} \end{array}$$

$$\mathbf{r}_{11} = \frac{.724\sqrt{.184}}{\sqrt{.108}} = .945$$

$$\mathbf{r}_{21} = \frac{-.689\sqrt{.024}}{\sqrt{.108}} = .325$$

$$\mathbf{r}_{12} = \frac{.689\sqrt{.184}}{\sqrt{.101}} = .930$$

$$\mathbf{r}_{22} = \frac{.724\sqrt{.024}}{\sqrt{.101}} = .353$$

Notice that when squared and summed, the correlations between x_1 and PC$_1$ and between x_1 and PC$_2$ approximate unity. That is, $r_{11}^2 + r_{21}^2 \cong 1.00$ and $r_{12}^2 + r_{22}^2 \cong 1.00$. The deviations from 1.00 are attributable to rounding error.

EIGENVECTOR ROTATION

The correlations between variables (x_1 and x_2) and principal components (PC$_1$ and PC$_2$) presented above are of only modest interest in the present case. Notice that both variables are strongly correlated with the first principal component. This is because the first component accounts for a much larger share of variance. Note that the first eigenvalue ℓ_1 was 0.184 and the second ℓ_2 was 0.024. Further, note that

$$\ell_1 + \ell_2 = s_1^2 + s_2^2$$

$$\mathbf{S} = \begin{bmatrix} 0.108 & 0.080 \\ 0.080 & 0.101 \end{bmatrix} \qquad \mathbf{L} = \begin{bmatrix} 0.184 & 0 \\ 0 & 0.024 \end{bmatrix}$$

$$0.108 + 0.101 = 0.209 \qquad 0.184 + 0.024 = 0.208$$

The slight difference between the two values is attributable to rounding error.

Rotating principal components involves the use of a transformation matrix Θ, which has the following structure for two variable examples:

$$\Theta = \begin{bmatrix} \cos(\theta) & -\sin(\theta) \\ \sin(\theta) & \cos(\theta) \end{bmatrix}$$

The objective of a vector rotation is typically "simple structure" (Thurstone 1947). The primary characteristics of a principal components matrix rotated toward simple structure are as follows:

- At least one *row* of the rotated matrix contains at least one zero. The implication of this is that (at least) one variable is perfectly uncorrelated with one PC.

- Each *column* of the rotated matrix contains at least k zeros (see Jackson 1991, 156).

- For each pair of columns in the rotated matrix, there should be at least several variables that have near-zero entries for one PC and near -1.00 entries for the other PC.

It should be clear that the objectives of simple structure include the derivation of a new rotated matrix **B** that has reapportioned variance in a fashion that facilitates interpretation of the component structure. This is somewhat analogous to *clustering* the variables based on their covariance with one another.

Several rotation techniques are available to achieve simple structure. Each can be considered to belong to either the orthogonal rotation methods or the oblique rotation methods. The former preserve the orthogonal nature of the PCs, while oblique methods permit the PCs to correlate.

Matrix algebra remains a very useful tool for researchers. It represents a powerful shorthand for many analyses. Virtually all advanced books on multivariate statistical analysis assume the reader has a fundamental understanding of matrix algebra. This appendix cannot provide a comprehensive treatment of the subject. We hope that the examples presented will spark or rekindle an interest in the subject.

Glossary of Terms

affective loyalty component: One of two components that can be identified when loyalty is considered to be an attitude with behavioral outcomes. The affective component of loyalty is presumed to reflect emotional ties to the service or product supplier. See also cognitive loyalty component.

American Customer Satisfaction Index (ACSI): An index sponsored by ASQ and the University of Michigan's National Quality Research Center. It relies upon a 100-point scale and benchmarks performance across more than 160 companies. Over 50,000 interviews are conducted annually as part of the ongoing study.

attrition risk: A number frequently assigned to individual customers based upon the possibility of relationship termination. Survival analysis is often used to calculate the probability of a given customer's mortality— that is, the probability that he or she will sever his or her relationship with the product or service provider.

Baldrige Award: See Malcolm Baldrige National Quality Award.

beta coefficient: An optimized weight encountered in dependence models, such as regression analysis, that is indicative of the magnitude of effect a given predictor variable has on the outcome variable.

bivariate statistics: Any measure used to summarize the relationship between two variables regardless of their measurement level (nominal, ordinal, interval, or ratio).

canonical correlation: The correlation between two sets of variables. One is generally considered to be the predictor set, and the other is considered to be the outcome set. A single coefficient represents the extent to which the two sets of variables are linearly dependent.

causal modeling: A family of analytical techniques (such as path analysis) that employ cross-sectional data and make inferences concerning the causal relations among variables. While causality is not proven, researchers can conclude that relations in the data are consistent with the causal hypotheses.

cognitive loyalty component: One of two components that can be identified when loyalty is considered to be an attitude with behavioral outcomes. The cognitive component of loyalty is believed to reflect rational considerations with respect to a service or product supplier. These might include justifications such as price and proximity. See also affective loyalty component.

collinearity: A mathematical problem that is especially troublesome in dependence models; also called "ill conditioning." It occurs when the relationships among predictor variables are very strong, resulting in an unstable model. Manifestations of this condition include sign reversals associated with beta coefficients and large standard errors around beta estimates.

condition index: A means of diagnosing the extent to which collinearity may be degrading a dependence model. Levels greater than 90 indicate substantive problems.

confirmatory analysis: Any analysis that requires the researcher to specify *a priori* the hypothesized outcome. Factor analysis, for example, can be exploratory or confirmatory. In the latter case, the researcher specifies which variables are expected to load on which factor(s).

control chart (Six Sigma): A chart that tracks processes by plotting data over time. Deviations from the center line are of special importance because they can reflect process irregularities. When deviations exceed the upper control limit or lower control limit, the indication is that a statistically significant deviation has occurred.

correlation: A relation between variables that tend to be associated. A wide variety of correlations exist in different data situations. All bivariate correlations reflect the extent to which two variables covary. Correlation does not by any means imply or demonstrate causality.

cross-sectional data analysis: A form of analysis in which the data are collected at one point in time. It can be differentiated from longitudinal or time series data analysis, which involves data collected over a period of time at equal intervals, such as months. Typically, survey research is cross-sectional in nature. See also longitudinal data analysis.

customer satisfaction: A summary metric that ostensibly reflects the extent to which the customer's expectations are being met. Its quantification typically involves a score on a multipoint scale.

customer value management: An approach to understanding why consumers buy certain products. It assumes that consumers weigh the price and quality of competing products or services and make summary conclusions about the value each presents. Rational consumers presumably purchase the choice that offers the greatest value.

data matrix: A matrix composed of rows and columns that contains all of the information used in statistical analyses. The rows typically correspond to individual respondents, and the columns represent the variables. An individual cell in a data matrix is the score provided by a given respondent on a single variable.

dependence model: A model that involves the extent to which a single variable or set of variables is dependent upon a set of one or more predictor variables.

dependent variable: In dependence models, the outcome variable. It is considered to be dependent upon one or more predictor variables. See also endogenous variable.

derived importance: An evaluation of importance based upon leveraging the covariation between a critical outcome variable such as overall satisfaction and specific, actionable predictor variables. Typically, derived importance implies the use of multiple regression analysis, but this need not be the case. Derived importance should be differentiated from stated importance measures, in which respondents are asked to indicate how important various product and service issues are to them.

earnings per share: One of the most familiar financial metrics used to evaluate a company's performance. Earnings per share is equal to net income divided by the number of shares outstanding.

eigenanalysis: A means of decomposing a symmetric matrix such as a correlation or covariance matrix. This technique is used in principal components analysis.

employee satisfaction: Typically, a summary metric that ostensibly reflects the degree to which an employee is satisfied with his or her job. It is frequently referred to as "job satisfaction." There are a variety of inputs that affect employee satisfaction. These range from pay and benefits to upward mobility, coworkers, and role ambiguity.

endogenous variable: An outcome or dependent variable. Overall customer satisfaction is frequently an endogenous variable—it is dependent upon a variety of service and product quality variables.

EQS: A computer program for developing structural equation models.

exogenous variable: A predictor or independent variable. Service and product quality are typically used as exogenous variables in dependence models characterized by some measure of overall satisfaction as the outcome variable.

goodness-of-fit statistic: Used in confirmatory analyses such as confirmatory factor analysis and path analysis to assess the extent to which the data are consistent with the hypothesized structural or measurement models.

heteroscedasticity: In regression analysis, a condition that reflects an undesirable distribution of the residuals. For example, as the values of one or more of the predictor variables increase, the residual value (the error in prediction) increases. This violates one of the fundamental assumptions of regression analysis.

hierarchical linear model (HLM): An analytical approach designed for situations in which the independent variables differ among themselves in terms of the organizational level being referenced; for example, a situation in which some variables pertain to the managers of retail outlets while other variables pertain to individual employees within those retail outlets.

house of quality: See quality functional deployment (QFD).

identification: A term frequently used in structural equation modeling that refers to the relation between the number of available observations and parameters to be estimated. A just-identified (saturated) model has as many observations as parameters. More problematic is the underidentified model, in which there are more parameters than observations, making estimation impossible.

ill conditioning: See collinearity.

imputation: A process conducted to rectify problems associated with missing values in multivariate data. A variety of approaches to imputing missing values are available. These range from rather simplistic mean substitution techniques to more sophisticated regression-based procedures.

independent variable: In dependence models, a variable that is presumed to affect one (or more) outcome variables.

influential observation: With respect to multiple regression analysis, an observation that exerts excessive influence over the beta coefficients. Removal of influential observations can sometimes substantively change the regression equation.

interval-level data: Typically, endpoint-anchored Likert-type scale data that employ five or more points. The characteristics that distinguish interval-level data include valid inferences concerning the distances between the scale points. With interval-level data, one can reasonably conclude that a score of 4 represents twice the level of a given attribute that a score of 2 does. Interval-level (or ratio-level) data are assumed to be on the dependent side of a multiple regression equation.

Job Descriptive Index (JDI): A popular standardized employee satisfaction questionnaire developed in the 1970s. It contains 72 items that fall into five categories: work, pay, promotion, supervision, and coworkers.

key driver analysis: Generally, any dependence model designed to assess the effect of various predictor variables on a single outcome variable. Examples include regression analysis, logistic regression analysis, and discriminant analysis.

Kruskal's relative importance: A dependence model technique known to be robust with respect to collinearity. The technique produces a metric that represents the average squared partial correlation over all permutations of independent variables.

latent variable: A variable that is inherently unobservable. Factor analysis and other similar procedures are frequently used to facilitate the understanding of latent variable structure. Examples of latent variables include intelligence and motivation. These are typically measured using test instruments in the form of questionnaires with predetermined scales that ostensibly reflect the underlying latent constructs.

level of analysis: The level at which an analysis is conducted. For example, employee satisfaction data may be considered at a variety of levels, including organization, department, work group, and individual.

Likert-type scale: Typically, attitudinal scales employed in applied customer satisfaction research. These may be endpoint anchored ("very dissatisfied" to "very satisfied") or fully anchored, in which case each point on the scale has a label. It may be argued that the fully anchored Likert-type scale yields ordinal-level data while the endpoint-anchored Likert-type scale yields interval-level data.

LISREL: A software application developed by Jöreskog and Sörbom specifically for latent variable path model applications.

logistic regression analysis: A dependence model appropriate for binary dependent variables. Such cases violate a fundamental assumption of ordinary least squares regression—that the dependent variable is normally distributed. Logistic regression employs a nonlinear link that permits more robust model development using binary outcome variables.

longitudinal data analysis: A form of analysis that involves examining relationships among variables across time. Data are typically recorded in terms of uniform periods of time such as months, quarters, or years. Of concern is how variables and their relationships with one another vary over time. See also cross-sectional data analysis.

lower control limit (LCL): In a Six Sigma control chart, the line that reflects the level of a given process parameter that is outside (below) the center line, which is the desired level. See also upper control limit (UCL).

loyalty: A latent construct that is frequently and erroneously confused with its behavioral manifestations. Loyalty is an attitudinal state focused on an organization, service, or product that results in desirable behaviors such as repurchase and tenure as a customer. Measuring the behaviors is not the same as measuring the attitude.

Malcolm Baldrige National Quality Award: A national award related to service and product quality. Customer satisfaction plays a large role in this reward, as do quality and operational results, leadership, process quality, and human resources management.

manifest variable: A variable that is tangible, in contrast to a latent variable. The actual questions in survey instruments represent manifest variables. Techniques such as factor analysis permit us to understand the latent dimensions underlying sets of manifest variables.

matrix: A "block" of numbers characterized by n rows and r columns. In customer satisfaction research, a matrix is typified by n rows (where n = number of observations) and k columns, each of which relates to a specific variable. Using matrix algebra, complex analyses can be conducted and communicated in an especially parsimonious fashion. Ordinary least squares regression, for example, is represented as $\mathbf{b} = (\mathbf{X'X})^{-1}\mathbf{X'Y}$, which produces a vector of beta weights.

matrix algebra: A type of algebra used extensively in modern statistical analysis and applied customer satisfaction research. It is a very convenient way to express complex statistical formulae.

measurement model: In structural equation modeling with latent variables, a model that represents the confirmatory factor analytic portion of the architecture. The measurement model specifies the relationships between the manifest and latent variables.

Minnesota Satisfaction Questionnaire (MSQ): A standardized test relating to employee satisfaction. The test was available in two forms, one containing 20 questions, and the other, 100 questions.

missing values: A problematic issue in multivariate analyses because most statistical packages exclude any observation that does not have valid data for every variable in a given multivariate procedure. Missing values occur when respondents fail to answer a question, when "skip" patterns force a respondent not to answer certain questions, when keypunching errors occur, and for a variety of other reasons.

multicollinearity: See collinearity.

multiple correlation coefficient: Represented with an uppercase *R* to differentiate it from the simple bivariate correlation coefficient, a coefficient that, when squared, plays a pivotal role in assessing the efficacy of multiple regression analyses. The multiple correlation coefficient is analogous to the simple bivariate correlation coefficient, but it reflects the extent to which a series of variables covaries with a single "outcome" measure.

multivariate data analysis: A form of data analysis that subsumes all statistical techniques that operate on more than two variables per observation simultaneously. Thus, factor analysis, multiple regression analysis, and path analysis all represent multivariate statistical techniques, despite their rather divergent objectives.

nominal data: Data that are categorical in nature. There is no inherent ordering associated with values of a nominal-level variable. Examples of nominal variables include eye color and body type.

nonlinear regression: A form of multiple regression analysis that accommodates nonlinear relationships between the predictor and dependent variables.

nonrecursive causal model: A casual model in which reciprocal causation is permitted. In this case, we may permit two variables to cause one another. In a recursive model, in which casuality is typically assumed to have a unidirectional flow, product and service quality affect overall satisfaction (y_1), which in turn causes customer loyalty (y_2). To make this a nonrecursive model, we would estimate an additional path from loyalty to satisfaction. The implication of this is that satisfaction causes loyalty and loyalty also causes satisfaction. Such reciprocal causal relationships are not uncommon in the modeling of psychological phenomena. Nonrecursive structural equation models are somewhat problematic from an identification perspective (see identification).

operationalize: To construct questionnaire items that purportedly measure a concept in marketing research.

ordinal data: Data that are ordered. Inferences may be made concerning the order of ordinal data values but not their absolute position. For example, if all the students in a class were assigned a rank with respect to their height, these would be ordinal data. We could conclude that one student was taller than another but not how much taller.

ordinary least squares (OLS): The most frequently encountered form of estimation in simple linear or multiple linear regression analysis. It involves the estimation of a regression line that minimizes the sum of squared deviations between the observed and predicted values of a dependent measure.

overidentified model: A model that permits parameter estimation and is desirable, as is the just-identified model. In confirmatory analyses where goodness of fit must be assessed, model identification plays a pivotal role.

path analysis: A technique developed in the early 1900s by Sewall Wright that represents the structural foundation for latent variable path modeling. It is included in the broad class of techniques known generally as causal modeling.

path coefficient: A coefficient in path analysis that is equivalent to a standardized beta coefficient and reflects the extent to which one variable "influences" another.

principal components analysis (PCA): A dimension-reducing technique used frequently in customer satisfaction research to reduce collinearity attributable to too many variables or variables that are too highly intercorrelated. The technique is conceptually and mathematically similar to factor analysis but does not assume that variables can be decomposed into their unique and common variances. As a result, PCA does not suffer from the factor indeterminacy problem associated with the estimation of communalities in common factor analysis. Component scores are frequently used subsequently in regression analysis due to their orthogonality (see principal components regression).

principal component regression (PCR): A technique that involves the use of PCA to reduce a set of predictor variables into a more manageable, smaller group of orthogonal component scores. With orthogonal components on the predictor side of the regression equation, there is no concern that collinearity will degrade the model. This approach is frequently used to circumvent the degrading effects of ill-conditioned data and, less commonly, to reduce a predictor variable set to a more manageable number.

profit margin on sales: A profitability metric equal to net income divided by net sales for a given period.

proportional hazards regression: A survival analysis technique that models the hazard function based on a set of predictor variables.

psychometric: Relating to the science of measuring attitudes.

quadrant chart: A type of chart that is used extensively in customer satisfaction research. The quadrant chart typically has a *y* axis (vertical) that indicates importance (derived or stated) and an *x* axis (horizontal) that reflects performance level in terms of respondent satisfaction. Thus, four quadrants based upon the integrated importance-performance data are possible. Each represents a different combination of importance and performance (for example, high importance and low importance). The strategic implications with respect to the product or service quality issues that fall into each quadrant can help organizations to maximize customer satisfaction.

quality function deployment (QFD): A set of quality management tools that is very customer oriented. It is frequently referred to as the "house of quality" because the primary diagram used in this approach resembles a house. QFD helps organizations to convert customer needs into process and product designs.

rate of return on assets: A metric that combines the profit margin on sales with asset turnover. The rate of return on assets is equal to net income divided by net sales (profit margin on sales) times net sales divided by total average assets (asset turnover).

rate of return on common stock equity: A metric that is equal to net income after preferred dividends are divided by average common stockholders' equity.

ratio-level data: The richest type of data from an analytical standpoint. They are ordered, inferences can be made about the relative magnitude of different values, and perhaps most important, there is a natural zero. Income represents a ratio-level variable.

recursive causal model: A type of structural equation model in which causal flow is assumed to be unidirectional. For example, consider a simple path model with two independent and two dependent variables. The independent variables (product and service quality) are assumed to affect the first dependent variable (overall satisfaction), which in turn affects the second dependent variable (loyalty). In the recursive model environment, we cannot permit the second dependent variable to "loop back" and affect the first. To do so would be to posit a nonrecursive causal model.

regression analysis: A dependency model that is used to assess the extent to which a set of predictor variables affects a single interval- or ratio-level outcome variable.

relative importance: In the realm of key driver (multiple regression) analysis, a metric that will permit interval- or ratio-level inferences concerning the relative effects of two predictor variables. Note that in evaluating beta weights it is only possible to make ordinal-level (rank-order) judgments about how two competing variables affect an outcome variable.

return on quality (ROQ): A program that focuses on the financial returns associated with quality improvement initiatives. The approach emphasizes the links between quality, customer satisfaction, customer retention, and profitability.

ridge regression: A special form of multiple regression analysis employed when collinear data are especially problematic. Ridge regression involves using a *ridge estimator* value (usually between zero and one) that is added to the data matrix. The resulting regression equation is generally more stable.

R-*square (R^2) statistic:* In regression analysis, the coefficient that represents the proportion of dependent variable variance accounted for by the set of predictor variables. In applied customer satisfaction research, it is not uncommon to encounter R^2 statistics greater than .80. R^2 is the multivariate equivalent of the bivariate correlation coefficient squared (r_{ij}^2).

SAS: Statistical Analysis System; a comprehensive programming and statistical package used extensively in marketing research generally and customer satisfaction research specifically.

saturated model: In causal modeling, a model in which all possible paths are estimated. No exogenous variables are constrained to zero with respect to any of the dependent variables. A saturated model is able to exactly replicate the original data covariance of a matrix and therefore has perfect goodness of fit.

SERVQUAL scale: A multi-item scale that is considered to be one of the first attempts to operationalize the customer satisfaction construct. The SERVQUAL scale focused on the performance component of the service quality model in which quality was defined as the disparity between expectations and performance. The battery of items used in the SERVQUAL scale is still used today as a foundation upon which instrument development is often based.

simple linear regression: A regression equation characterized by a numeric outcome variable and a single predictor variable. This is differentiated from multiple regression analysis, which includes more than one predictor variable.

Six Sigma: An empirically driven system that places emphasis on root cause analysis and closed-loop business processes. The primary objective of the Six Sigma process is to reduce variance around critical business measures relating to service or product quality. Reducing process variation yields improved products and services. Services or products that are produced at the optimum Six Sigma level yield a mere four defects per million.

SPSS: Statistical Package for the Social Sciences; an advanced statistical analysis program used extensively in marketing research and customer satisfaction research.

stated importance: A metric of importance that relies upon the respondent's introspective capacity to communicate which product and service quality issues are important. This is typically achieved through the use of survey instruments that ask respondents to indicate how important various issues are to them. Stated importance has been criticized on several grounds. Among these are respondents' tendency to indicate that all issues are important, thus minimizing the variance of responses across items.

stepwise selection: A purely mechanical procedure used extensively in multiple regression analysis when collinearity is problematic. Stepwise selection checks the residual sum of squares as each variable is entered into the equation. Variables that fail to meet the entry criterion (frequently referred to as the "*F*-to-enter") are dropped from the model since their unique contribution to accounting for variance in the dependent variable is trivial. Stepwise selection can be forward or backward. The latter refers to a reversal of the procedure in which an "*F*-to-remove" is calculated for each variable and those that do not exceed the criterion are dropped. It is possible for a variable to be initially included in the model selection process and subsequently dropped as other variables are added.

structural equation modeling (SEM): A family of techniques that includes integrated confirmatory factor analysis and path analysis in a causal model that demonstrates the linkages between latent constructs.

structural model: In SEM, a model that depicts the causal relationships among latent variables. The structural model is rooted in path analysis, which was developed in the early 1900s by Sewall Wright.

survival analysis: A longitudinal statistical technique that focuses on variables that are predictive of mortality. When survival analysis is applied to human mortality, key predictor variables might include smoking, age, cholesterol level, and weight. When applied to customer relationships, survival analysis might suggest that tenure, complaints, and purchase patterns are indicative of risk level. See also proportional hazards regression.

top-box score: The top-box and top-two-box scores are metrics that are frequently employed in presenting univariate customer satisfaction data. Many organizations track the proportion of respondents who rate their product or service in a Likert-type scale's top one or two numeric categories. The top-box score when a 5-point Likert-type scale is being used is the proportion of respondents who indicated that their satisfaction level was a 5.

underidentified model: A model that is characterized by too many estimable parameters in relation to the number of observations. This situation precludes model estimation and must be reexamined. In confirmatory analyses where goodness of fit must be assessed, model identification is critical.

univariate statistics: A type of analysis that focuses on individual variables and their distributions. Deriving univariate profiles is an excellent idea prior to undertaking more complex multivariate analyses. Univariate examination will reveal any pathological conditions at this level and can lead to correction through various transformations.

upper control limit (UCL): In a Six Sigma control chart, the line that reflects the level of a given process parameter that is outside (above) the center line, which is the desired level. See also lower control limit (LCL).

variance inflation factor: An indicator of the extent to which collinearity in a regression model is degrading. Variance inflation factors help statisticians diagnose the collinearity problem and assess the extent to which different variables contribute to the condition. See also condition index.

Bibliography

Agho, A., C. Mueller, and J. Price. "Determinants of Employee Job Satisfaction." *Human Relations* 46, no. 8, 1993.

Allen, D., and T. Rao. *Analysis of Customer Satisfaction Data.* Milwaukee: ASQ Quality Press, 2000.

Allison, P. *Survival Analysis.* Cary, NC: SAS Institute, 1995.

Anderson, E., and C. Fornell. "Foundations of the American Customer Satisfaction Index." *Journal of Total Quality Management,* 2000.

Anderson, E., C. Fornell, and R. Rust. "Customer Satisfaction, Productivity, and Profitability: Differences between Goods and Services." *Marketing Science* 16 (1997): 129–45.

Anderson, E., and C. Fornell. "Customer Satisfaction, Market Share, and Profitability." *Journal of Marketing* 58 (1994): 53–67.

Asher, H. B. *Causal Modeling.* Newbury Park, CA: Sage Publications Quantitative Applications in the Social Sciences Series, 1983.

Ashkanasy, N., C. Wilderom, and M. Peterson. *Handbook of Organizational Culture and Climate.* Thousand Oaks, CA: Sage Publications, 2000.

Auh, S., and M. Johnson. "The Complex Relationship between Customer Satisfaction and Loyalty for Automobiles." In *Customer Retention in the Automotive Industry: Quality, Satisfaction, and Loyalty.* Wiesbaden, Germany: Gabler, 1997: 141–66.

Barsky, J. *Finding the Profit in Customer Satisfaction.* Chicago: Contemporary Books, 1999.

Bartlett, M. "The Goodness of Fit of a Single Hypothetical Discriminant Function in the Case of Several Groups." *Annals of Eugenics* 16 (1951): 199–214.

Basilevsky, A. *Statistical Factor Analysis and Related Methods.* New York: John Wiley and Sons, 1994.

Bearden, W., and J. Teel. "Selected Determinants of Consumer Satisfaction and Complaint Reports." *Journal of Marketing Research* 20 (1983): 21–28.

Belsley, D., E. Kuh, and R. Welsch. *Regression Diagnostics.* New York: John Wiley and Sons, 1980.

Bernhardt, K., N. Donthu, and P. Kennett. "A Longitudinal Analysis of Satisfaction and Profitability." *Journal of Business Research* 47, no. 2 (2000).

Birkes, D., and Y. Dodge. *Alternative Methods of Regression.* New York: John Wiley and Sons, 1993.

Bhalla, G., and L. Lin. "Cross-Cultural Marketing Research: A Discussion of Equivalence Issues and Measurement Strategies." *Psychology & Marketing* 4, no. 4 (1987): 275–85.

Bhote, K. R. *Beyond Customer Satisfaction to Customer Loyalty.* New York: AMA Management Briefing, 1996.

Blakeslee, J. "Implementing the Six Sigma Solution." *Quality Progress* (1999): 77–85.

Blalock, H. M., Jr. *Causal Inferences in Non-Experimental Research.* Chapel Hill: University of North Carolina Press, 1964.

Bloom, P., and P. Kotler. "Strategies for High Market Share Companies." *Harvard Business Review* 63 (1975): 8–27.

Bollen, K. A. *Structural Equations with Latent Variables.* New York: John Wiley and Sons, 1989.

Boulding, W., A. Kalra, R. Staelin, and V. Zeithaml. "A Dynamic Process Model of Service Quality: From Expectations to Behavioral Intentions." *Journal of Marketing Research* 30 (1993): 7–27.

Breyfogle, F. W. *Implementing Six Sigma: Smarter Solutions Using Statistical Models.* New York: John Wiley and Sons, 1999.

Brooke, P., and J. Price. "The Determinants of Employee Absenteeism." *Journal of Occupational Psychology* 62 (1989): 1–19.

Bryant, B., and J. Cha. "Crossing the Threshold: Some Customers Are Harder to Please Than Others." *Marketing Research* 8, no. 4 (1996).

Bryk, A., and S. Raudenbush. *Hierarchical Linear Models.* Thousand Oaks, CA: Sage Publications, 1992.

Bullock, H. E., L. L. Harlow, and S. A. Mulaik. "Causation Issues in Structural Equation Modeling." *Structural Equation Modeling: A Multidisciplinary Journal* 3 (1994): 253–67.

Buzzell, R., and B. Gale. *The PIMS Principles.* New York: The Free Press, 1987.

Chin, W. W. "The Partial Least Squares Approach to Structural Equation Modeling." In *Modern Methods for Business Research,* ed. George A. Marcoulides. Mahwah, NJ: Lawrence Erlbaum Associates, 1998.

Churchill, G., and C. Surprenant. "An Investigation into the Determinants of Customer Satisfaction." *Journal of Marketing Research* 19 (1982): 491–504.

Council on Financial Competition. *Service Quality.* Council on Financial Competition, 1987.

Cox, D. "Regression Models and Life Tables." *Journal of the Royal Statistical Society* B34 (1972): 187–220.

Crampton, S., and J. Wagner. "Percept-Percept Inflation in Micro-Organizational Research: An Investigation of Prevalence and Effect." *Journal of Applied Psychology* 79 (1994): 67–76.

Cronin, J., and S. Taylor. "Measuring Service Quality: A Reexamination and Extension." *Journal of Marketing* 56 (1992): 55–68.

Crosby, L. "Toward a Common Verbal Scale of Perceived Quality." In *The Race Against Expectations.* Amsterdam: 45th ESOMAR Congress, Joint Session on Customer Satisfaction and Quality Management, 1992.

Danaher, P., and R. Rust. "Indirect Financial Benefits from Service Quality." *Quality Management Journal* 3 (1996): 63–75.

Deshpandé, R. *Developing a Market Orientation.* Thousand Oaks, CA: Sage Publications, 1999.

Deshpandé, R., and J. Farley. "Understanding Market Orientation." In *Developing a Market Orientation.* Thousand Oaks, CA: Sage Publications, 1999.

Deshpandé, R., J. Farley, and F. Webster. *Factors Affecting Organizational Performance: A Five-Country Comparison.* Cambridge, MA: Marketing Science Institute, 1997.

Deshpandé, R., and F. Webster. "Organizational Culture and Marketing: Defining the Research Agenda." *Journal of Marketing* 53 (1989): 53–62.

Dick, A., and K. Basu. "Customer Loyalty: Toward an Integrated Conceptual Framework." *Journal of the Academy of Marketing Science* 22 (1994): 99–114.

Dillon, W. R., and M. Goldstein. *Multivariate Analysis: Methods and Applications.* New York: John Wiley and Sons, 1984.

Dillon, W. R., J. B. White, V. R. Rao, and D. Filak. "Good Science: Use Structural Equation Models to Decipher Complex Customer Relationships." *Marketing Research* (Winter 1997): 23–31.

Draper, N. R., and H. Smith. *Applied Regression Analysis.* New York: John Wiley and Sons, 1998.

Eckes, G. *The Six Sigma Evolution.* New York: John Wiley and Sons, 2001.

Elandt-Johnson, R. C., and N. L. Johnson. *Survival Models and Data Analysis.* New York: John Wiley and Sons, 1980.

England, G., and I. Harpaz. "Some Methodological and Analytic Considerations in Cross-National Comparative Research." *Journal of International Business Studies* (Fall 1983): 49–59.

Eves, H. *Elementary Matrix Theory.* Toronto: General Publishing, 1966.

Fornell, C. "The Quality of Economic Output: Empirical Generalizations about Its Distribution and Relationship to Market Share." *Marketing Science* 14 (1995): 203–11.

———. American Customer Satisfaction Index. Q3: 1999 Commentary, 1999.

———. American Customer Satisfaction Index. Q1: 2001 Commentary, 2001.

Fornell, C., E. Johnson, W. Anderson, J. Cha, and B. Bryant. "The American Customer Satisfaction Index: Nature, Purpose and Findings." *Marketing Research* 8 (1996): 4.

Fuller, H. T. "Observations about the Success and Evolution of Six Sigma at Seagate." *Quality Engineering* 12 (2000): 311–15.

Garfield, E. "100 Most Cited Papers of All Time." *Current Conditions* 12 (1990).

Gayle, B. *Managing Customer Value.* New York: The Free Press, 1994.

Glick, W. "Response: Organizations Are Not Central Tendencies." *Academy of Management Review* 13, no.1 (1988): 133–37.

Hackman, J., and G. Oldham. "Motivation through the Design of Work." *Organizational Behavior and Human Performance* 16 (1976): 250–79.

Hahn, G. T., N. Doganaksoy, and R. Hoerl. "The Evolution of Six Sigma." *Quality Engineering* 12 (2000): 317–26.

Hammermesh, M., M. Anderson, and J. Harris. "Strategies for Low Market Share Businesses." *Harvard Business Review* 63 (1975).

Hartigan, J. *Bayes Theory.* New York: Springer-Verlag, 1983.

Hatcher, L. *A Step-by-Step Approach to Using the SAS System for Factor Analysis and Structural Equation Modeling.* Cary, NC: SAS Institute, 1994.

Hayes, B. E. *Measuring Customer Satisfaction.* Milwaukee: ASQ Quality Press, 1998.

Heskett, J., E. Sasser, and L. Schlesinger. *The Service Profit Chain.* New York: The Free Press, 1997.

Hoerl, A. "Application of Ridge Analysis to Regression Problems." *Chemical Engineering Progress* 58, no. 3 (1962): 54–59.

Hoerl, A., and R. Kennard. "Ridge Regression: Biased Estimation for Non-Orthogonal Problems." *Technometrics* 12 (1970): 55–67.

Hoppock, R. *Job Satisfaction.* New York: Arno Press, 1935.

Hosmer, D. W., and S. Lemeshow. *Applied Logistic Regression.* New York: John Wiley and Sons, 1989.

Hu, L., and P. M. Bentler. "Evaluating Model Fit." In *Structural Equation Modeling*, ed. Rick Hoyle. Thousand Oaks, CA: Sage Publications, 1995.

Hughes, G. *Demand Analysis for Marketing Decisions.* Homewood, IL: Richard D. Irwin, 1973.

Hulin, C., M. Roznowski, and D. Hachiya. "Alternative Opportunity and Withdrawal Decisions." *Psychological Bulletin* 97 (1985): 233–50.

Iaffaldano, M., and P. Muchinsky. "Job Satisfaction and Job Performance: A Meta-Analysis." *Psychological Bulletin* 97 (1985): 251–73.

Jackson, J. *A User's Guide to Principal Components.* New York: John Wiley and Sons, 1991.

Jain, S. *Marketing Planning and Strategy.* Cincinnati: South-Western Publishing, 1990.

James, L., W. Joyce, and J. Slocum. "Comment: Organizations Do Not Cognize." *Academy of Management Review* 13, no. 1 (1988): 133–137.

Jaworski, B., and A. Kohli. "Market Orientation: Antecedents and Consequences." *Journal of Marketing* 57 (1993): 53–70.

Johnson, M., F. Herrmann, and A. Gustafsson. "An Introduction to Quality, Satisfaction, and Retention: Implications for the Automotive Industry." In *Customer Retention in the Automotive Industry: Quality, Satisfaction, and Loyalty.* ed. M. Johnson, A. Herrmann, and A. Gustafsson. Wiesbaden, Germany: Gabler, 1997: 1–17.

Johnson, R., A. Ryan, and M. Schmit. "Employee Attitudes and Branch Performance at Ford Motor Credit." In *Linking Employee Survey Data to Organizational Outcome Measures.* Nashville: Society for Industrial and Organizational Psychology, 1994.

Jöreskog, K. G., and D. Sörbom. *LISREL 8: User's reference guide.* Chicago: Scientific Software International, 1993.

Kanungo, R. *Work Alienation.* New York: Praeger, 1982.

Keiningham, T., and A. Zahorik. "Getting Return on Quality." *Journal of Retail Banking* 16, no. 4 (1995): 7–13.

Kendall, M., and A. Stewart. *The Advanced Theory of Statistics.* Vol 1. New York: Hafner, 1958.

Kieso, D., and J. Weygandt. *Intermediate Accounting.* New York: John Wiley and Sons, 1977.

Kohli, A., and B. Jaworski. "Market Orientation: The Construct, Research Propositions, and Managerial Implications." *Journal of Marketing* 54 (1990): 1–16.

Kohli, A., B. Jaworski, and A. Kumar. "MARKOR: A Measure of Market Orientation." *Journal of Marketing Research* 30 (1993): 467–77.

Kornhauser, A., and A. Sharp. "Employee Attitudes: Suggestions from a Study in a Factory." *Personnel Journal* 10 (1932): 393–401.

Kreft, I., and J. DeLeeuw. *Introducing Multilevel Modeling.* Thousand Oaks, CA: Sage Publications, 1998.

Lee, E. T. *Statistical Methods for Survival Data Analysis.* New York: John Wiley and Sons, 1992.

Li, S. "Survival Analysis." *Marketing Research* 7 (1995): 17–25.

Liou, K., R. Sylvia, and G. Brunk. "Non-Work Factors and Job Satisfaction Revisited." *Human Relations* 43, no. 1 (1990): 77–86.

Locke, E. "The Nature and Causes of Job Satisfaction." In *Handbook of Industrial and Organizational Psychology,* ed. M. D. Dunnette. Chicago: Rand McNally, 1976.

Love, F. "Six Sigma, What Does It Really Mean?" *Automotive Excellence,* 2000.

Mannheim, B., Y. Baruch, and J. Tal. "Alternative Models for Antecedents and Outcomes of Work Centrality and Job Satisfaction of High-Tech Personnel." *Human Relations* 50, no. 12 (1997): 1537–62.

Marsh, H. W., J. R. Balla, and K. Hau. "An Evaluation of Incremental Fit Indices: A Clarification of Mathematical and Empirical Properties." In *Advanced Structural Equation Modeling,* ed. G. A. Marcoulides and R. E. Schumacker. Mahwah, NJ: Lawrence Erlbaum Associates, 1996.

McCauley, D., and M. Colberg. "Transportability of Deductive Measurement Across Cultures." *Journal of Economic Measurement* 20, no. 3 (1983): 267–98.

McCullagh, P., and J. Nelder. *Generalized Linear Models.* London: Chapman Hall, 1983.

Michaels, C., and P. Spector. "Causes of Employee Turnover." *Journal of Applied Psychology* 67 (1982): 53–59.

Mobley, W., S. Horner, and A. Hollingsworth. "An Evaluation of Precursors of Hospital Employee Turnover." *Journal of Applied Psychology* 63 (1978): 408–14.

Mowday, R., L. Porter, and R. Steers. *Organizational Linkages: The Psychology of Commitment, Absenteeism, and Turnover.* San Diego: Academic Press, 1982.

Mowday, R., R. Steers, and L. Porter. "The Measurement of Organizational Commitment." *Journal of Vocational Behavior* 14 (1979): 224–47.

Narver, J., and S. Slater. "The Effect of a Market Orientation on Business Profitability." *Journal of Marketing* (October 1990): 20–35.

Narver, J., R. Jacobson, and S. Slater. *Market Orientation and Business Performance: An Analysis of Panel Data.* Marketing Science Institute Report No. 93-121. 1993.

Naumann, E., and S. Hoisington. *Customer Centered Six Sigma.* Milwaukee: ASQ Quality Press, 2001.

Nelson, E., and R. Rust. "Do Patient Perceptions of Quality Relate to Hospital Financial Performance?" *Journal of Health Care Marketing* 12 (1992): 6–12.

Oliver, R. "A Cognitive Model of the Antecedents and Consequences of Satisfaction Decisions." *Journal of Marketing Research* 42 (1980): 460–69.

Ostroff, C. "Comparing Correlations Based on Individual-Level and Aggregated Data." *Journal of Applied Psychology* 78, no. 4 (1993): 569–82.

Parasuraman, A., L. Berry, and V. Zeithaml. "A Conceptual Model of Service Quality and Its Implications for Future Research." *Journal of Marketing* 14 (1985): 41–50.

———. "SERVQUAL: A Multiple-Item Scale for Measuring Customer Perceptions of Service Quality." *Journal of Retailing* 16 (1988): 12–40.

Pelham, A. "Influence of Environment, Strategy, and Marketing Orientation on Performance in Small Manufacturing Firms." *Journal of Business Research* 45 (1999): 33–46.

Perlis, S. *Theory of Matrices.* New York: Dover Publications, 1991.

Petty, M., G. McGee, and J. Cavender. "A Meta-Analysis of the Relationships between Individual Job Satisfaction and Individual Performance." *Academy of Management Review* 9 (1984): 712–21.

Porter, L., and P. Smith. "Employee Commitment." *Journal of Applied Psychology* 34: 34–41.

Price, J., and C. Mueller. *Absenteeism and Turnover among Hospital Employees.* Greenwich, CT: JAI Press, 1981.

Reichheld, R. *The Loyalty Effect.* Boston: Harvard Business School Press, 1996.

Reichheld, F., and W. Sasser. "Zero Defections: Quality Comes to Services." *Harvard Business Review* 68 (1990): 105–111.

Rigdon, E. E. "Structural Equation Modeling." In *Modern Methods for Business Research.* ed. G. A. Marcoulides. Mahwah, NJ: Lawrence Erlbaum Associates, 1998.

Roethlisberger, F., and W. Dickson. *Management and the Worker.* Cambridge: Harvard University Press, 1939.

Rousseau, D. "Issues of Level in Organizational Research." *Research in Organizational Behavior* 7 (1985): 1–37.

Rucci, A., S. Kirn, and R. Quinn. "The Employee–Customer–Profit Chain at Sears." *Harvard Business Review* 76, no. 3 (1998): 83–97.

Rust, R., and A. Zahorik. "Customer Satisfaction, Customer Retention, and Market Share." *Journal of Retailing* 69 (1993): 193–215.

———. "Return on Quality (ROQ): Making Service Quality Financially Accountable." *Journal of Marketing* 59, no. 2 (1995): 58–71.

Rust, R., A. Zahorik, and T. Keiningham. *Return on Quality (ROQ): Making Service Quality Financially Accountable.* Cambridge, MA: Marketing Science Institute, 1994.

Ryan, A., M. Schmit, and R. Johnson. "Attitudes and Effectiveness." *Personnel Psychology* 49 (1996): 853–82.

Schneider, B., and D. Bowen. "Employee and Customer Perceptions of Service in Banks: Replication and Extension." *Journal of Applied Psychology* 70 (1985): 423–33.

Schneider, B., D. Bowen, M. Ehrhart, and K. Holcombe. "The Climate for Service: Evolution of a Construct." In *Handbook of Organizational Culture and Climate,* ed. N. Ashkanasy, C. Wilderom, and M. Peterson. Thousand Oaks, CA: Sage Publications, 2000.

Schneider, B., J. Parkington, and V. Buxton. "Employee and Customer Perceptions of Service in Banks." *Administrative Science Quarterly* 25 (1980): 252–67.

Schneider, B., S. White, and M. Paul. "Linking Service Climate and Customer Perceptions of Service Quality." *Journal of Applied Psychology* 83, no. 2 (1998): 150–63.

Schumacker, R. E., and R. G. Lomax. *A Beginner's Guide to Structural Equation Modeling.* Mahwah, NJ: Lawrence Erlbaum Associates, 1996.

Scott, K., and G. Taylor. "An Examination of Conflicting Findings on the Relationship between Job Satisfaction and Absenteeism." *Academy of Management Journal* 28 (1985): 599–612.

Searle, S. R. *Matrix Algebra Useful for Statistics.* New York: John Wiley and Sons, 1982.

Slater, S., and J. Narver. "The Positive Effect of a Market Orientation on Business Profitability: A Balanced Replication." *Journal of Business Research* 48 (2000): 69–73.

Smith, P., J. Kendall, and C. Hulin. *Measurement of Satisfaction in Work and Retirement.* Chicago: Rand McNally, 1969.

Spector, P. *Job Satisfaction.* Thousand Oaks, CA: Sage Publications, 1997.

Steiger, J. "Structural Model Evaluation and Modificantion: An Interval Estimation Approach." *Multivariate Behavioral Research* 25 (1990): 173–80.

Steinberg, D. I. *Computational Matrix Algebra.* New York: McGraw-Hill, 1974.

Tornow, W., and J. Wiley. "Service Quality and Management Practices." *Human Resource Planning* 14 (1991): 105–16.

Tukey, J. W. *Exploratory Data Analysis.* Reading, MA: Addison-Wesley, 1977.

Van de Vijver, F., and Y. Poortinga. "Cross-Cultural Generalization and Universality." *Journal of Cross-Cultural Psychology* 13, no. 4 (1982): 387–408.

Webb, D., C. Webster, and A. Krepapa. "An Exploration of the Meaning and Outcomes of a Customer-Defined Market Orientation." *Journal of Business Research* 48 (2000): 101–12.

Weiss, D., R. Dawis, G. England, and L. Lofquist. *Manual for the Minnesota Satisfaction Questionnaire.* Minneapolis: University of Minnesota Press, 1967.

Wiley, J. "Linking Survey Results to Customer Satisfaction and Business Performance." In *Organizational Surveys: Tools for Assessment and Change.* San Francisco: Jossey Bass, 1996.

Wiley, J., and S. Brooks. "The High-Performance Organizational Climate." In *Handbook of Organizational Culture and Climate,* ed. N. Ashkanasy, C. Wilderom, and M. Peterson. Thousand Oaks, CA: Sage Publications, 2000.

Wittink, D., and L. Bayer. "Statistical Analysis of Customer Satisfaction Data: Results from a Natural Experiment with Measurement Scales." Working paper 94-04, Cornell University Johnson Graduate School of Management, 1994.

Wright, S. "On the Nature of Size Factors." *Genetics* 3 (1918): 367–74.

———. "Correlation and Causation." *Journal of Agricultural Research* 20 (1921): 557–85.

———. "Path Coefficients and Path Regressions: Alternative or Complementary Concepts." *Biometrics* 16 (1960): 189–202.

Zeithaml, V., L. Berry, and A. Parasuraman. "The Behavioral Consequences of Service Quality." *Journal of Marketing* 60 (1996): 31–46.

Index

A

B